RODALE'S

NATURALLY DELICIOUS DESSERTS AND SNACKS

RODALE'S

NATURALLY DELICIOUS DESSERTS AND SNACKS

BY FAYE MARTIN

Photography:
Carl Doney
Sally Ann Shenk
and
Laura Hendry

Editor:
Charles Gerras

Jacket and
Book Design:
John Landis

Rodale Press
Emmaus, Pennsylvania

Printed in the United States of America

Library of Congress Cataloging in Publication Data

Martin, Faye.
  Rodale's Naturally delicious desserts and snacks.

  Includes index.
  1. Desserts. 2. Snack foods. I. Gerras, Charles. II. Title.
III. Title: Naturally delicious desserts and snacks.
TX773.M273   641.8′6   78-9145
ISBN 0-87857-211-2

6 8 10 9 7 5

Dedication

To the memory of my mother and friends who, through the years, taught me to know and appreciate good food.

Acknowledgments

My sincere thanks to all those whose special services contributed to the production and completion of this work, with particular gratitude to:

Marion Zimmerman
Molly and Fred Gearhart
Karen Bell

Appreciation to

Cinruss Creations and C. Leslie Smith of Allentown, Pennsylvania and Colonial Manor Gift Shop of Emmaus, Pennsylvania for their generous cooperation.

CONTENTS

IT'S TIME
FOR A FRESH ATTITUDE
TOWARD DESSERTS

NATURALLY DELICIOUS DESSERTS AND SNACKS

Dessert—for some people it's the best part of any meal. Unfortunately, today's commercially prepared cakes and pies bear little resemblance to the fresh-baked treats mother used to make. The products that appear on the shelves or in the freezers of the supermarkets are usually too sweet, and often greasy. They sometimes taste of the chemicals added at the factory for freshness, flavor, and color. The box cakes, the instant pies, and the slice-and-bake cookies you can "make" in a jiffy have the same drawbacks. And don't try to fool anyone into thinking you've served the real thing. It doesn't take a gourmet to spot a mix.

Even those who would never accept outside help with their cooking and baking are faced with considerations that can dim the pleasure of serving desserts and snacks to the family. What sensible person can ignore growing scientific evidence of sugar's negative effects on nerves and circulation? Who wouldn't prefer to avoid the empty calories of white flour with all its bleaches and preservatives? And why risk the allergy problems so many chocolate eaters encounter?

If such concerns have turned you or your family away from desserts and other goodies entirely, or if you are looking for desserts which taste wonderful and manage to sidestep these problems at the same time, this book is for you!

It will show you how to prepare a wide variety of treats which have real food value in them. The selection runs the gamut from very simple to fancy to delightfully exotic dishes. You'll find choices for every occasion—a quick snack with TV as well as magical presentations that will thrill sophisticated dinner guests.

Shortly after I became interested in getting better nutrition into my life, I stopped using sugar and bleached flour in any type of cooking. As a result, I noticed after a while that I was making desserts less frequently. For that little sweet at the end of a meal, or for that between-meal snack you crave sometimes, I was using mostly fresh fruits.

As time went on, I had a yen, every so often, for the goodies of the past. That's when I made up my mind to try substituting honey and other natural sweeteners for sugar and whole wheat flour for so-called cake flour in some of my recipes. It turned out to be easier than I expected. Gradually I was able to adapt just about all of my old favorite recipes to natural ingredients. Surprisingly, the resulting dishes were comparable in flavor to the originals, sometimes even better.

I've collected recipes for years (used them, too, of course), starting with my mother's very old cookbooks, and I've gleaned many recipes from friends, so when I browse through the file it is a nostalgic experience. I'm delighted to find that some of those recipes are just what we're searching for today.

I've sorted out the best of the old-time favorites and have adapted them to natural ingredients. You will soon see how you can turn your own favorites into goodies that are good as gold for you and your family.

Along with the old-timers I have created hundreds of new recipes that call for only natural ingredients. Some of them were take-a-chance experiments that turned out so successfully that even I was surprised at their fine quality and superb flavor.

The recipes in this book call for some natural ingredients that might be unfamiliar to you. They are not exotic or difficult to use if you follow instructions carefully and understand the characteristics of each ingredient. Here is some of the basic information you should know.

Flour

Whole wheat flour is a natural flour made from hard wheat; it contains all the bran and wheat germ of the original grain. Since it has not been bleached, it is golden brown in color, and the final product will have that rich, earthy color, too. Because of the bran content, the flour is somewhat heavy. To lighten it, either stir it with a whisk or sift it. Then return the bran which remains in the sifter to the flour.

Whole wheat flour is used mostly for the preparation of yeast doughs and for general thickening purposes.

Whole wheat pastry flour is made from soft wheat and, though it, too, contains the natural bran and wheat germ, the flour is ground very fine and is lighter than whole wheat flour. It should be sifted or whisked to fluff it before it is mixed into a dough or batter.

Whole wheat pastry flour is used for cakes, pies, and some delicate cookies. It produces a very pleasing texture.

Leavening

For leavening, the recipes in this book call for either *yeast, eggs,* or *baking soda*—or a combination of yeast and eggs or eggs and soda. I never use baking powder because most of the ones on the market contain aluminum sulphate, an undesirable additive in terms of good health.

When using baking soda (which is alkaline), it is necessary to add to the recipe an acid ingredient which will neutralize the soda and start the leavening process. Molasses, buttermilk, sour cream, or yogurt may be used. (In the old-time recipes natural sour milk or thick milk were often specified.) For example, when you adapt a recipe which calls for baking powder and sweet milk you can substitute soda and buttermilk for those ingredients.

Sweeteners

Honey is the sweetener used most frequently to replace sugar in desserts. It is a worthy substitute because it adds a very pleasant, mild flavor to foods. However, there are many different types of honey ranging from light and delicate to dark and strong. Usually, the darker it is, the more sweetness it gives. By experimenting, you will find a kind of honey just right for your taste, or you might want to stock several kinds to be used for different purposes. The trick is to use enough honey to add the right amount of sweetness without allowing the taste of honey to predominate.

Honey has twice the sweetening power of sugar, so we use half as much; honey is semiliquid so we use less liquid—one tablespoon less per cup—in the recipe. Also, we warm the honey to thin it before adding it to the recipe. (Just set the jar in a small pan of hot water.) That makes the honey easier to measure accurately, and the thin honey is more readily creamed with the butter and eggs.

Using honey in place of sugar will change the consistency of most recipes. In puddings, custards, cakes, cookies, pies, fruit desserts, and sauces, the conversion is very easy; just follow the formula above. Cakes and cookies will have a little coarser texture when made with honey, and they will be moist and soft. You will notice, also, that honey enhances the keeping qualities of most baked products.

If stored properly, honey keeps indefinitely. A dark cupboard is good—the cold of a refrigerator or exposure to bright light will cause it to granulate. If that happens, just warm it and the honey will regain its original consistency.

Maple syrup is sometimes substituted for sugar in about the same proportion as honey. If you use it, just be sure to buy *pure* maple syrup which is free of additives and retains its natural nutrients. The flavor is mild and distinctive and is a pleasant change in some desserts.

Molasses comes in basically two forms: unsulphured and blackstrap. Unsulphured molasses has a rather mellow flavor, and blackstrap is quite strong and bitter. Each is manufactured in a different way, but both types retain the same original beneficial elements; namely iron, calcium, and phosphorus. Both types blend very well with spices and are generally used for gingerbread and any other spice cake.

Natural fruit juices, such as orange, apple, prune, and pineapple, can be used to add a subtle and delightful sweetness to many desserts. Once you get into the habit of using juice to replace the milk or water plus sugar in a recipe, you'll be encouraged to make such substitutions often, and you will see how very easy it is.

Chocolate Flavor

Carob, made from a plant sometimes called St. John's Bread, is a delicious food in its own right but also has become very popular as a substitute for chocolate and cocoa. When I started to use carob, I found it added an unpleasant graininess to the texture of the dish in which it was used. By experimenting, I discovered that this problem can be avoided by using carob in the following ways:

As a substitute for *melted bitter chocolate*, I prepare a BASIC CAROB SYRUP (see Index), cooking the carob powder with an equal amount of water. I use one-quarter cup of this syrup for every two squares of melted bitter chocolate. *Carob syrup, sold commercially, cannot be substituted for this ingredient.*

As a substitute for *melted semisweet chocolate* or *chocolate bits*, I use the BASIC CAROB SYRUP plus honey and butter in the proportion of one-quarter cup of carob syrup, two tablespoons honey, and one tablespoon of butter to take the place of one-third cup melted semisweet chocolate.

As a substitute for cocoa, use an equal amount of carob powder.

All the "chocolate" recipes in this book have been based on the above substitutions.

If you and your family are fond of chocolate, prepare the BASIC CAROB SYRUP and keep it on hand in a covered container in the refrigerator. It will keep for weeks.

In addition to the general tips above, you will find helpful suggestions included in the recipes throughout this book.

It is with every confidence that I welcome you to a new approach to desserts. Think of them as an exciting and delectable addition to your good diet, instead of a bad-for-you, but obligatory final course to a meal. No need to give up desserts to stay fit. In fact, if you follow the recipes in this book, eating desserts can be part of your good-health program.

CHAPTER 1

FROZEN AND CHILLED DESSERTS

FROZEN AND CHILLED DESSERTS

The widespread revival of the old-time ice cream parlor is a fresh indication of the universal popularity this type of dessert enjoys. Of course, ice cream can be made successfully at home, as it originally was made, in a hand-crank freezer. You can also use today's electrically powered freezer, or just a refrigerator-freezer tray.

Making your own ice cream is fun and it gives you the opportunity to enjoy any unusual flavors that are your special favorites. It also carries with it the assurance that this luscious dessert contains no sugar, no artificial filler or flavoring, nor chemicals of any kind. Upon checking commercial ice cream products, I found none which listed all ingredients, leaving to your imagination exactly what has gone into their production.

The best ice cream is the velvety, smooth-as-satin kind which can be produced only in a freezing churn, turned either by hand or electrically.

There are two types of ice cream: plain ice cream, which is made without eggs and contains relatively small amounts of flavoring, and French ice cream, which uses whole eggs or egg yolks as a major ingredient. The eggs lend a custard flavor and usually require some precooking.

In making fruit ice cream, the fruit is usually pureed and added to the mix · at the start; the fruit might also be mashed or chopped and added after the processing and before the hardening.

Of all the frozen desserts, French-type ice cream is the richest. Plain ice cream is next in flavor and richness. After that come other frozen desserts:

Sherbets are thickened only with the basic syrup.

Parfaits are made with a boiled syrup base, frozen right in the mold and never beaten or stirred.

Fruit ices are the simplest form of frozen desserts (shaved ice and fruit juice), delicious because of their pure fruit flavor.

In the same family of desserts we have those which are thoroughly chilled, but not actually frozen:

Mousses are made either with eggs or whipped cream.

Iced souffles are usually thickened with eggs and/or gelatin. The egg whites give these souffles their fluff and the yolks or gelatin help them hold their shape.

Since the success of homemade ice cream depends so much upon the churning, refrigerator ice creams lack the smoothness of a perfect ice cream. However, if you do not have an ice cream freezer, you can experiment with the refrigerator-tray type of ice cream and come up with a thoroughly acceptable product. Select only the recipes in this book which are thickened with either gelatin, egg yolks, flour, or cornstarch. This type is less apt to become icy.

Ice Milk

Ice milk can be made from the same recipes as ice cream, substituting milk for the cream. Whole milk or 99 percent fat-free milk may be used. The texture and taste of the product will be different, but a satisfactory result can be obtained. The recipe provided is for low-calorie ice milk, similar to the type produced commercially. A softer, creamier ice milk results from using a custard ice cream recipe, with milk instead of cream.

Frozen Yogurt

Frozen yogurt is a variation of ice milk or sherbet in which most or all of the milk is replaced by yogurt, which gives the product a characteristic tangy flavor. Frozen yogurt enjoys great popularity, since it is relatively low in calories, and high in nutrition and flavor.

Sherbet

All sherbet mixtures must be made with a light syrup. If you use a mechanical freezer, from time to time scrape the inside of the container to loosen any sherbet sticking to the sides of the can, but do not stir.

Sherbets are seasoned with fruits, liqueurs, or heavy wines.

Ices

Ices, like ice creams, benefit from the steady beating of the churn freezer. To attain the same smooth texture in the refrigerator tray, the ice must be beaten well and often during the freezing process. Starting one hour after the mixture has been put into the freezer tray, when the ice is set around the sides but still mushy in the center, the beating should take place every half-hour until the ice is frozen solid. Ices include neither eggs nor milk, they are simple water ices, made with pure fruit juice, perhaps some honey, and crushed ice—all blended together, then frozen in a churn or a refrigerator tray.

Parfait

A parfait should freeze without stirring and always begins with a boiled syrup to which flavoring is added, often in the form of crushed fruit. Usually it is poured into a mold or parfait glasses and frozen.

Bombe

The first *bombes* were spherical, which accounts for the name. Today this layering of frozen desserts may be molded into any desired shape, provided the mold can be covered.

Mousse

A mousse can be made with eggs or whipped cream or both. It is light and usually delicate, and almost any flavor works well. It can be set in a large mold or individual molds or in sherbet glasses or *pot de creme* cups and chilled for about four hours before serving.

Cold Souffle

This dessert is remarkably similar in its aura of elegance and festiveness to a hot souffle. The ingredient that makes the difference is gelatin. In a hot souffle it is eggs alone that provide the volume.

Basic Procedure for Churned Ice Cream

☐ Chill the cream mixture and pour it into the freezer can, filling it no more than two-thirds full—this allows for expansion. Cover securely.

☐ Fill the tub one-third full of crushed ice cubes, then layer ice and rock salt (or regular household salt) to a level slightly above the level of the mixture in the can.

☐ Process (work the churn) until the ice cream is smooth and thick. In an electric freezer, when this point is reached, the freezer turns off automatically.

☐ Remove the dasher from the can and pack the ice cream down solidly with a wooden spoon.

☐ The ice cream is now ready to be hardened. This can be done by repacking the tub of the freezer, surrounding the can with more ice and salt and then covering the whole machine with burlap or newspapers; or the container may be removed from the tub, covered, and placed in a freezer to harden. If you prefer, spoon ice cream into a plastic container with a tight-fitting lid. Whatever system you use, the ice cream should be allowed to mellow and harden for two or three hours before serving.

☐ If you make up your mixture well ahead of time and prechill for an hour or two in your refrigerator, the subsequent processing time will be reduced.

☐ The texture of the finished product depends largely on how fast it is processed. The slower the freezing process, the smoother the texture. You can easily control the processing rate, and hence the finished texture, by varying the amount of salt you use. Using about three-fourths of a standard 26-ounce box of salt will result in a reasonably fast freezing action and produce a relatively smooth-textured finished product. Use of up to a full box of salt will shorten the processing time and produce a coarser, more granular texture.

Basic Procedure for Refrigerator Tray Ice Cream

☐ Prepare the mixture as directed and pour into a refrigerator tray without the dividers. Place the tray in the freezer compartment of your refrigerator (or a deep freeze if you have one) for about an hour, or until the mixture is mushy but not solid.

☐ Transfer the ice cream from the tray to a chilled bowl and beat it rapidly (with a chilled rotary beater) until the mixture is smooth. Work as quickly as possible to prevent melting.

☐ Return the mixture to the tray and when it has frozen almost solid, remove and beat again until smooth.

☐ Cover the tray with plastic wrap to prevent ice crystals from forming on the top of the cream. Place in the freezer again to complete setting.

1 quart OLD-FASHIONED VANILLA
CUSTARD ICE CREAM (see Index)
1 cup BLUEBERRY SAUCE (see Index)

Process vanilla ice cream in churn freezer until thick and smooth. Remove from container and place in bowl.

Fold BLUEBERRY SAUCE into ice cream just enough to produce marbleized swirl effect. Pack in covered container and place in deep freeze several hours to harden.

Yield: 4 to 6 servings

Blueberry Ripple Ice Cream

3 tablespoons honey
1 tablespoon lemon juice
4 cups peeled and sliced peaches
½ teaspoon unflavored gelatin
1 cup heavy cream, whipped

Mix honey and lemon juice and drizzle over peaches. Cover and set aside for 2 hours.

Drain fruit and combine ¾ cup of the juice with gelatin. Place over low heat until gelatin is completely dissolved.

Put peaches in the container of a blender. Add gelatin mixture and process at medium speed until peaches are chopped fine. Refrigerate.

When mixture begins to thicken, fold in whipped cream and pour into container of ice cream freezer. Process until thick and creamy. Transfer to covered container and place in deep freeze to harden.

Yield: 6 servings

Peach Ice Cream

Frozen and
Chilled
Desserts

Avocado
Ice Cream

In a saucepan, combine milk, honey, and salt. Bring to boiling. Pour about ¼ cup of the hot mixture over eggs. Mix well, then pour back into the hot milk mixture, stir well, and cook for about 1 minute. Remove from heat, stir in cream and lemon juice, and cool thoroughly.

Add avocado and mix well. Pour into container of ice cream freezer and process until thick and smooth. Put into covered container and place in deep freeze to harden.

Yield: about 1 quart

2 cups milk
¼ cup honey
¼ teaspoon salt
2 eggs, well beaten
1 cup heavy cream
2 teaspoons lemon juice
1 cup sieved avocado

Frozen and
Chilled
Desserts

French Carob Ice Cream

In a medium-size saucepan, combine honey, carob syrup, flour, and salt. Place over low heat and gradually add the half-and-half. Cook and stir until mixture begins to thicken.

In a small bowl, beat eggs until fluffy. Add slowly to hot mixture and cook for 1 minute longer. Remove from heat, cool, and chill.

Stir in cream and vanilla. Pour mixture into cream can of churn freezer, chill thoroughly, then process in freezer until thick and smooth. Place in covered plastic container and put into deep freeze to harden.

Yield: about 8 servings

½ cup honey
8 tablespoons BASIC CAROB SYRUP (see Index)
2 tablespoons whole wheat flour
⅛ teaspoon salt
2 cups half-and-half
2 eggs
2 cups light cream
1½ teaspoons vanilla

Carob Swirl Ice Cream

Process vanilla ice cream in churn freezer until thick and smooth. Remove from container and place in bowl. Fold in carob sauce with a wooden spoon, stirring just enough to produce marbleized effect. Pack in container, cover, and place in deep freeze to harden.

Yield: 4 to 6 servings

1 quart OLD-FASHIONED VANILLA CUSTARD ICE CREAM (see Index)
1 cup BASIC CAROB SAUCE (see Index)

Frozen and
Chilled
Desserts

Sprinkle pistachios with almond extract. (Almond is a powerful flavoring—be careful not to use too much.)

Process ice cream as usual in churn freezer until thick and smooth. Remove from container and place in a bowl.

1 cup ground pistachios
¼ teaspoon almond extract
1 quart OLD-FASHIONED VANILLA CUSTARD ICE CREAM (see Index)

Fold nuts into ice cream and mix well. Place in covered container and put into deep freeze to harden.

Yield: 4 to 6 servings

Commercially made pistachio ice cream is usually light green in color. If you wish, AVOCADO ICE CREAM (see Index) may be substituted for vanilla in this recipe to produce the pale green color and for an unusual and delightful flavor combination.

Pistachio Ice Cream

Process vanilla ice cream in churn freezer until thick and smooth. Remove from container and place in bowl.

1 quart OLD-FASHIONED VANILLA CUSTARD ICE CREAM (see Index)
1 cup peanut butter
1 cup cream or milk

Mix peanut butter and cream or milk, beating until very soft and smooth. Fold into ice cream just enough to produce marbleized effect. Pack in covered container and place in deep freeze for several hours to harden.

Yield: 4 to 6 servings

Peanut Butter Whirl Ice Cream

Frozen and Chilled Desserts

½ cup honey
2 tablespoons whole wheat flour
⅛ teaspoon salt
2 cups milk
2 eggs
3 tablespoons instant powdered coffee
2 cups light cream
1½ teaspoons vanilla

French Coffee Ice Cream

In a saucepan, combine honey, flour, and salt. Mix well, then add milk. Cook and stir over low heat until mixture begins to thicken. Add eggs slowly, cooking and stirring for 1 minute longer.

Dissolve coffee in ¼ cup of light cream; add to hot mixture. Stir in remaining cream and vanilla.

Pour mixture into cream can of ice cream freezer, chill in refrigerator for about 1 hour, then process. Transfer to deep freeze for hardening.

Yield: 8 servings

Frozen and
Chilled
Desserts

1½ cups milk
1 tablespoon arrowroot
⅛ teaspoon salt
1 cup RUM-RAISIN SAUCE (see Index)
1 cup heavy cream, whipped

Scald milk in heavy-bottom saucepan. Add arrowroot and salt. Stir with wire whisk until smooth, then cook slowly until thickened. Cool.

Add RUM-RAISIN SAUCE to cold milk mixture. Fold in whipped cream.

Process in ice cream freezer until thick and creamy. Pack in covered container and place in deep freeze to harden.

Yield: 8 servings

Rum-Raisin Ice Cream

3 cups chopped honeydew melon
1 cup chopped papaya
2 tablespoons lime juice
½ teaspoon unflavored gelatin
⅓ cup apple juice
1 cup heavy cream, whipped

Combine melon, papaya, and lime juice. Cover and allow to set for several hours.

Soak gelatin in apple juice. Place over low heat until gelatin is dissolved.

In a blender, combine fruit and its juice and the dissolved gelatin. Blend at medium speed until fruit is chopped fine but not pureed. Chill.

When mixture begins to thicken, fold in whipped cream and pour into container of ice cream freezer. Process until smooth and thick. Transfer to covered container and place in deep freeze to harden.

Yield: 6 servings

Tropical Ice Cream

Frozen and
Chilled
Desserts

Old-Fashioned Vanilla Custard Ice Cream

In a heavy-bottom saucepan, scald milk.

In a medium bowl, beat egg yolks lightly. Gradually add honey and arrowroot. Slowly stir the hot milk into the egg mixture. Return to saucepan, place over medium heat, and cook until thick. Cool, then chill for several hours.

When ready to freeze, add the vanilla. Beat egg whites and fold gently into the mixture.

Process in ice cream freezer until thick and creamy. Pack in covered container and place in deep freeze to harden.

Yield: 4 to 6 servings

1 quart milk
4 egg yolks
½ cup honey
1 teaspoon arrowroot
2 teaspoons vanilla
4 egg whites

Vanilla Ice Milk

In a saucepan, combine all ingredients. Stir over low heat until honey is dissolved. Cool, then chill in refrigerator or freezer.

Pour mixture into cream container of churn freezer and process until thick and smooth. Pack in covered container and place in deep freeze to harden.

Yield: 4 to 6 servings

1 quart milk
⅓ cup honey
1½ teaspoons vanilla
⅛ teaspoon salt

Frozen and
Chilled
Desserts

Spoon yogurt into cream can of ice cream freezer.

Puree fruit in an electric blender, add honey, then add the mixture to yogurt in the can.

Fruit Frozen Yogurt

Process for about 20 minutes, or until yogurt is thick and smooth. Remove from churn and place in plastic container, tightly covered. Put into deep freeze for several hours to harden.

Yield: 2 quarts

In using berries or any fruit which has small seeds, strain the pureed fruit before adding to the yogurt.

2 pints unflavored, natural yogurt
(homemade preferred)
¼ to ⅓ cup honey
1 cup fresh fruit of your choice (or frozen, unsweetened, thawed)

Combine water and honey in a small saucepan and boil for 5 minutes. Cool thoroughly.

Mix grapefruit juice, apricot puree, and lemon juice. Stir into the cold syrup. Pour into the container of an ice cream freezer and freeze to the consistency of soft mush.

Apricot-Grapefruit Sherbet

Remove lid from the container and stir in egg white. Re-cover and continue processing until stiff enough to serve.

If not serving immediately, store in freezer until about 15 minutes before serving.

Yield: 4 to 6 servings

Since the acidity of fruit varies, it is always wise to taste a sherbet before freezing to make sure it is sweet enough to suit the individual taste. Add honey if necessary.

1 cup water
⅔ cup honey
1¼ cups grapefruit juice
(freshly squeezed)
1 cup apricot puree
1 tablespoon lemon juice
1 egg white, beaten stiff

Frozen and Chilled Desserts

Cook cranberries with water until berries pop and become quite soft (about 15 minutes).

Soak gelatin in cold water.

Cranberry Sherbet

Force cranberries through a sieve, then add softened gelatin and honey. Stir until well blended. Cool. Add juice and chill until jelled. Beat in the milk.

Pour into ice cube trays and place in freezer until partly frozen. Remove from tray, beat again, and fold in egg whites. Return to tray and place in deep freeze for several hours.

Remove from freezer about 15 minutes before ready to serve.

Yield: 6 to 8 servings

1 pound cranberries (4 cups), fresh or frozen
2 cups water
1 envelope unflavored gelatin
¼ cup cold water
1 cup honey
2 cups unsweetened apple or grape juice
1 quart milk
2 egg whites, stiffly beaten

Frozen and Chilled Desserts

Put all ingredients into an electric blender, cover, and blend at medium speed until smooth. Pour mixture into a 9-inch-square baking pan, cover and freeze 1 to 2 hours, until mixture is frozen around the edge of the pan.

Lemon-Lime Buttermilk Sherbet

With a fork, beat mixture until smooth. Cover and freeze several hours, until firm.

1 quart buttermilk
¼ cup honey
2 tablespoons lemon juice
2 tablespoons lime juice
1 teaspoon finely grated lemon peel
1 teaspoon finely grated lime peel

Remove from freezer 10 to 15 minutes before serving to soften slightly.

Yield: 6 to 8 servings

This sherbet is very tangy in flavor. If you like the taste of buttermilk, you will find it very refreshing; if you prefer something sweet, skip this one.

Raspberry Sherbet

Mix all ingredients except egg whites and pour into can of freezer, churn until partly frozen, then fold in egg whites and continue to freeze. Pack in covered container and place in deep freeze for several hours.

Yield: 4 to 6 servings

2 cups fresh raspberries, mashed (or 2 cups frozen, unsweetened berries, thawed, drained, and mashed)
2 tablespoons honey
½ cup orange juice
1 quart whole milk
2 egg whites, stiffly beaten

Frozen and
Chilled
Desserts

2 cups light cream
⅓ cup RED CURRANT GLAZE
(see Index)
3 egg yolks
¼ cup honey
⅓ cup Cassis liqueur
1½ cups heavy cream

Scald the light cream in a saucepan. Add currant glaze and stir over medium heat until glaze is dissolved.

In a medium-size bowl, beat egg yolks until light and fluffy. Gradually add honey and beat until thick and smooth. Slowly pour the hot cream mixture into the egg mixture, stirring with a whisk. Beat until well blended.

Return mixture to saucepan, place over medium heat, stirring constantly until thick and smooth (about 5 to 7 minutes). Cool, then chill in a freezer for about 10 minutes. Stir in Cassis and refrigerate until cold.

Whip cream and fold into the mixture. Pour into container of ice cream freezer and process until thick and smooth. Spoon into tightly covered container and put into deep freeze to harden.

Yield: 4 to 6 servings

Cassis Sherbet

Grape
Ice

Put grape juice, lemon, and honey into bowl of blender. Blend on medium speed until lemon is pureed. Then add ice cubes and process at high speed until mixture is a snowy consistency.

Serve at once.

Yield: about 2 cups

1 cup unsweetened red grape juice
1 tablespoon chopped lemon, with peel
1 teaspoon honey
1 cup ice cubes (about 6)

Grapefruit
Ice

In a saucepan, combine water and honey. Bring to a boil and simmer 5 minutes. Add grapefruit juice, grapefruit peel, and lemon juice. Mix thoroughly and freeze either in refrigerator trays or in ice cream freezer.

Yield: 8 to 10 servings

3 cups water
1 cup honey
2 cups grapefruit juice
1 tablespoon grated grapefruit peel
½ cup lemon juice

Frozen and
Chilled
Desserts

1 cup orange juice
½ cup lemon juice
1 tablespoon chopped orange,
with peel
1 tablespoon chopped lemon, with peel
1 tablespoon honey
1½ cups ice cubes (about 9)

Put orange juice, lemon juice, orange pieces, lemon pieces, and honey in a blender and blend until fruit is pureed. Then add ice cubes and process at high speed until mixture is a snowy consistency.

Serve at once.

Yield: about 3 cups

Orange-Lemon Ice

¾ cup maple syrup
3 egg yolks
⅛ teaspoon salt
3 egg whites
1½ cups heavy cream, whipped
1 teaspoon vanilla

Heat syrup to boiling point in small saucepan. Beat egg yolks in a small bowl, then add about ¼ cup of the syrup to the yolks. Mix well and return mixture to hot syrup in pan. Over low heat, beat mixture until it is thick and light in color. Remove from heat.

Add salt to egg whites and beat stiff. Fold into syrup mixture. Chill for 1 hour.

Fold in whipped cream and vanilla. Pour into individual molds or ice cube tray and freeze without stirring. Remove from freezer and allow to stand at room temperature for 30 minutes before serving.

Yield: 6 servings

Frozen Maple Parfait

Frozen and Chilled Desserts

Basic Procedure for Making a *Bombe*

Chill the mold well before filling it. Line it with a one-inch-thick layer of ice cream, sherbet, or water ice, spreading it as evenly as possible. Add another flavor or type of ice in the same manner, then add a third flavor as a filling, spooning into the center until mold is completely filled. Cover and place in deep freeze for several hours to allow the *bombe* to harden and mellow.

When ready to serve, dip the mold quickly into very hot water. Dry the mold and invert it on a chilled serving platter. Garnish and serve immediately. Slice with a heated silver knife.

Vanilla-Carob-Raspberry *Bombe*

Line a well-chilled *bombe* mold with a 1-inch layer of OLD-FASHIONED VANILLA CUSTARD ICE CREAM (see Index). Add a second 1-inch layer of FRENCH CAROB ICE CREAM (see Index). Fill the center with RASPBERRY SHERBET (see Index).

Cover and freeze as directed in the Basic Procedure for Making a *Bombe*, above.

When ready to serve, unmold *bombe* and garnish it with raspberries marinated in Kirsch or Framboise.

Frozen and Chilled Desserts

Cut oranges in half crosswise and scoop out fruit. Freeze rind for about 4 hours.

Spread several tablespoons of vanilla ice cream in bottom of each orange half. Freeze again for 4 hours.

Stuffed Frozen Oranges

Place ½ teaspoon Cointreaux over ice cream in each half. Freeze again for 4 hours.

Cover with vanilla ice cream to within ¼ to ½ inch of top of rind. Freeze.

Fill to heaping with mound of ice or sherbet. Freeze.

When ready to serve, garnish with mint.

Yield: 6 servings

This attractive dessert is easy to make but it must be prepared in five steps to permit proper freezing.

3 large oranges
1 pint OLD-FASHIONED VANILLA CUSTARD ICE CREAM (see Index)
3 teaspoons Cointreaux
¾ cup ORANGE-LEMON ICE (see Index) or APRICOT-GRAPEFRUIT SHERBET (see Index)
fresh mint sprigs for garnish

Banana Cream Freeze

Mash the bananas and sprinkle them with lemon juice and honey. Blend together.

Whip the cream just until stiff.

Fold the banana mixture through the whipped cream. Pour into an ice cube tray and freeze until firm but not hard. Do not stir.

Yield: 4 servings

2 very ripe bananas
2 tablespoons lemon juice
1 to 2 tablespoons honey, to taste
1 cup heavy cream

Apricot Mousse

In a small saucepan, combine apricots, water, honey, and lemon. Bring to a boil, cover, and simmer for 20 minutes or until apricots are tender. Cool.

Place apricots and their juice in a blender, set at medium speed, and process until completely pureed.

Fold apricot puree into whipped cream, then spoon into individual dessert dishes, sherbet glasses, or *pot de creme* cups. Chill several hours.

Yield: 6 servings

1½ cups dried apricots
1 cup water
¼ cup honey
1 very thin slice of lemon with rind
1 cup heavy cream, whipped

Frozen and
Chilled
Desserts

4 bananas, mashed, about 1 to 1¼ cups
3 tablespoons lime juice
1½ to 2 tablespoons honey, to taste
1 teaspoon vanilla
1½ cups heavy cream, whipped
2 tablespoons natural cookie crumbs (optional)

Mash bananas and sprinkle with lime juice. Add honey and vanilla. Mix well.

Whip cream. Gently blend in the banana mixture.

Pour into sherbet glasses or *pot de creme* cups. Refrigerate at least 4 hours.

When ready to serve, top with cookie crumbs (if desired).

Yield: 6 servings

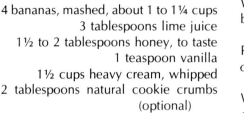

Banana Mousse

¼ cup honey
½ cup slivered almonds
4 eggs
¼ cup warmed honey
2 cups heavy cream, whipped

In a small, heavy skillet, heat honey. Add almonds and cook until mixture is golden brown, about 5 minutes. Spread mixture on plastic wrap, and allow to cool to room temperature. Chop into small pieces either by hand or in blender.

In the top of a double boiler, beat eggs lightly, then gradually add honey, a teaspoon at a time. Set over hot water and cook until thick, stirring with whisk or wooden spoon. Remove from heat and cool.

Stir in chopped almond mixture, then fold in whipped cream. Spoon into individual souffle cups or parfait glasses, and freeze for at least 4 hours. When ready to serve, allow to soften at room temperature for 5 or 10 minutes.

Yield: 6 or 8 servings

Toasted Almond Mousse

Frozen and Chilled Desserts

33

Put the egg yolks, honey, lime peel, and juice into the top of a double boiler. Mix well, then place over simmering water and cook 10 to 15 minutes, or until mixture is thick and smooth. Stir occasionally during cooking. Remove boiler from hot water and cool, then place in refrigerator for about 30 minutes.

Fresh Lime Mousse

In a large bowl, beat egg whites until stiff. Stir about one-quarter of the egg white into the chilled lime mixture. Then gently fold the lime mixture into the remaining egg white.

Fold cream into the mousse. Pour into a large serving bowl or into 6 individual sherbet or small parfait glasses. Cover and refrigerate several hours or overnight.

When ready to serve top with chopped nuts.

Yield: 6 servings

4 egg yolks
⅓ to ½ cup honey
2 tablespoons finely grated fresh lime peel
½ cup fresh lime juice
4 egg whites
1 cup heavy cream, whipped
¼ cup (about 1 ounce) chopped nuts (pistachios, cashews, or walnuts)

Frozen and
Chilled
Desserts

Basic Procedure for Making a Souffle Collar

For cold souffles, the wax paper collar and the souffle dish should be oiled; this is to permit easy unmolding if you choose to serve your souffle that way. The paper collar is made from a length of wax paper long enough to go around the dish with some overlap. Fold the paper in half lengthwise and brush the inside of the collar with oil. Attach the collar with string or with paper clips, fitting it securely and extending it about two inches above the dish.

Cold Fruit Souffle

1 envelope unflavored gelatin
2 tablespoons lemon juice
6 egg yolks
⅓ cup honey
1 cup pureed fruit (strawberries, raspberries, peaches, apricots or any seasonal fruit)
2 tablespoons Grand Marnier liqueur
6 egg whites, beaten stiff
1 cup heavy cream, whipped
fresh fruit for garnish

Prepare 1-quart souffle dish with collar (see the Basic Procedure for Making a Souffle Collar, above.

Soften gelatin in lemon juice.

In the top of a double boiler, beat egg yolks and honey until smooth and thick. Place over hot water, add softened gelatin, and continue to beat.

Add fruit puree and liqueur and stir until mixture thickens. Cool.

Fold in egg whites, then whipped cream. Spoon into prepared souffle dish and chill for at least four hours.

When ready to serve, remove collar and garnish with fruit.

Yield: 6 servings

In small saucepan, soften gelatin in water. Add lemon rind and juice, then honey. Stir over low heat until gelatin is dissolved. Chill until mixture starts to jell.

Prepare a 1-quart souffle dish with a collar of wax paper (see the Basic Procedure for Making a Souffle Collar on page 35).

Cold Lemon Souffle

Beat egg whites until stiff but not dry. Fold into the gelatin mixture, stirring carefully but thoroughly.

Fold the whipped cream into the mixture, reserving about ⅓ cup for decoration. Spoon mixture into prepared souffle dish and chill.

When ready to serve, remove paper collar, and decorate with a border of whipped cream, mint leaves, a sprinkling of crumbs, and the lemon slices.

Yield: 6 servings

1 envelope unflavored gelatin
2 tablespoons water
grated peel of 4 lemons (about ½ cup)
½ cup lemon juice, strained (this is the juice of 2 lemons)
½ cup honey
7 egg whites (about 1 cup)
1 cup heavy cream, whipped
mint leaves, 2 tablespoons natural cookie crumbs, and 7 or 8 very thin lemon slices for decoration

Frozen and
Chilled
Desserts

CHAPTER II

FRUIT AND FRUIT DESSERTS

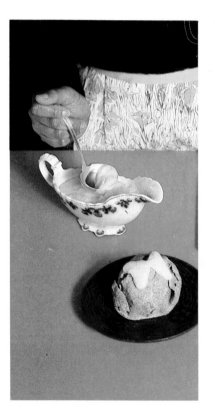

FRUIT AND FRUIT DESSERTS

I believe there is no finer treat than fresh, ripe fruit! It can bring pleasure to any part of the day—refreshing at breakfast, welcome as an accompaniment or dessert at lunch or dinner, and always perfect as a snack. The generous food values in fruits are famous. Who has not heard of the rich deposit of vitamin C in oranges, the potassium packed into bananas, the iron in raisins? These and many more essential nutrients appear in an easily assimilated form. Compared with most other desserts, fruits are also low in calories.

Uncooked sliced fruit is sometimes enhanced by adding a touch of honey or maple syrup or a well-chosen liqueur. The zest of lemon or orange may be added to bring out flavor.

A beautiful bowl of fresh fruits, carefully prepared and combined, makes a very attractive and nutritious dessert. Here are some appetizing combinations to try: grapefruit and orange sections with pears and grapes; pineapple cubes with strawberries; peaches, pears, and raspberries; and melon balls with pineapple cubes.

For a truly elegant and luscious finale to a fine meal, adopt the popular European custom of serving a beautiful bowl of fresh fruit with cheese. This tasty combination of flavors can also be used as a quick and elegant snack for unexpected guests.

In making up your fruit bowl be sure to include colorful combinations. Among the many choices open to you are grapes in tiny bunches; strawberries with stem or hull; pineapple peeled and sliced into quarter-rounds with core remaining for a finger-hold; apples cored but unpeeled, cut into wedges; pears, peaches, and apricots in season; and melon wedges.

Although any kind of cheese may be served with fruit, the semihard cheeses are probably the most satisfactory. Serve a variety so the individual can make a choice. Some of the most compatible ones are: Port Salut, Bel Pease, Reblochon, Chevre, or Munster. Roquefort or Blue Cheese, though powerful, also can be used.

Store cheese carefully to keep it in good condition. Soft cheeses and cream cheeses can be kept up to a week in the refrigerator. Most other cheeses should be kept in a cool—not cold—place or in the warmest part of the refrigerator. Semisoft cheeses should be wrapped tightly in a damp cloth, then put into a plastic bag. Blue cheese should be kept in an airtight container.

Always serve cheeses at room temperature; in fact, they should be brought out of their cool storage place and allowed to stand at room temperature for an hour or two to reach the height of flavor.

The wide variety of recipes which follow are representative of the many delightful desserts you can make using fruits. Always use fresh fruit when it is available; when it is not, I use frozen (unsweetened) or dried fruit. I use very little canned fruit, but when I do I choose unsweetened brands or drain the syrup from the sweetened ones.

Due to fast shipping techniques every kind of fresh fruit is available during most of the year. Pineapple, melon, apples, strawberries, and citrus fruit are shipped very successfully and can be ripened at room temperature at home. Place them loosely (so fruits are separated) in partially closed paper bags. Check them twice daily and when ripe, store in refrigerator.

Frozen fruit is improving in quality and availability and some companies are packing it without syrup. Unsweetened rhubarb, blueberries, strawberries, cranberries, and apricots can be found quite readily.

Dried fruit is now being packed sun-dried and unsulphured, making it a perfect natural food.

Stewed Apples in White Wine

Peel and core apples and cut into thick wedges. Melt butter in skillet which has a lid. Add apples and saute until golden; drizzle honey over apples. Add water, wine, salt, lemon peel, and nutmeg. Cover and simmer until apples are just tender, about 20 minutes. Cool.

Cover and refrigerate.

Yield: 6 to 8 servings

2 pounds apples
¼ cup butter
2 tablespoons honey
½ cup water
½ cup dry white wine
½ teaspoon salt
1 teaspoon grated lemon peel
¼ teaspoon ground nutmeg

Fruit and
Fruit Desserts

Soften yeast in lukewarm water. Add butter, honey, and salt. Blend in egg. Add flour and mix until dough is well blended and soft.

Roll out on well-floured board to ⅛-inch thickness. Cut into 8 6-inch squares.

Mix the honey, nuts, raisins, and cinnamon for filling.

Fill each apple with filling and dot with butter.

Apple Dumplings

Place an apple in the center of each square of dough; moisten edges, bring corners together, and seal at the top. Place on greased baking sheet, cover with cloth, and let rise in warm place for 45 minutes.

Preheat oven to 350° F.

Bake dumplings for 1 hour in preheated oven.

Serve immediately, topped with LEMON CUSTARD SAUCE (see Index).

Yield: 8 servings

Basic Dough
1 package yeast
½ cup lukewarm water
⅓ cup melted butter
2 tablespoons honey
2 teaspoons salt
1 egg
2 cups whole wheat flour

8 apples, peeled and cored

Filling
¼ cup honey
¼ cup chopped nuts
¼ cup raisins
1 teaspoon cinnamon
butter

Fruit and
Fruit Desserts

Apple and Grapefruit Dessert

In a medium-size saucepan, bring apple juice to a boil. Add apples, bring again to a boil, and cook 2 minutes. Remove from heat and cool.

Add grapefruit and chill.

Serve in individual dessert dishes or sherbet glasses and garnish with sprigs of fresh mint.

Yield: 6 servings

(One medium-size apple yields 1 cup chopped apple)

1½ cups unsweetened apple juice
4 cups diced apples (peel only if skins are tough)
2 grapefruit, cut into sections
fresh mint for garnish

Apples Stuffed with Prune-Nut Filling

Cook prunes in water in covered pan for about 25 minutes.

Cool, drain, and pit prunes. Pour cooking juice into the bowl of a blender, add prunes, and puree. Transfer to a mixing bowl and add walnuts, honey, butter, lemon juice, and spices.

Wash and core apples and place in an 8- or 9-inch round, flat-bottom casserole.

Preheat oven to 300° F.

Place about 2 tablespoons of the prune filling in cavity of each apple. Combine water and honey and pour into pan around apples. Bake in preheated oven for about 1 hour, or until apples are tender.

Serve with pan juice.

Yield: 6 servings

1 cup prunes
water to cover
¼ cup chopped walnuts
1 tablespoon honey
1 tablespoon softened butter
1 teaspoon lemon juice
¼ teaspoon cinnamon
⅛ teaspoon ginger
⅛ teaspoon ground cloves
6 large baking apples
1½ cups water
⅓ cup honey

For a specially appealing flavor, add 2 tablespoons peanut butter to filling.

2 cups fresh whole-grain bread crumbs
⅓ cup melted butter
4 medium-size bananas, thinly sliced
2 tablespoons honey
½ teaspoon nutmeg
½ teaspoon cinnamon
1 tablespoon grated lemon peel
2 tablespoons lemon juice
½ cup grated, unsweetened coconut
1 cup light cream

Preheat oven to 375° F. and grease a 1½-quart casserole.

Mix bread crumbs with butter. Arrange a third of the crumbs in the bottom of the prepared casserole. Cover with half of the bananas. Mix honey, nutmeg, cinnamon, and lemon peel. Drizzle half the mixture over the bananas.

Layer another third of the crumbs, then the remaining bananas, and the rest of the honey mixture. Pour lemon juice over the whole mixture.

Combine the remaining crumbs with coconut and sprinkle over the top of the casserole.

Bake, uncovered, for about 35 minutes or until golden brown.

Serve warm with light cream.

Yield: 6 servings

Banana-Coconut Betty

How to Select and Prepare a Fresh Coconut

Select a coconut which is a rich brown color, then shake it to make sure it is full of liquid. This means it is moist and fresh.

To open the coconut, puncture the indentations (which are sometimes called "eyes") with an ice pick. Invert the coconut over a large tumbler or bowl and allow the liquid to drain into the container. Reserve this liquid to be used later as a drink or as the base for dessert sauce.

Heat the punctured coconut in a heavy saucepan or in a 400° F. oven for about 15 minutes. Remove from the heat, and place on a heavy cutting board, then split with a mallet or hammer. The dry shell will fall away from the moist meat.

With a very sharp knife, peel away the thin, brown skin from the coconut meat and grate on a medium-fine grater.

If you want to keep the fresh coconut for a few days after it is grated, place it in a jar, cover it with the coconut liquid, seal and store in the refrigerator until ready to use. Drain off the liquid and use as recipe directs.

Fruit and
Fruit Desserts

With a sharp knife, peel oranges, taking off the outside membrane. Slice crosswise into very thin slices.

Peel and core pears, and cut into slices about ¼ inch thick. Peel and core pineapple slices, and cut into pieces about 1½ inches wide. Peel and slice bananas about ¼ inch thick.

4 navel oranges
3 ripe pears
6 ½-inch slices fresh pineapple
3 bananas
1 cup orange juice
¼ teaspoon almond extract or
3 tablespoons Strega
1 cup grated, fresh coconut

In a large serving bowl, layer fruit, ending with oranges. Mix orange juice and flavoring, pour over fruit, and chill for several hours to allow flavors to blend.

When ready to serve, top with a generous layer of coconut.

Yield: 6 to 8 servings

Fresh Fruit Ambrosia

Baked Bananas

Preheat oven to 350° F. and butter a shallow baking dish.

Peel bananas and cut in half horizontally. Arrange in the prepared baking dish. Sprinkle with mixture of butter, honey, lemon juice, and peel. Bake in preheated oven for 15 to 20 minutes.

Yield: 4 servings

Baked bananas are very rich; they can be served at the end of the meal or as a side dish with chicken or pork.

4 medium-size bananas
1 tablespoon butter, softened
1 tablespoon honey
1 teaspoon lemon juice
½ teaspoon grated lemon peel (optional)

Blueberry Buckle

Preheat oven to 350° F. and grease an 8 × 8-inch pan.

Cream together butter, honey, egg, and salt. Add flour, soda, and buttermilk or yogurt. Mix well.

Spread in prepared pan and cover with berries.

Mix butter, honey, flour, and cinnamon into crumbs. Spread over blueberries.

Bake in preheated oven for about 40 minutes. Cut into squares.

Yield: 6 to 8 servings

¼ cup butter
¼ cup honey
1 egg
dash of salt
1 cup whole wheat pastry flour
1 teaspoon soda
⅓ cup buttermilk or yogurt
1 pint blueberries (2 cups fresh or frozen)
¼ cup butter
2 tablespoons honey
⅓ cup whole wheat pastry flour
½ teaspoon cinnamon

Fruit and
Fruit Desserts

1 envelope unflavored gelatin
¼ cup cold water
3 tablespoons honey
1 tablespoon BASIC CAROB SYRUP
(see Index)
¼ teaspoon salt
1 cup hot coffee
1 tablespoon lemon juice
1 cup sliced dates
¼ cup chopped walnuts
½ cup cream, whipped
½ teaspoon vanilla

Soak gelatin in cold water. Add honey, carob, salt, hot coffee, and lemon juice. Stir until gelatin is dissolved. Chill.

When gelatin begins to thicken, add dates and nuts. Fold in the vanilla and half of the whipped cream. Chill.

When ready to serve, unmold onto fancy plate and garnish with remaining whipped cream.

Yield: 6 servings

Molded Date Delight

Preheat oven to 325° F. and grease a 9- or 10-inch round baking dish.

Arrange fruit in casserole, alternating to mix flavors.

8 fresh peach halves, peeled and pitted
8 fresh pear halves, peeled and cored
2 cups fresh pineapple cubes
⅓ cup butter
2 teaspoons curry powder
⅓ cup honey

Melt butter; add curry and honey. Spoon over fruit and bake in preheated oven, uncovered, for about 1 hour.

Serve warm.

Yield: 6 to 8 servings

Curried Fruit Bake

This dish is an excellent dessert or a very tasty accompaniment to hot or cold meat. It can be made with frozen or canned fruit but, of course, fresh is best. If you must use frozen, be sure to use unsweetened fruit; if canned, drain off the syrup.

Fruit and Fruit Desserts

Southwestern Fruit Cup

Combine fruit. Pour apple or grape juice over all. Chill.

When ready to serve, drain fruit, reserving ½ cup of liquid, and put fruit into sherbet or large wine glasses. Combine reserved juice with lemon juice and salad oil. Drizzle over the fruit in each glass and garnish with fresh mint leaves.

Yield: 6 servings

1½ cups fresh pineapple cubes
¾ cup avocado balls
1½ cups grapefruit segments
1 cup unsweetened apple or white grape juice
1 tablespoon lemon juice
2 tablespoons salad oil
fresh mint leaves for garnish

Grapes in Sour Cream

Stem grapes, wash, and drain. Place in large bowl. Add sour cream and toss until grapes are coated. Chill.

When ready to serve, spoon into individual dessert dishes, sherbet glasses, or large wine glasses. Garnish with mint leaves.

Yield: 6 servings

3 cups seedless green grapes
½ to ¾ cup sour cream
fresh mint leaves for garnish

Fruit and
Fruit Desserts

54

Cover prunes with cold water and soak overnight. Simmer in the same water until tender and plump. Remove prunes from juice and pit.

1 cup prunes
1 tablespoon honey
½ cup orange juice
6 unpeeled kumquats, sliced

In a saucepan, combine honey, ½ cup of the cooking juice from prunes, orange juice, and the kumquats. Simmer about 5 minutes, then add prunes. Toss to combine fruits. Serve hot or cold.

Yield: 4 servings

Stewed Kumquats and Prunes

In a small saucepan, sprinkle gelatin over cold water. Add honey, place over low heat, and stir until gelatin is dissolved. Remove from heat. Add orange juice, lemon juice, and wine. Chill until mixture starts to jell, then fold in melon and grapes. Pour into 6-cup ring mold and chill until firm.

2 envelopes unflavored gelatin
2 cups cold water
½ to ⅔ cup honey, to taste
1 cup orange juice
¼ cup lemon juice
⅓ cup Port wine
2 cups cantaloupe balls
1 cup seedless green grapes
fresh mint leaves for garnish

Unmold and decorate with fresh mint leaves.

Yield: 6 to 8 servings

Melon Ball Ring

Fruit and
Fruit Desserts

Orange Charlotte

Soak gelatin in cold water. Add boiling water and stir until gelatin is dissolved. Add honey, lemon juice, and orange juice. Mix well. Chill.

Beat egg whites until stiff. Fold into mixture as it begins to set.

Whip cream until stiff. Fold into gelatin mixture. Pour into sherbet glasses and chill for several hours.

Garnish with mint leaves.

Yield: 6 servings

1½ envelopes unflavored gelatin
¼ cup cold water
½ cup boiling water
½ cup honey
¼ cup lemon juice
1 cup orange juice
3 egg whites
1 cup heavy cream
mint leaves for garnish

Oranges Amandine

Peel oranges, section or slice, and place in a serving bowl.

Sprinkle with orange juice and maple syrup. Chill for about 2 hours.

When ready to serve, top with almonds.

Yield: 6 servings

6 large oranges
¼ cup orange juice
½ teaspoon maple syrup
⅓ cup slivered, toasted almonds

Fruit and
Fruit Desserts

4 cups sliced fresh peaches
2 tablespoons honey
1 egg, well beaten
1 tablespoon tapioca granules
1 cup whole wheat pastry flour
1 teaspoon soda
¼ teaspoon salt
1 tablespoon butter, softened
⅓ cup buttermilk

Combine peaches, honey, egg, and tapioca.

Preheat oven to 425° F. and grease a 9-inch round baking dish.

Spread peach mixture evenly over bottom of baking dish.

Combine flour, soda, salt, butter, and buttermilk. On a well-floured board, roll dough to ½-inch thickness. Prick dough with a fork and place loosely over peaches. Bake in preheated oven for 20 to 30 minutes.

Serve warm, topped with CUSTARD SAUCE (see Index).

Yield: 6 servings

Peach Cobbler

2 packages frozen raspberries (unsweetened), thawed
8 fresh peach halves or 1 29-ounce can, drained
3 egg whites
1 tablespoon warmed honey

Put raspberries on the bottom of a large, flat serving dish. Prepare peaches.

Beat egg whites until stiff but not dry. Add honey slowly and continue to beat until smooth and glossy.

Preheat oven to 450° F. and grease a shallow baking dish.

Place peaches, cut side up, in the prepared baking dish, top each with a mound of egg whites, and bake in preheated oven for 4 to 5 minutes.

Remove peaches carefully and float on the raspberries in the serving dish.

A beautiful presentation!

Yield: 8 servings

Peach Meringue with Raspberries

Fruit and
Fruit Desserts

Baked Pears with Almonds and Yogurt

Preheat oven to 350° F. and grease a 9-inch baking dish.

Core and slice pears (do not peel unless skins are tough or if you want the dessert to be especially fancy). Arrange the slices of pears in attractive rows in the prepared dish. Mix honey and vanilla and drizzle over pears; top with the almonds and dot with butter. Bake in preheated oven 10 to 15 minutes or until pears are tender. Baste frequently during the baking, using the accumulated juice.

Serve hot or cold, topped with yogurt.

Yield: 6 servings

6 firm, ripe pears
¼ to ⅓ cup honey, depending on sweetness of pears
1 teaspoon vanilla
½ cup slivered almonds
2 tablespoons butter
1 cup yogurt

Ginger-Baked Pears and Apricots

Preheat oven to 325° F.

Drain pears and apricots, reserving liquid.

In a 2-quart round casserole, arrange pears around the edge with cut side down and narrow end toward the center. Fill in center of casserole with apricots.

Mix ginger, honey, and cornstarch and ¾ cup of the fruit juice. Pour over fruit. Top with lemon slices. Bake, uncovered, for about 30 minutes. Chill.

Yield: 6 servings

1 1-pound 14-ounce can unsweetened pear halves
1 1-pound 14-ounce can unsweetened apricots (or 2 cups frozen)
½ teaspoon ground ginger
1 tablespoon honey
1 teaspoon cornstarch
4 very thin lemon slices, with peel

Fruit and
Fruit Desserts

1 quart fresh strawberries
1 cup heavy cream
1 teaspoon honey
1 tablespoon rum or brandy or a
liqueur such as Kirsch, Framboise,
Chartreuse, or Cointreau

Wash berries, hull, and drain on paper towels.

Whip cream, add honey, then fold in liqueur.

When ready to serve, fold berries into cream and spoon into individual dessert dishes or one large serving bowl.

Yield: 6 servings

Chantilly is technically fresh, sweet cream whipped and lightly sweetened. It can be flavored with vanilla but using a liqueur gives it a subtle elegance which enhances the flavor of the fruit.

Strawberries Chantilly

In the top of a double boiler, with a hand beater or an electric beater set at medium speed, beat egg yolks until thick. Gradually add honey, beating until mixture is light and thick. Place over hot water, continue to beat, and slowly add the Grand Marnier. Continue beating for about 5 minutes, or until mixture is fluffy.

4 egg yolks
1 tablespoon honey
¼ cup Grand Marnier
⅓ cup heavy cream, whipped
1 quart fresh strawberries, washed,
hulled, and dried on paper towel

Remove from heat and set boiler in pan of ice water. Beat until custard mixture is cool. Fold in whipped cream, cover, and chill.

Place prepared berries in a large serving bowl or individual dessert dishes. Stir chilled sauce and pour over the fruit.

Yield: 6 servings

Strawberries Sabayon

Pineapple Fruit Basket

Select ripe pineapples, allowing one-half or one-quarter per person, depending on size of pineapple. Cut in half or quarters lengthwise, including top. Scoop out pulp and cut into cubes or small wedges, leaving shell intact. Combine pineapple pieces with:

melon balls
orange segments
strawberries, blueberries, or raspberries
avocado slices

Heap mixed fruit in pineapple shells, piling high.

Serve topped with APRICOT SAUCE (see Index) or FOAMY SAUCE (see Index).

Fruit and
Fruit Desserts

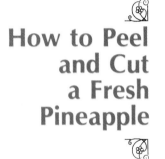

How to Peel and Cut a Fresh Pineapple

Select a pineapple which is golden brown in color, soft to the touch and which smells sweet.

With a large, sharp knife, cut the pineapple into 1-inch slices, starting at the bottom to enable you to use the top as a hand-hold.

Using a smaller sharp knife, peel each slice and remove any eyes which might remain. Cut in half and remove core. Use in half-slices or cut into 1-inch cubes, as desired.

If your pineapple is ripe and the knives sharp, this whole process can be completed in 5 minutes.

Fruit and
Fruit Desserts

Broiled Fresh Pineapple

1 whole, fresh pineapple
2 teaspoons honey
2 teaspoons butter

Slice pineapple, skin and all, into ½-inch slices. Peel the slices and cut out the eyes. Place on a buttered baking sheet, drizzle honey over the slices, and dot with butter.

Broil about 5 to 7 minutes, or until slightly browned.

Yield: about 4 servings
(allowing 2 slices for each serving)

Fresh Pineapple Melba

3 cups chopped, fresh pineapple
3 cups white seedless grapes
½ cup RASPBERRY SAUCE (see Index)
fresh mint leaves for garnish

Combine pineapple and grapes, and chill.

When ready to serve, put fruit into individual dessert dishes or sherbet glasses, cover with RASPBERRY SAUCE, and garnish with mint.

Yield: 6 servings

Fruit and
Fruit Desserts

63

Preheat oven to 350° F. and grease 8 × 8 × 2-inch baking pan.

Arrange rhubarb in prepared pan. Mix orange juice and honey and drizzle over rhubarb. Dot with butter.

Rhubarb Sweetie

In a medium-size mixing bowl, combine egg, honey, vanilla, and sour cream. Mix flour, salt, and soda and add to egg mixture.

Spread batter over rhubarb and bake in preheated oven for about 30 minutes, or until nicely browned.

Yield: 6 to 8 servings

3 cups diced, fresh rhubarb (or 3 cups frozen, thawed)
2 tablespoons orange juice
⅓ cup honey
1 tablespoon butter
1 egg, beaten
¼ cup honey
1 teaspoon vanilla
2 tablespoons sour cream
1 cup whole wheat pastry flour
¼ teaspoon salt
½ teaspoon soda

Grind cranberries in food grinder and combine with honey. Cover and chill overnight. Add apples, grapes, walnuts, and salt. Fold in whipped cream; chill for several hours.

Cranberry Waldorf

Serve garnished with clusters of green grapes and whole, fresh cranberries, if desired.

Yield: 6 to 8 servings

2 cups (½ pound) fresh cranberries
⅓ cup honey
2 cups diced, tart apples, unpared
1 cup seedless green grapes, halved
½ cup chopped English walnuts
¼ teaspoon salt
1 cup heavy cream, whipped

Fruit and Fruit Desserts

2 cups fresh cranberries
(or frozen, thawed)
½ cup honey
1 teaspoon ground cinnamon
1 teaspoon grated orange peel
½ cup water
4 egg yolks
3 tablespoons warmed honey
¼ cup whole wheat pastry flour
1 teaspoon vanilla
4 egg whites, beaten stiff

Preheat oven to 375° F., and butter a 9-inch pie or flan pan.

In a saucepan, combine cranberries, honey, cinnamon, orange peel, and water. Bring to boiling and cook, uncovered, until berries pop open, about 5 minutes. Let cool, then lift out cranberries and place them in the prepared pan. Reserve juices.

Beat egg yolks until light and fluffy, then add honey and beat again. Sift in flour, then add vanilla and mix gently until smooth. Carefully fold in egg white.

Pour custard over berries, and bake in preheated oven for 25 minutes, until lightly browned. Serve immediately.

Serve reserved juices in a small pitcher to be poured over each serving if desired.

Yield: 4 to 6 servings

Baked Cranberry Puff

In a medium-size bowl, mix the almonds, honey, flour, wheat germ, and salt. Add butter and work into the mixture with your fingers until well blended and crumbly. Refrigerate while preparing the fruit.

Plum Crisp

Preheat oven to 400° F. and butter a 9 x 9-inch baking dish.

Arrange the plums cut side up in the baking dish. Sprinkle them with the lemon juice and honey. Spoon the almond mixture over the fruit and bake on the middle shelf of the oven for 35 to 40 minutes, or until top is crisp and lightly browned. Cool 15 minutes or longer before serving. Serve with yogurt or sour cream.

Yield: 6 to 8 servings

½ cup chopped, blanched almonds
1 tablespoon honey
½ cup whole wheat flour
2 tablespoons wheat germ
¼ teaspoon salt
¼ cup butter, diced
2 pounds fresh red or purple plums, pitted and sliced
1 tablespoon lemon juice
1 tablespoon honey, or more (to taste)
1 cup plain yogurt or sour cream

Fruit and
Fruit Desserts

CHAPTER III

CUSTARDS, PUDDINGS, AND SOUFFLES

CUSTARDS, PUDDINGS, AND SOUFFLES

Milk and eggs combined and prepared in different ways are the foundation for a variety of popular, nutritious, inexpensive, and interesting desserts.

Custards

There is no mystery about custards, but, somehow, inexperienced cooks are timid when it comes to working with them. The techniques are simple. Basically, custard is a mixture of beaten eggs and milk, flavored in many different ways and cooked slowly (mostly over hot water) or baked in an oven. The surest way to make a perfect custard on the top of the stove is to use a double-boiler. The water in the bottom of the boiler should always be very hot but not boiling. A heavy-bottom stainless steel saucepan can be used successfully, too, if you are very careful to keep the heat low and stir constantly.

If your custard curdles, it is because the water boiled or the custard was overcooked. To correct this, simply beat with a whisk or hand beater; the custard will be thinner than usual but will be smooth.

If you are baking your custard in an oven, place the mold, casserole, or custard cups in a pan and pour boiling water around the mold to a depth of about one inch. The water will provide the very slow, steady heat it takes to make a perfect custard.

To save fuel, custards can be baked in a skillet. Put a double thickness of paper towels in the bottom of a heavy skillet which has a tight-fitting cover. Pour in cold water to a depth of about three-quarters of an inch. Set the container of custard in the water, cover the skillet, and bring the water to a boil. Then turn the heat off immediately and allow custard to steam until set (about 15 to 20 minutes).

Puddings

Puddings—like custards—are usually prepared in the top of a double boiler or in a saucepan which has a heavy bottom. These are the utensils which best provide for very slow cooking, which is important. The base of every pudding is milk, but the thickening agents might be cornstarch, arrowroot, whole wheat flour, and (occasionally) gelatin. Grains, such as rice, tapioca, and barley or meals, such as farina and cornmeal, can also be used for thickening.

Puddings are quick and simple to prepare and need no special equipment or technique. The only precaution is to cook slowly and stir constantly.

Steamed Puddings

A steamed pudding for dessert is especially appealing in cold weather. Sometimes these puddings are made with suet, particularly by the English, which gives them a hearty and distinctive flavor. You can easily get suet for this purpose from your butcher or the supermarket meat section.

The textures of steamed puddings vary from light and delicate to sturdy and filling; all are wholesome and nutritious.

Hot Souffles

A souffle has only a few fleeting moments of perfection. It must be served as soon as it is baked or it will fall. It is said that a souffle which is sturdy enough to stand long without falling is not delicate enough to be great.

The base of a souffle may be made well in advance and stored, covered, so a dry skin cannot form on the surface. At the last moment all you need do is fold in the egg whites and place the souffle in the oven while you are having your dinner. The hot souffle can be carried right to the table—a most spectacular presentation.

To make an even, fairly firm souffle, bake at 325° F. for 30 to 40 minutes. To make a souffle with a crusty top and soft center, bake at 375° F. for 20 minutes.

4 eggs
1 quart milk, scalded
2 cups cottage cheese
¼ cup honey
1 teaspoon vanilla
3 tablespoons whole wheat flour
½ teaspoon salt

Preheat oven to 325° F. and grease an 8-inch round, glass baking dish.

In a medium-size bowl, beat eggs lightly. Add scalded milk and stir until well blended.

Put cottage cheese through a sieve, then add it to the milk-egg mixture. Add honey and vanilla.

Mix flour and salt and add to the custard. Pour into baking dish, set dish in larger pan, and pour boiling water into the pan to a level of about 1½ inches.

Bake in preheated oven for about 1½ hours or until a knife inserted in center of custard comes out clean. Cool.

Yield: 6 to 8 servings

Cheese Custard

Custards,
Puddings,
and Souffles

Put milk into a large saucepan, add barley, cover, and cook slowly for about 30 minutes or until barley is tender.

Preheat oven to 350° F.

Barley-Prune Custard

Beat eggs, add honey, vanilla, salt, and chopped prunes.

Slowly stir egg mixture into barley and cook over very low heat for 5 minutes, stirring constantly. Put mixture into individual custard cups and sprinkle lightly with cinnamon.

Bake in preheated oven 10 to 15 minutes or until custard is set. Cool and refrigerate.

Yield: 4 to 6 servings

1 quart milk
¼ cup barley
2 eggs
2 tablespoons honey
½ teaspoon vanilla
pinch of salt
¼ cup chopped prunes
cinnamon for decoration

Put milk in a medium-size saucepan. Add gelatin, carob, honey, and salt. Place over medium heat until gelatin is completely dissolved, stirring constantly. Remove from heat and add vanilla. Stir briskly with a wire whisk until well blended.

Carob Chiffon Pots

Pour mixture into a blender, add ice cubes, and blend at medium speed until ice cubes have melted. Stir once or twice to be sure mixture is completely blended. Allow to stand for about 5 minutes until pudding starts to jell.

1½ cups milk
2 envelopes unflavored gelatin
3 tablespoons carob powder
4 teaspoons honey
pinch of salt
2 teaspoons vanilla
1 cup ice cubes (6 to 8)
¼ cup heavy cream, whipped
1 tablespoon finely chopped nuts

Spoon into *pots*, custard cups, or parfait glasses. Chill. When ready to serve, top with whipped cream and finely chopped nuts.

Custards, Puddings, and Souffles

Yield: 4 to 6 servings

3 cups milk
3 tablespoons cornstarch
2 egg yolks
⅓ cup honey
3 tablespoons BASIC CAROB SYRUP
(see Index)
3 tablespoons whole wheat flour
1 teaspoon vanilla
1 tablespoon butter
2 egg whites, beaten stiff

Mix ½ cup milk with cornstarch. In a saucepan, heat remaining milk. Meanwhile, in a small bowl, mix egg yolks, honey, carob syrup, and flour. Blend well, then add to heated milk. Add cornstarch mixture and cook until thick (about 8 minutes), stirring constantly.

Remove from heat and add vanilla and butter. Cool and transfer to oven-proof dish. Cover with beaten egg whites and set under broiler for about 5 minutes, or until meringue browns slightly.

Yield: 6 servings

Carob Cream

6 egg yolks
½ cup honey
6 tablespoons whole wheat flour
2 tablespoons Madeira
5 cups milk, scalded
1 teaspoon grated lemon peel
1 teaspoon vanilla
⅛ teaspoon salt
2 tablespoons butter
½ cup natural cookie crumbs

In the top of a double boiler, beat egg yolks until light and fluffy. Add honey, flour, and Madeira. Place over hot water and slowly add the milk. Blend well. Add lemon peel, vanilla, and salt. Cook, stirring constantly until mixture thickens. Remove from heat and stir in butter. Cool.

Spoon into sherbet glasses and chill. When ready to serve, sprinkle crumbs over each serving.

Yield: 8 servings

Cookie crumbs make an attractive topping for most puddings and custards. Save all your broken bits and crumbs, place in a jar in the refrigerator, and use as needed for decoration and a tasty touch.

Madeira Custard Cream

Custards, Puddings, and Souffles

75

Preheat oven to 350° F. and butter a 2-quart casserole.

Prepare peaches.

In the top of a double boiler, over hot but not boiling water, heat milk.

Peach-Rice Custard

In a small bowl, beat eggs lightly. Add honey, salt, nutmeg, and cinnamon. Add slowly to hot milk and cook, stirring constantly with a wooden spoon or wire whisk, for 15 minutes or until it starts to thicken. Remove from heat and add rice. Mix well.

Pour half the rice mixture into the prepared casserole, top with half the peaches, then cover with another layer of rice and then the remaining peaches.

Bake in preheated oven for 10 to 15 minutes, until custard is set.

Serve warm or cold, with pouring cream or milk, if desired.

Yield: 6 servings

4 cups sliced fresh peaches (or frozen, unsweetened and well drained)
1½ cups milk
2 eggs
2 tablespoons honey
½ teaspoon salt
½ teaspoon nutmeg
½ teaspoon cinnamon
2 cups cooked brown rice

Custards,
Puddings,
and Souffles

Rice Custard

Preheat oven to 350° F. and oil 6 individual custard cups.

Combine eggs, salt, and honey. Add milk slowly, stirring constantly, until mixture is smooth.

Add vanilla, rice, lemon peel, and raisins. Pour into custard cups and sprinkle nutmeg on top of each. Place in pan of hot water and bake in preheated oven 30 to 40 minutes, or until knife inserted in center of custards comes out clean.

Yield: 6 servings

3 eggs, lightly beaten
¼ teaspoon salt
⅓ cup honey
3 cups scalded milk
½ teaspoon vanilla
1 cup cooked brown rice
½ teaspoon grated lemon peel
½ cup raisins
dash of nutmeg for decoration

Pennsylvania Dutch Potato Custard

Preheat oven to 350° F. and grease a 1-quart casserole.

In a medium-size bowl, combine potatoes, butter, honey, and salt; stir to a creamy consistency. Add egg yolks, milk, lemon peel, and juice. Mix well, then fold in egg whites.

Pour into casserole and bake in preheated oven for about 25 minutes.

Yield: 4 servings

1½ cups mashed potatoes, freshly cooked or warmed
2 tablespoons butter, softened
⅓ cup honey
⅛ teaspoon salt
2 egg yolks, beaten
½ cup milk
grated peel of ½ lemon
juice of ½ lemon
2 egg whites, stiffly beaten

Custards,
Puddings,
and Souffles

Sherry Bavarian Cream

1 envelope unflavored gelatin
1¾ cup milk
2 to 3 tablespoons sherry
1 to 2 tablespoons honey
⅛ teaspoon almond extract
2 egg whites

In a medium-size saucepan, over low heat, combine gelatin and milk. When gelatin is dissolved, remove from heat and pour into mixing bowl. Stir in sherry, honey, and almond extract. Chill until mixture begins to thicken. Beat egg whites until stiff and fold into gelatin mixture. Chill.

Yield: 4 servings

Strawberry Cream

¼ cup cold milk
2 envelopes unflavored gelatin
½ cup unsweetened apple or grape juice, heated
2 tablespoons honey
1 quart fresh strawberries, or 1 16-ounce package, frozen (unsweetened)
2 egg yolks
1 cup heavy cream
1 cup ice cubes

Pour cold milk into blender container, add gelatin and hot juice. Cover and process at low speed for about 1 minute. Remove cover and add honey, berries, and egg yolks. Process until berries are pureed. Add the cream and ice, then process at medium speed until ice is completely liquified.

Pour immediately into individual dessert dishes or sherbet glasses. Allow to set for at least 5 to 10 minutes before serving.

Yield: 6 to 8 servings

The blender system is very easy and quick, and produces a dessert which is attractive and delicious. Combining the ice with the mixture hastens the jelling process and makes the pudding very smooth.

Custards,
Puddings,
and Souffles

Spanish Cream

In the top of a double boiler, scald milk. Slowly add gelatin and honey. Pour a few tablespoonfuls over egg yolks, then add egg mixture to the milk mixture in the boiler. Place over hot water and cook until thick and smooth. Remove from heat. Add salt and vanilla, then fold in egg whites. Pour into a large mold and chill.

The mixture will form two layers as it sets. When ready to serve, invert mold onto a large serving plate. Cover mold with a cloth dipped in hot water and wrung out. Allow to stand until molded cream drops onto plate.

Yield: 6 to 8 servings

3 cups milk
1½ envelopes unflavored gelatin
¼ cup honey
3 egg yolks, slightly beaten
¼ teaspoon salt
1 teaspoon vanilla
3 egg whites, beaten stiff

Custards,
Puddings,
and Souffles

Buttermilk Pudding

In a small bowl, soften gelatin in cold water. Add boiling water and stir until dissolved.

Combine egg, honey, and buttermilk, then blend with the gelatin mixture. Chill until it starts to thicken. Fold in whipped cream. Pour into a 1½-quart casserole and refrigerate until set.

Yield: 4 to 6 servings

2 envelopes unflavored gelatin
¼ cup cold water
¼ cup boiling water
1 egg, beaten
¼ cup honey
1½ cups buttermilk
½ cup heavy cream, whipped

Coconut Rice Pudding

In a 1½-quart casserole, combine milk, rice, salt, lemon peel, and molasses or honey. Bake, uncovered, at 300° F. for about 3 hours. Stir occasionally with a fork. After the second hour, add the coconut and butter. Serve hot or cold in individual dessert dishes.

Yield: 6 servings

Fresh coconut makes this pudding superb; if you prefer, it can be made with dried, unsweetened coconut.

4 cups milk (or 3 cups milk and 1 cup coconut milk)
¼ cup raw brown rice
½ teaspoon salt
grated peel of half a lemon
⅓ cup molasses or honey
1 cup grated, fresh coconut
1 tablespoon butter

Custards,
Puddings,
and Souffles

Preheat oven to 400° F.

Place milk in saucepan; add carob and salt. Heat over low heat and beat with hand beater or whisk until well blended.

In a large bowl, put 1 whole egg and 2 yolks (put 2 whites in small bowl and set aside for meringue). Beat the eggs slightly, then add honey. Gradually add carob mixture and vanilla. Add bread cubes and let stand for about 10 minutes. Turn mixture into a 1½-quart casserole and set in a pan of hot water which comes halfway up the sides of the casserole. Bake in preheated oven 1 hour.

3¾ cups milk
3 tablespoons carob powder, sifted
½ teaspoon salt
3 eggs
⅓ cup honey
1 teaspoon vanilla
4½ cups stale whole-grain bread cubes
½ teaspoon warmed honey

Carob-Cream Bread Pudding

Beat egg whites until foamy. Add warmed honey very slowly and continue to beat until stiff. Pile meringue in mounds on top of pudding. Return to oven and bake another 5 to 10 minutes or until lightly browned. Serve warm or cold.

Yield: 4 to 6 servings

Custards,
Puddings,
and Souffles

In the top of a double boiler, scald milk, then add dates.

Date Caramel Cream

Mix cornstarch, cold milk, and salt. Add to hot milk and cook over simmering water until thickened, stirring constantly. Cover and continue to cook for 10 minutes. Mix eggs and honey and add to hot mixture. Cook 1 minute longer.

Remove from heat, add nuts and vanilla, and pour into individual serving dishes. Chill.

Yield: 4 to 6 servings

1¾ cups milk
½ cup sliced dates
⅓ cup cornstarch
¼ cup cold milk
¼ teaspoon salt
1 egg, beaten lightly
2 tablespoons honey
¼ cup chopped nuts
½ teaspoon vanilla

Maple Walnut Tapioca Pudding

In the top of a double boiler, combine milk, tapioca, salt, and maple syrup. Cook over hot water for 15 minutes, stirring frequently. Stir a few spoonfuls of the hot mixture into the beaten egg yolk. Mix well, then add to the rest of the hot pudding. Cook and stir for about 3 minutes, then remove from the hot water and cool. Add chopped nuts and fold in egg whites. Cool and refrigerate.

Yield: 6 servings

If desired, this pudding may be topped with whipped cream, sour cream, or yogurt.

2 cups milk
¼ cup tapioca granules
¼ teaspoon salt
⅓ to ½ cup maple syrup, according to taste
1 egg yolk, beaten
½ cup chopped walnuts
1 egg white, beaten stiff

Custards, Puddings, and Souffles

Preheat oven to 350° F. and butter a 2-quart ring mold.

In a heavy-bottom saucepan, combine milk, honey, butter, vanilla bean, and salt. Bring the mixture to a boil and slowly sprinkle in the farina, stirring constantly. Cook slowly for about 20 minutes, stirring from time to time. Turn the mixture into a bowl and remove the vanilla bean. Add 2 tablespoons butter and the egg yolks. Mix well, then fold in egg whites.

1 quart milk
¼ cup honey
3 tablespoons butter
1-inch piece of vanilla bean
½ teaspoon salt
1 cup farina
2 tablespoons butter
6 egg yolks, well beaten
4 egg whites, beaten stiff

Farina Pudding

Sprinkle the prepared mold with a little dry farina and fill it with the pudding. Set the mold in a pan of boiling water and place in the preheated oven. Bake for about 25 minutes.

Allow pudding to stand for 10 minutes, then unmold onto a serving plate. Serve with SOUR CREAM ORANGE SAUCE (see Index).

Yield: 6 to 8 servings

Custards,
Puddings,
and Souffles

Preheat oven to 350° F.

In a medium-size bowl, beat egg yolks lightly. Add butter and honey. Stir in flour, then add lemon juice and milk. Fold in egg whites.

Lemon Cake-Top Pudding

Pour into 5 ungreased, individual custard cups. Place cups in baking pan, pour water into the pan around the cups to a level of about halfway up the sides of the cups. Bake in preheated oven for about 35 minutes.

Yield: 5 servings

2 egg yolks
1 tablespoon softened butter
⅓ cup honey
2½ tablespoons whole wheat flour
¼ cup lemon juice
1 cup milk
2 egg whites, beaten stiff

Custards,
Puddings,
and Souffles

Peach Delight

Preheat oven to 375° F.

In a 1½-quart casserole, stir together peaches, honey, salt, nutmeg, cinnamon, lemon juice, and tapioca. Add boiling water or juice.

Bake in preheated oven for 30 minutes, or until tapioca is soft and clear, stirring occasionally during cooking.

Serve warm or cold, topped with whipped cream.

Yield: 4 servings

3 cups sliced, fresh peaches
2 teaspoons honey
¼ teaspoon salt
⅛ teaspoon nutmeg
¼ teaspoon cinnamon
2 tablespoons lemon juice
¼ cup tapioca granules
1 cup boiling water or fruit juice
⅓ cup heavy cream, whipped

Pineapple Rice Cream

In the top of a double boiler, combine rice, milk, honey, and salt. Mix well. Place over hot, not boiling, water. Cover and cook slowly until rice is soft and creamy (about 1¼ hours). Stir occasionally during cooking.

Remove from heat and cool. Add pineapple chunks and mix well. Cover and refrigerate at least several hours.

When ready to serve, fold in whipped cream and vanilla.

Turn into large serving bowl.

Yield: 8 to 10 servings

1 cup raw brown rice
4 cups milk
¼ cup honey
⅛ teaspoon salt
1 small can (8¼-ounce) pineapple chunks, drained
½ cup heavy cream, whipped
1 teaspoon vanilla

Custards,
Puddings,
and Souffles

½ pound prunes
2 cups hot water
⅓ cup honey
⅛ teaspoon salt
½ teaspoon cinnamon
½ cup boiling water
⅓ cup cornstarch
¼ cup cold water
1 tablespoon lemon juice
1 cup light cream

Place prunes in a saucepan, cover with hot water, and let stand for 1 hour. Place over low heat and simmer until soft. Remove pits, then return prunes to cooking water. Add honey, salt, cinnamon, and boiling water. Simmer 10 minutes.

Mix cornstarch with cold water to make a smooth paste. Add to prune mixture and cook for 5 minutes, stirring constantly. Add lemon juice.

Pour into a large serving dish and chill. Serve with light cream on the side.

Yield: 6 servings

Norwegian Prune Pudding

⅓ cup butter
4 cups grated, raw sweet potato
¼ teaspoon salt
⅔ cup honey
1½ cups milk
½ cup chopped nuts
1 cup raisins or chopped prunes
½ teaspoon cloves
1 teaspoon allspice
1 teaspoon cinnamon
3 eggs, well beaten
1½ cups light cream (optional)

Preheat oven to 350° F. and grease a 2-quart casserole.

In a medium-size saucepan, melt butter. Add sweet potatoes, salt, honey, milk, nuts, raisins or prunes, and spices. Place over low heat, and stir until mixture is well heated. Add eggs slowly, stirring constantly.

Pour mixture into the prepared casserole and bake in preheated oven for 30 to 40 minutes.

Serve hot or cold, with light cream, if desired.

Yield: 8 servings

Grated Sweet Potato Pudding

Custards,
Puddings,
and Souffles

89

Creamy Peanut Butter Pudding

In a small bowl, mix cornstarch with ½ cup milk.

In a medium-size saucepan, over moderate heat, heat remaining 1½ cups milk. When milk is just under boiling, add peanut butter, honey, and salt. Mix thoroughly, then stir in cornstarch mixture and continue cooking about 5 minutes, until thick and creamy. Pour about ½ cup of the hot mixture into the beaten egg, then return this mixture to the saucepan and cook 1 minute longer.

Remove pan from heat, add vanilla, and beat about 1 minute. Cool.

Pour into individual dessert dishes, cover, and refrigerate several hours before serving.

Yield: 4 servings

2 tablespoons cornstarch
½ cup milk
1½ cups milk
¼ cup peanut butter
¼ cup honey
⅛ teaspoon salt
1 egg, beaten
1 teaspoon vanilla

Custards,
Puddings,
and Souffles

To prepare a steamed pudding you need a large pudding mold or a casserole which has a lid. If you prefer to use individual molds, they may be covered with parchment paper or aluminum foil (but the cover must *not* touch the pudding). Coffee cans can also be used.

Whatever type of container you decide to use, butter the inside of it lightly and fill it only about two-thirds full to allow for rising and expansion.

For steaming, select a pot at least four inches larger than your pudding containers so you will have about two inches of space on each side of the mold. Place a rack or steamer basket in the pot and then put the mold or molds on the rack. Pour boiling water into the pot, around the mold, until it comes halfway up the sides of the mold. Cover the large pot and adjust the heat so that the water remains at the boiling point throughout the steaming period. Steam the length of time suggested in the recipe.

Basic Procedure for Steamed Pudding

Steamed Blueberry Pudding

Mix flour, soda, and salt, then add oil, bread crumbs, and honey. Add egg and milk and mix thoroughly.

Fold in blueberries, pour into a greased 1-quart mold, cover tightly, and steam for 2 hours (see Basic Procedure for Steamed Pudding on page 91).

Serve with MAPLE SYRUP PUDDING SAUCE (see Index).

Yield: 6 servings

1 cup whole wheat pastry flour
1 teaspoon baking soda
½ teaspoon salt
½ cup oil
½ cup dry whole-grain bread crumbs
¼ cup honey
1 egg, well beaten
⅔ cup buttermilk or yogurt
1½ cups blueberries

Custards,
Puddings,
and Souffles

In a medium-size bowl, cream together butter and honey, then add buttermilk and coconut. Fold in egg whites.

Mix flour, soda, and salt and add to first mixture.

Coconut Mounds

Butter 4 or 5 custard cups and fill about ⅔ full with the batter. Steam in covered pot (see Basic Procedure for Steamed Puddings on page 91) for about 20 minutes.

Unmold immediately onto individual serving plates. Serve hot or cold covered with APRICOT SAUCE (see Index) or RASPBERRY SAUCE (see Index).

Yield: 4 or 5 servings

½ cup butter, softened
¼ cup honey
¼ cup buttermilk
½ cup grated, unsweetened coconut
2 egg whites, beaten stiff
1 cup whole wheat pastry flour
½ teaspoon soda
¼ teaspoon salt

Steamed Fig Pudding

Chop the suet and figs and mix them together with a wooden spoon or with your hands. Soak the bread crumbs in milk and add to the suet mixture. Beat in the eggs, add honey, and mix thoroughly. Pour into a mold which has a tight-fitting lid. Cover and place in steamer (see Basic Procedure for Steamed Pudding on page 91). Cover and steam for 3 hours.

Unmold the hot pudding by inverting the mold on a serving plate. Serve with RUM-RAISIN SAUCE (see Index) or HONEY BRANDY SAUCE (see Index).

Yield: 4 to 6 servings

½ cup ground beef suet
2 cups dried figs
3 cups fresh whole-grain bread crumbs
½ cup milk
3 eggs
⅓ cup honey

Steamed Fruit Pudding

In a large bowl, combine egg, honey, salt, butter or oil, and pineapple juice. Stir in raisins, nuts, dates, and vanilla. Mix well.

Mix together flour, nutmeg, and cinnamon. Add to the first mixture. Mix soda and yogurt and add to the batter.

Pour into a well-greased 1-quart mold, cover and steam for 1 hour (see Basic Procedure for Steamed Pudding on page 91).

Remove from steamer and transfer to a 250° F. oven. Bake for 1 hour.

Unmold the pudding by inverting the mold onto a large serving plate.

Serve with FOAMY SAUCE (see Index).

Yield: 6 servings

1 egg, well beaten
¼ cup honey
½ teaspoon salt
3 tablespoons butter or oil
1 cup unsweetened pineapple juice
½ cup chopped raisins
½ cup chopped nuts
1 cup chopped dates
1 teaspoon vanilla
1½ cups whole wheat flour
¼ teaspoon nutmeg
1 teaspoon cinnamon
¾ teaspoon soda
¼ cup yogurt

Custards,
Puddings,
and Souffles

To prepare pudding

In a small saucepan over very low heat, combine milk and raisins and heat for 20 minutes. Allow to cool to room temperature.

Sift together flour, soda, salt, nutmeg, and cinnamon.

In a large bowl, beat eggs until light. Gradually add honey and beat until smooth. Add bread crumbs and suet, and mix well. Stir in milk-raisin mixture, then add yogurt. With wooden spoon, fold in flour mixture.

Grease a 2-quart pudding mold which has a tube. Pour in batter (batter will be stiff), cover tightly, and steam for 2 hours (see Basic Procedure for Steamed Puddings, page 91).

Remove mold from pot. Let stand for about 10 minutes. With a knife, loosen pudding around edges and tube and turn out onto a large serving plate. Serve immediately, topped generously with sauce (see below).

Yield: 10 servings

To prepare sauce

In the top of a double boiler, beat butter until creamy. Add honey and continue to beat until light. Set over hot water.

Beat in egg, cream, and nutmeg. Cook, stirring constantly, until smooth and thick.

Remove from heat and stir in whiskey. Serve warm or cold.

Yield: 2 cups

Pudding
1 cup milk
1½ cups raisins, chopped
1½ cups whole wheat pastry flour
1 teaspoon soda
½ teaspoon salt
1 teaspoon nutmeg
½ teaspoon cinnamon
3 eggs
½ cup honey
1½ cups fresh whole-grain bread crumbs
1 cup grated suet
½ cup yogurt

Sauce
¼ cup soft butter
½ cup honey
1 egg
1 cup light cream
dash of nutmeg
¼ cup Irish whiskey

Steamed Raisin Pudding
with
Irish Whiskey Sauce

Custards,
Puddings,
and Souffles

Basic Procedure for Hot Souffles

In spite of its reputation for being a difficult and temperamental dish, a souffle is simple to make. The secret is in the egg whites—how they are beaten and how they are folded into the base. Always have whites at room temperature and beat them by hand so you can beat more air into them and make them fluffier. Beat only until moist, not stiff and dry.

Fold the eggs in by moving the spoon down through the mixture along the bottom of the pan toward you, lifting the sauce from the bottom to the top. Continue the process until sauce and egg whites are well mixed.

To bake a souffle it is important to use a straight-sided baking dish to encourage the souffle to rise easily as it cooks. For hot souffles, do not butter the dish. Fill two-thirds full if you want the souffle to just fill the dish. For an impressive effect, use a smaller souffle dish, tie a 3- to 4-inch collar of wax paper around the top edge of it, and fill to the top of the dish. During the baking, the souffle will rise in the collar. When baking is completed, remove the collar carefully and serve immediately.

Another system (which is the one I prefer) is to make a deep cut all around the souffle mixture about an inch from the edge of the dish. Do this just before placing the souffle in the oven. As the souffle bakes, the center will rise higher than the edge, forming a crown somewhat like a man's hat.

Bring the water to a boil in a large saucepan. Stir in ½ teaspoon salt and the rolled oats. Cook for 5 minutes over moderate heat, stirring constantly. Remove from heat, cover, and let stand for 5 minutes.

Meanwhile, heat oven to 400° F., and butter a 2-quart souffle dish.

3 cups water
1 teaspoon salt
1⅓ cups rolled oats
4 egg yolks
2 tablespoons honey
1½ tablespoons freshly grated lemon peel
4 egg whites

With a wooden spoon, beat egg yolks into rolled oats, 1 at a time. Add the remaining salt, the honey, and the lemon peel.

In a clean, dry bowl, beat the egg whites until stiff peaks form when beater is lifted. Gently fold egg whites into rolled oats mixture. Turn mixture into prepared souffle dish and bake 30 to 35 minutes, until puffed and beginning to brown.

Yield: 4 to 6 servings

Oatmeal Souffle

Custards,
Puddings,
and Souffles

In a medium-size saucepan, melt butter and stir in flour. Blend well, then add scalded milk, mix well, and remove from heat. Add egg yolks, one at a time and beat in carefully. Add honey, carob syrup, coffee, and brandy or rum. Return to low heat and cook for 1 minute. Cool.

Preheat oven to 325° F.

Beat egg whites until stiff but not dry. Carefully fold whites into mocha mixture. Pour into unbuttered 1½-quart souffle dish, or a collared 1-quart souffle dish. Bake on the center rack of preheated oven for about 35 to 40 minutes. Serve immediately.

Yield: 6 servings

Mocha Souffle

3 tablespoons butter
3 tablespoons whole wheat pastry flour
1 cup milk, scalded
6 egg yolks
¼ cup honey
2 tablespoons BASIC CAROB SYRUP (see Index)
2 tablespoons instant powdered coffee
2 tablespoons brandy or rum
7 egg whites

Custards,
Puddings,
and Souffles

In the top of a double boiler, heat carob syrup, honey, and butter. Place over hot water and mix until smooth. Stir in the flour and salt, then gradually add the milk. Cook to the boiling point, stirring constantly.

Remove from heat and pour over egg yolks. Beat well and set aside to cool.

Carob Souffle

When it is time to bake the souffle, preheat oven to 325° F.

Beat egg whites until stiff but not dry. Add vanilla. Fold into the souffle mixture and pour into a collared 1-quart souffle dish (see Basic Procedure for Hot Souffles on page 98). Bake in preheated oven for 30 to 40 minutes.

Serve with whipped cream.

Yield: 4 or 5 servings

4 tablespoons BASIC CAROB SYRUP (see Index)
2 tablespoons honey
2 tablespoons butter
2 tablespoons whole wheat pastry flour
¼ teaspoon salt
¾ cup milk
3 egg yolks, well beaten
3 egg whites
½ teaspoon vanilla
½ cup heavy cream, whipped

Irish Coffee Dessert

Soak gelatin in cold water. Add honey, coffee, and whiskey. Pour into coffee cups or *pot de creme* cups and chill until set.

When ready to serve, top with a dollop of whipped cream.

Yield: 4 to 6 servings

2 envelopes unflavored gelatin
½ cup cold water
3 to 4 tablespoons honey, to taste
2 cups strong coffee
1 cup Irish whiskey
½ cup cream, whipped, for topping

Custards,
Puddings,
and Souffles

½ cup melted butter
¼ cup molasses
1 tablespoon honey
1 egg, lightly beaten
1 cup grated raw carrots
1 teaspoon grated lemon peel
½ cup golden raisins
½ cup chopped prunes or dates
1¼ cups whole wheat pastry flour
½ teaspoon salt
½ teaspoon nutmeg
½ teaspoon ginger
1 teaspoon soda
¾ cup APRICOT SAUCE (see Index)

Preheat oven to 350° F. and butter 6 individual custard cups or molds.

In a medium-size bowl, mix butter, molasses, honey, egg, carrots, lemon peel, raisins, and prunes or dates.

Sift together remaining ingredients, except APRICOT SAUCE, then stir into first mixture. Spoon into molds, and bake in preheated oven for 30 to 35 minutes.

Unmold onto individual dessert plates, top with APRICOT SAUCE, and serve immediately.

Yield: 6 servings

This spicy pudding is very much like a steamed pudding but takes only a short time to prepare and bake.

Baked Carrot Pudding

Custards,
Puddings,
and Souffles

CHAPTER IV

CAKES

CAKES

Cake recipes, more than most other kinds, are traditionally cherished and passed down from generation to generation with pride and love. Techniques and equipment may change, but the basic, appetizing, soul-satisfying results that follow when baking ingredients are properly combined, remain as pleasurable as they have been for hundreds of years.

Those who enjoy baking know that skill and accuracy are much more important in cake baking than in any other dessert preparation. First, the recipe must be balanced perfectly, then the measurements must be exact. I think it's wise to read the recipe carefully before starting anything. That way you know exactly what you're getting into.

Assemble the ingredients and be sure you have the size pan the recipe calls for. If it is different, the given baking time will be wrong. It isn't necessary to have a lot of fancy equipment, but you do need measuring cups and spoons so that you can measure with assurance: too much shortening, sweetening, or leavening may cause a cake to fall; too much flour or too little liquid will make a cake rise unevenly and become tough and dry.

Be sure all cake ingredients are at room temperature when you add them; eggs will have greater volume and butter will cream faster and become fluffier.

If you are new to natural cooking a few of the cake ingredients might be different from what you've been using: we use butter or vegetable oil, never processed shortening or margarine; honey, molasses, or maple syrup in place of sugar; whole wheat or whole wheat pastry flour for bleached flour; and carob instead of cocoa or chocolate. Cooking with these ingredients is not difficult and, in many cases, they are used in the same way as the less desirable ingredients would be.

The old-fashioned method of adding the dry ingredients to the batter alternately with the liquid is still a good one. It blends the ingredients well without overmixing and will produce an even-textured cake.

If recipe calls for beaten egg whites they are usually folded into the batter last. Never beat them in, always use a folding, under-over motion and do not overfold.

Pour or spoon the batter into the prepared pans, making sure it covers the area completely. Spread the batter toward the sides and into the corners, leaving the center slightly lower. This will guarantee a flat-topped cake. Fill pans about two-thirds full.

The oven should be preheated to the desired temperature before the cake is put in. Assemble the ingredients and utensils for mixing and baking the cake, then turn on the oven just before mixing. This method has the advantage that once the mixing process has begun, it need not be interrupted.

Butter cakes should be allowed to stand in the pan for about five minutes after removing from the oven. They should then be taken from the pan carefully and allowed to cool right-side-up on a wire rack. If wax paper is used, it should be removed as soon as cakes are taken from the pan.

Store cakes in a covered container away from other foods which might absorb the moisture.

Icebox or refrigerator cakes are really cake-like molded desserts, made with gelatin and either sponge cake or cake crumbs.

Tortes are rich, rather heavy cakes, with only eggs for leavening. They are made up of thin layers, each separated by fruit glaze or whipped cream. They may or may not be iced.

Upside-down cakes are made by covering the bottom of the baking pan with a light syrup and fruit base, then topping that with a simple moist batter. To serve, these cakes are usually cut into squares, fruit side up, and topped with whipped cream.

Angel and sponge cakes give the illusion of richness but, actually, they are made without shortening and without leavening; the air beaten into the eggs serves as the leavening agent.

Buns and most breakfast cakes are made from yeast dough. Usually, they are neither very sweet nor rich and go well with coffee. You will find recipes for a few unusual ones, popular in particular areas and certainly worth trying.

Doughnuts are an American favorite. To avoid deep-frying, we've created a recipe for baked doughnuts. Add more sweetening if you wish, or a combination of mace and orange peel. For a new and delicious flavor try dipping the doughnuts into a mixture of maple syrup and cinnamon while they are still hot.

Muffins are distinguished from biscuits by their slight sweetness. They may be served with any meal or at snack time or teatime. To give muffins a special flavor, drop a teaspoon of peanut butter into muffin tins before pouring in the batter, or top with a teaspoon of fruit sauce before placing them in the oven.

Icings and Cake Fillings
Icing a cake can be fun! Children love to do it. The cake should always be cooled thoroughly before it is iced and loose crumbs should be brushed away. Crumbs in the frosting make it look lumpy. Use a flexible spatula for spreading the frosting. Frost between the layers, then the sides of the cake, then pile the remaining icing on top and spread to the edges in attractive swirls and dips.

Many cakes are complete without an icing, but for some icing or filling greatly complements the flavor. Particular icings are suggested for some of the cakes in this section, but you should feel free to make your own selection from the recipes given.

Basic Procedure for Natural-Ingredient Cakes

First, cream butter, then *add warmed honey* and beat with wire whisk, hand beater, or electric mixer. (I like to use a whisk—it is so easy and blends ingredients so quickly to a smooth mixture.) Add eggs and beat until the mixture is thick, fluffy, and quite pale in color. *Using honey will make the mixture just a little thinner than it would be with sugar, but it will be very smooth, light, and creamy.*

This is the point in cake mixing where it is impossible to overbeat, so be sure to beat until you have the desired texture and color. Flavoring may be added at this time.

The whole wheat flour must be lightened in body before it is measured and added to the batter. This can be done by stirring lightly with a whisk or by sifting. In sifting whole wheat flour you might find a lot of bran particles left in the sifter. Don't let that worry you, simply put them back into the flour or add them directly to the batter after the flour has been added.

The benefits of sifted flour are so important to the accuracy of measurement and to the texture of the cake, this little extra step is well worth the effort. If salt, soda, and spices are indicated, they should be sifted with the flour.

If carob is used in a recipe, it is added either in powdered form, the way you would use cocoa, or it is added as BASIC CAROB SYRUP (see Index), which is very easy to blend into any batter. In the latter form it is used to replace melted bitter chocolate.

1 envelope unflavored gelatin
¼ cup cold water
3 egg yolks, beaten
1 cup canned, crushed pineapple
with juice
2 tablespoons lemon juice
1 teaspoon grated lemon peel
2 tablespoons honey
½ teaspoon salt
1 cup dry cottage cheese (not creamed)
1 cup natural cookie crumbs
2 tablespoons honey
3 tablespoons melted butter
3 egg whites, beaten stiff

Soften gelatin in cold water.

In the top of a double boiler, combine egg yolks, pineapple, lemon juice and peel, honey, and salt. Cook over hot water until thick, stirring constantly. Add softened gelatin and stir until dissolved. Remove from heat and add cottage cheese. Chill until partially set.

Mix cookie crumbs, honey, and butter and press into a greased 6 x 10-inch pan, saving a few crumbs for top.

Fold egg whites into partially set dessert, then pour into crumb-lined casserole. Sprinkle remaining crumbs on top. Chill.

Yield: 6 servings

Canned pineapple must be used; fresh or frozen pineapple cannot be used with gelatin.

Pineapple Refrigerator Cake

Dessert Cakes and Small Cakes

Soak gelatin in water. Split ladyfingers and line bottom and sides of a straight-sided one-quart baking dish with the split halves (or with slices of sponge cake).

In the top of a double boiler, with wire whisk or fork, beat egg yolks until thick and lemon colored. Gradually add honey, lemon peel, and juice. Add boiling water slowly. Place over boiling water and cook to custard stage (until thick and smooth). Remove from hot water. Add gelatin which has been soaked in water. Stir with whisk until gelatin is dissolved completely. Allow to cool slightly.

Lemon Icebox Cake

Beat egg whites until stiff but not dry; fold them into custard. Pour lemon filling into cake-lined mold and set in refrigerator several hours or overnight.

Just before serving, unmold onto large plate, and cover the top and sides of the dessert with whipped cream or sour cream, spreading as you would to ice a cake. Garnish with the fruit.

Yield: 6 servings

If you serve this dessert on a lovely, fancy, crystal plate, you can serve it right at the dinner table. It looks very appetizing and luscious, and yet it is light enough to be served after a heavy meal. Another plus is that it can be prepared a whole day ahead.

1 envelope unflavored gelatin
2 tablespoons cold water
12 LADYFINGERS or thin slices of SPONGE CAKE (see Index)
4 egg yolks
⅓ cup honey
grated peel of 1 lemon
juice of 1 lemon
4 tablespoons boiling water
4 egg whites
1 cup heavy cream, whipped, or 2 cups sour cream
1 pint fresh strawberries, raspberries, or pitted, red, sweet cherries

Dessert Cakes and Small Cakes

Using heavy-bottom skillet which has a tight-fitting lid, on medium low heat (or use an electric skillet set at 250°), melt butter. Then stir in honey and simmer until well mixed and beginning to thicken. Arrange apricots over the mixture, with cut side down. Cover with nuts.

Apricot Upside-Down Skillet Cake

Cream butter and honey together, then add eggs one at a time, beating until smooth. Add vanilla. Combine buttermilk or yogurt with soda. Add to creamed mixture. Add flour and mix well.

Pour batter over the apricots, spreading evenly. Cover with lid (with vent open) and bake for 40 to 50 minutes. Remove immediately by inverting a large cake plate over pan and turning upside down.

Serve warm or cold, topped with sour cream, if desired.

Yield: 6 to 8 servings

3 tablespoons butter
¼ cup honey
2 cups fresh apricot halves (or 8-ounce package frozen halves, thawed)
¼ cup chopped nuts
½ cup butter or oil
⅔ cup honey
2 eggs
1 teaspoon vanilla
¼ cup buttermilk or yogurt
½ teaspoon soda
1¾ cups whole wheat pastry flour
½ cup sour cream for garnish (optional)

Dessert Cakes and
Small Cakes

Grease an 8 x 8-inch pan and line with parchment paper.

Cream butter or oil with honey. Blend in 1 tablespoon orange peel and ½ teaspoon vanilla. Spread in prepared pan. Coarsely chop cranberries (in blender or food grinder) and mix with 2 tablespoons honey and the orange juice. Spread over the mixture in the pan.

Preheat oven to 350° F.

Mix flour, soda, and salt. Mix honey, oil, buttermilk, orange peel, and vanilla. Add to flour mixture. Mix well and add egg. When completely blended, pour over cranberries in pan.

Bake in preheated oven for about 30 minutes.

Remove from pan immediately by inverting onto serving plate. Peel off parchment paper.

Serve warm or cold.

Yield: 6 to 8 servings

Cranberry Upside-Down Cake

¼ cup butter or oil
⅓ cup honey
1 tablespoon grated orange peel
½ teaspoon vanilla
1½ cups fresh cranberries
    (or frozen, thawed)
2 tablespoons honey
2 tablespoons orange juice
1 cup plus 1 tablespoon whole
    wheat flour
1 teaspoon soda
½ teaspoon salt
⅓ cup honey
¼ cup oil
½ cup buttermilk
1 tablespoon grated orange peel
1 teaspoon vanilla
1 egg

Dessert Cakes and
Small Cakes

Preheat oven to 350° F. and grease a deep 9-inch pie pan or casserole.

Sift flour, soda, and salt. Cut in butter with 2 knives, sharp spoon, or pastry blender. Beat egg, honey, and buttermilk; stir lightly into flour mixture. (Dough will be stiff.)

Dutch Apple Cake

Place apples in baking pan, sprinkle with honey and cinnamon. Dot with remaining butter and spread dough over them.

Bake in preheated oven for 45 minutes. Loosen cake from sides and bottom and turn out onto a cake plate immediately.

Serve warm, topped with LEMON CUSTARD SAUCE (see Index).

Yield: 6 servings

Fresh peaches, pears, or cherries may be substituted for apples in this recipe. Follow the same procedure, but change the amount of honey if necessary.

2 cups whole wheat pastry flour
1 teaspoon soda
½ teaspoon salt
¼ cup butter
1 egg
2 tablespoons honey
1 cup buttermilk
3 cups thinly sliced apples
2 to 3 tablespoons honey, depending on sweetness of apples
1 teaspoon cinnamon
1 tablespoon butter

Dessert Cakes and Small Cakes

Preheat oven to 350° F. and butter 2 9-inch layer-cake pans, line with wax or parchment paper, and butter the paper.

In a medium-size bowl, beat egg yolks, add honey and vanilla. Continue to beat until mixture is thick and light in color, about 5 minutes.

5 egg yolks
¼ cup honey
½ teaspoon vanilla
¾ cup whole wheat pastry flour
5 egg whites, beaten stiff
2 tablespoons melted butter, cooled
1 quart fresh strawberries; hulled, washed, and drained, or 20 ounces frozen (unsweetened), thawed and drained
1 cup heavy cream, whipped
½ cup RED CURRANT GLAZE (see Index)

Sift flour into yolk mixture. Gently fold in egg whites, then add butter, stirring only until mixed—do not overmix.

Divide the batter into the prepared pans and bake in preheated oven for 10 to 15 minutes, until lightly browned.

Remove from oven and turn out onto cake rack. Cool about 5 minutes, then peel off paper. Cool completely.

Slice about 1 cup of berries and add to 1 cup of whipped cream. Place 1 layer of cake on a flat serving plate, spread with mixture of berries and cream. Place second layer of cake on top. Cover top and sides of cake with remaining whipped cream. Combine remaining berries and glaze and spread over top of whipped cream as garnish.

Chill torte for at least 1 hour before serving.

Yield: 8 to 10 servings

Strawberry Torte

Dessert Cakes and Small Cakes

Preheat oven to 350° F. and grease an 8 x 8-inch baking pan.

In a mixing bowl, beat egg yolks until light. Add honey, farina, crumbs, and nuts. Fold in egg whites. Pour batter into prepared pan and bake in preheated oven for 15 to 20 minutes or until lightly browned.

Farina Torte

Remove from oven and allow to cool. Butter a round 1-quart mold or small, deep bowl. Break cake into 1½-inch pieces and layer into mold alternately with whipped cream until all is used. Press lightly with a wooden spoon to fill mold solidly. Chill until ready to use.

Run a knife around sides of mold and invert over fancy cake plate. Cake should drop out easily. Cover top and sides with whipped cream and garnish with fruit or nuts.

Yield: 6 servings

3 egg yolks
¼ cup honey
⅜ cup farina
2 tablespoons dry, whole-grain
    bread crumbs
½ cup chopped nuts
3 egg whites, beaten stiff
1 cup heavy cream, whipped
½ cup heavy cream, whipped
    (additional for topping)
¾ cup chopped fruit, berries,
    or nuts for garnish

Preheat oven to 325° F.

Rinse a large mixing bowl in warm water and dry very thoroughly.

Separate eggs carefully, putting whites into warmed bowl. Beat with a wire whisk until frothy, then add salt and cream of tartar and continue to beat until whites are very smooth, shiny, and stiff but not dry. Add almond extract. Gradually beat in warmed honey and mix thoroughly.

Angel Food Cake

Sprinkle flour by tablespoonful over the surface of whites, using a spatula to fold flour into mixture. Do not overmix.

Spoon the batter into ungreased 9- or 10-inch tube pan. Set on middle rack of preheated oven and bake about 1 to 1¼ hours, or until top is lightly browned.

Invert pan on cake rack and allow to cool. When cooled completely, loosen with knife or spatula and turn onto cake rack.

Yield: 8 to 10 servings

Angel food keeps well. It may be served plain or with LEMON ICING (see Index).

10 egg whites (about 1⅓ cups)
    at room temperature
½ teaspoon salt
½ teaspoon cream of tartar
½ teaspoon almond extract
½ cup warmed honey
1 cup whole wheat pastry flour, sifted

Dessert Cakes and
Small Cakes

Preheat oven to 350° F. and grease 3 8-inch layer-cake pans.

Cream butter, add honey, and beat until smooth and light. Add eggs one by one, beating thoroughly after each addition. Add bananas and nuts.

Banana Nut Cake

Mix flour, soda, and salt and sift into mixture. Stir in yogurt and vanilla.

Pour batter into prepared pans and bake in preheated oven for 30 minutes. Cool layers slightly, then remove from pans and cool completely. Fill and ice with WHITE FROSTING or LEMON ICING (see Index).

Yield: 12 to 14 servings

¾ cup butter
¾ cup honey
3 large eggs
4 medium-size bananas, mashed
   (about 1¼ cups)
½ cup chopped nuts
3⅛ cups whole wheat pastry flour
1 teaspoon soda
½ teaspoon salt
⅓ cup yogurt
1 teaspoon vanilla

Preheat oven to 325° F., and grease 2 9-inch layer-cake pans.

In a medium-size bowl, cream butter until light and fluffy. Add honey, then BASIC CAROB SYRUP. Mix well.

Sour Cream Carob Cake

Mix flour, salt, and soda together and add to creamed mixture. Add sour cream and vanilla and beat until smooth. Fold in egg whites. Pour into prepared pans and bake in preheated oven for about 30 minutes.

Cool slightly, then remove from pans, and place on wire rack to cool completely.

Spread FRENCH COFFEE FROSTING (see Index) between layers and on top and sides of cake.

½ cup butter
1 cup honey
¾ cup BASIC CAROB SYRUP
   (see Index)
1¾ cups whole wheat pastry flour
½ teaspoon salt
½ teaspoon soda
½ cup sour cream
1 teaspoon vanilla
3 egg whites, beaten stiff

Dessert Cakes and Small Cakes

Yield: 8 to 10 servings

Preheat oven to 350° F. and grease and flour a 9-inch round springform pan.

In a mixing bowl, cream butter, add honey, and beat until light and smooth. Add buttermilk or yogurt.

Sift together the flour and carob powder. Add to the creamed mixture. Stir in vanilla. Mix soda with hot coffee and add to batter. Stir in nuts.

Pour batter into prepared pan and bake in preheated oven for 35 minutes. Allow to cool for 5 minutes, then remove ring and set cake on wire rack to cool completely.

Ice with MOCHA FROSTING (see Index).

Yield: 8 servings

For an unusual flavor and rich color, add ½ teaspoon ground cloves to the flour and carob mixture.

1 tablespoon butter
¾ cup warmed honey
1 cup buttermilk or yogurt
2 cups whole wheat pastry flour
½ cup carob powder
1 teaspoon vanilla
1 teaspoon soda
½ cup strong, hot coffee
½ cup chopped nuts

Carob-Nut Cake (no eggs)

Dessert Cakes and Small Cakes

Preheat oven to 350° F. and butter a shallow 10 x 14-inch baking pan, line with wax or parchment paper, and then butter the paper.

In a medium-size bowl, beat egg yolks with honey and vanilla until thick and light in color (this will take about 5 minutes).

In a small bowl, sift together carob and flour. Add to the yolk mixture. Gently fold in egg whites, then add the melted butter.

Carob Roll

Spread the batter evenly, about ½ inch thick, in the prepared pan, and bake in preheated oven for about 10 minutes.

Remove from oven, and immediately roll cake (along with paper) lengthwise.

Allow to cool slightly, then unroll, remove paper, and spread with LEMON CURD (see Index), or ½ recipe MADEIRA CUSTARD CREAM (see Index) or SHERRY BAVARIAN CREAM (see Index).

Reroll cake and frost with whipped cream. Garnish with dates and nuts.

Yield: 10 to 12 servings

5 egg yolks
¼ cup honey
½ teaspoon vanilla
3 tablespoons carob powder
¾ cup whole wheat pastry flour
5 egg whites, beaten stiff
2 tablespoons melted butter
1 cup heavy cream, whipped
1 cup finely chopped dates and nuts for garnish

Carrot Cake

Preheat oven to 300° F. and grease an 8 x 8-inch pan.

In a mixing bowl, beat eggs. Add honey, oil, and buttermilk. Beat until well blended. Stir in carrots and nuts.

In a separate bowl, sift together flour, salt, soda, and cinnamon. Fold into carrot mixture and mix well but do not beat. Pour batter into prepared pan and bake in preheated oven for 1 hour.

Remove from oven and allow to cool for 10 minutes. Cover with APRICOT GLAZE and allow to cool completely.

Yield: 6 to 8 servings

2 eggs
½ cup warmed honey or maple syrup
¾ cup oil
¼ cup buttermilk
1½ cups grated carrots
½ cup chopped nuts (pecans, almonds, or walnuts)
1¼ cups whole wheat pastry flour
1 teaspoon salt
1 teaspoon soda
1 tablespoon cinnamon
¾ cup APRICOT GLAZE (see Index)

Dessert Cakes and
Small Cakes

Fritz's Christmas Fruitcake

**Fruit mixture, to be prepared
in advance**

2 cups diced, sun-dried pineapple
1⅓ cups chopped, pitted dates
1⅓ cups dark, seedless raisins
2⅔ cups golden raisins
⅔ cup currants
2 cups chopped English walnuts
1⅓ cups finely chopped Brazil nuts
1 cup HONEYED MIXED CITRUS PEEL
    (see recipe below)
1 cup grated, unsweetened coconut

Batter

½ cup softened butter
½ cup dark honey
6 eggs
¼ cup brandy
2 teaspoons vanilla
3 cups whole wheat pastry flour
¼ teaspoon cloves
½ teaspoon cinnamon
½ teaspoon allspice
½ teaspoon soda
½ teaspoon salt

In a shallow dish, pour a small amount of boiling water over diced pineapple to barely cover it. Soak pineapple until soft, about 1 hour. Drain thoroughly.

In a very large bowl, combine fruits, nuts, and peels. Toss with the coconut, using a wooden spoon or hand to mix the ingredients thoroughly.

Preheat oven to 275° F. and grease and flour a large tube-cake pan.

In another bowl, beat together butter, honey, and eggs until light. Add brandy and vanilla.

Sift together dry ingredients, then add to honey mixture and mix until thoroughly combined. Pour batter over fruit and nut mixture and stir with a wooden spoon or mix by hand until fruits and nuts are evenly distributed in the batter. Spoon into prepared pan and press batter firmly to remove pockets of air. If desired, arrange pecan halves attractively on top. Bake in preheated oven for 3 to 3½ hours.

Remove cake from pan immediately and cool completely on wire rack.

Wrap in several layers of cheesecloth and saturate cloth with wine or brandy. Seal wrapped cake in airtight container and store in refrigerator for at least three weeks before slicing. (Fruitcakes improve with age.) Once a week during storage, resaturate cheesecloth with wine or brandy.

Yield: 1 fruitcake, about 5 lbs.

HONEYED MIXED CITRUS PEEL

1 cup chopped grapefruit peel
    (1 medium grapefruit)
1 cup chopped lemon peel
    (3 medium lemons)
¾ cup chopped orange peel
    (1 large orange)
¼ cup chopped lime peel
    (2 medium limes)
¾ cup honey
¾ cup water

Place all the peel in a heavy saucepan and cover with 2½ cups cold water. Bring to a boil and simmer 10 minutes. Drain and rinse with cold water. Repeat process 5 times.

In a saucepan, combine honey and water. Bring to a boil and cook about 3 minutes. Add peel and boil until syrup is completely absorbed by the peel. Store in jar in refrigerator.

Yield: about 2½ cups honeyed peel

This delightful and delicious ginger-bread is truly an old American recipe, dating back to 1784. Mary Washington's gingerbread was a favorite of her son, George, as well as his friend, General Lafayette. When Lafayette would make one of his visits, Mary would leave her old-fashioned garden and serve her son and his friend this spicy goodness (along with a tall, cold mint julep).

Here is the recipe, written as it was passed down through the generations:

Cut up in a pan ½ cup of nice sweet butter with ½ cup of brown sugar. Beat to a cream with a paddle. Add 1 cup of the very best India molasses and ½ cup of warm milk. To this add 2 teaspoons of finely powdered ginger and 1 heaping teaspoon of cinnamon, mace, and nutmeg (powdered and mixed), and 1 wine glass of brandy.

Beat 3 eggs till very light and thick, 3 cups of flour and 1 teaspoon of cream of tartar sifted with the flour and stirred alternately with the beaten eggs into the batter. Last, mix in the juice and grated rind of 1 large, ripe orange. Dissolve 1 teaspoon of soda in a little warm water and stir in. Beat until very light. A cup of large, seeded raisins is a good addition. Bake in a moderate oven until done. Serve with brandy or lemon sauce.

This gingerbread is the best I've ever eaten. Here's how to prepare it:

½ cup butter
¼ cup warmed honey
1 cup molasses
½ cup warm milk
2 teaspoons finely ground ginger
1 teaspoon cinnamon
1 teaspoon nutmeg
⅓ cup brandy
3 eggs, well beaten
2⅞ cups whole wheat pastry flour
1 teaspoon cream of tartar
juice of 1 large orange (about ⅓ cup)
grated peel of 1 large orange
(about 1 tablespoon)
1 teaspoon soda
1 tablespoon warm water
1 cup seeded raisins

Preheat oven to 350° F. and grease and flour a 9½-inch springform pan.

In a large mixing bowl, cream butter until light and fluffy, then add honey and beat until smooth. Add molasses and milk, then ginger, cinnamon, and nutmeg. Stir in brandy.

Beat eggs until light and thick.

Mix flour and cream of tartar and add to batter alternately with the eggs. Stir in orange juice and peel. Combine soda with warm water and add to batter. Last, add raisins and stir well.

Pour into prepared pan and bake in preheated oven for about 1 hour or until top of cake feels firm to the touch.

Serve plain or with HONEY BRANDY SAUCE (see Index) or LEMON SAUCE (see Index).

Yield: 12 to 14 servings

Mary Washington's Gingerbread

Dessert Cakes and Small Cakes

6 egg yolks
1 tablespoon grated orange peel
½ cup orange juice
½ cup warmed honey
1⅓ cups whole wheat pastry flour
¼ teaspoon salt
6 egg whites
1 teaspoon cream of tartar
2 tablespoons warmed honey

Basic Sponge Cake, Sponge Roll, or Ladyfingers

Preheat oven to 325° F.

In the bowl of an electric mixer, beat egg yolks at high speed for about 5 minutes. Add orange peel and orange juice and beat another 5 minutes. Gradually beat in honey, about 1 tablespoonful at a time. Continue to beat until mixture is very thick and smooth, about 12 to 15 minutes. Do not underbeat—the lightness of this sponge cake depends on this beating process.

Sift together flour and salt and fold into egg yolk mixture. Set aside.

Beat egg whites until foamy, then add cream of tartar and beat until mixture forms soft peaks. Gradually add honey and beat until mixture is stiff and fine.

Gently fold egg white mixture into egg yolk mixture, using a rubber spatula.

For a 3-layer sponge cake, pour batter into 3 ungreased 8-inch layer-cake pans and bake in preheated oven for 20 to 22 minutes or until tops of layers are lightly browned. Cool cake completely before removing from pans. Ice as desired.

For a sponge roll, place a sheet of parchment or wax paper in a 12 x 16-inch shallow pan. Pour in dough and bake in preheated oven for about 20 minutes. Cool for 10 minutes, then remove paper and follow directions for preparing roll.

For ladyfingers, place a piece of parchment paper on a cookie sheet and drop the batter by the tablespoonful onto the paper, forming into fingers about ¾ inch by 3 inches, spaced 2 inches apart. Bake in preheated oven for about 10 minutes. Cool 5 minutes, then remove from paper, and place on wire rack to cool completely. This yields 30 ladyfingers.

This very light, bright yellow cake is delightfully versatile. It can be used by itself or as a part of other desserts.

Pour boiling water over the rolled oats and let soak for 20 minutes. Mix butter, honey, vanilla, eggs, and yogurt. Beat with spoon or whisk until smooth and fluffy.

Cake

1¼ cups boiling water
1 cup rolled oats
½ cup butter
1 cup warmed honey
1 teaspoon vanilla
2 eggs
¼ cup yogurt
1¼ cups whole wheat pastry flour
1 teaspoon soda
1 teaspoon cinnamon
½ teaspoon salt

Topping

2 tablespoons butter
2 tablespoons warmed honey
2 tablespoons dry milk powder
½ cup grated, unsweetened coconut

Preheat oven to 325° F. and grease a 9-inch square pan.

Add oatmeal to honey-butter-egg mixture. Combine flour, soda, cinnamon, and salt. Add to batter. Pour into prepared pan and bake in preheated oven for about 55 minutes.

Remove cake from oven, turn on broiler, then mix topping, adding each ingredient as given. Spread over the hot cake, place under the broiler for about 5 minutes, until topping is bubbly and slightly brown. (Watch carefully so it does not burn.)

Yield: about 10 servings

This cake has a good flavor and sturdy texture. It is excellent for lunch boxes, and it freezes well.

Oatmeal Cake

Preheat oven to 375° F. and grease and flour 3 8-inch layer-cake pans.

In a large, deep bowl, cream butter thoroughly. Add honey and continue to beat until fluffy and light. Add eggs and beat well.

Party Cake

Sift flour, soda, and salt together, and add slowly to butter mixture, alternating with yogurt. Fold in vanilla, mixing only enough to blend well.

Pour batter into prepared pans and bake in preheated oven for about 20 minutes.

Cool on wire rack for 5 minutes, loosen edges, and invert on rack. Cool completely, then frost with WHITE FROSTING (see Index) between layers, on sides, and on top.

Yield: 10 to 12 servings

¾ cup butter
1 cup warmed honey
3 eggs
3 cups whole wheat pastry flour
1½ teaspoons soda
¾ teaspoon salt
1 cup yogurt
1 teaspoon vanilla

Dessert Cakes and
Small Cakes

134

Preheat oven to 300° F. and grease and flour a large tube pan, or a 9 x 5 x 3-inch loaf pan.

1 cup butter
1 cup warmed honey
4 eggs
2⅛ cups whole wheat pastry flour
¼ teaspoon salt
½ teaspoon soda
⅔ cup sour cream
1 teaspoon vanilla

Cream butter. Add honey and blend well. Add eggs one at a time, beating well. Mix flour, salt, and soda. Add alternately with sour cream; blend well. Fold in vanilla. Pour into prepared pan and bake in preheated oven for about 1½ hours, or until lightly browned on top.

Yield: 8 servings

As a change, add 1 cup freshly grated coconut to this basic pound cake.

Pound Cake

Preheat oven to 350° F. and grease an 8 x 8-inch square pan.

2 egg yolks
⅓ cup warmed honey
1 cup sour cream
1½ cups whole wheat pastry flour
1 teaspoon soda
¼ teaspoon salt
¼ teaspoon nutmeg
¼ teaspoon ground cloves
½ teaspoon cinnamon
½ cup chopped nuts (English walnuts, pecans, hickory nuts)
1 cup raisins
2 egg whites, stiffly beaten

Beat egg yolks well, add honey and sour cream, and blend thoroughly.

Combine flour, soda, salt, nutmeg, cloves, and cinnamon. Add to the first mixture, then fold in nuts and raisins. Do not overmix. Fold in egg whites.

Pour into prepared pan and bake in preheated oven for 35 to 45 minutes. Cool in pan on wire rack.

If frosting is desired, frost with MOCHA FROSTING (see Index).

Cut into 2-inch squares to serve.

Yield: 16 servings

Sour Cream Spice Cake

Dessert Cakes and Small Cakes

Prepare SPONGE ROLL and while it is baking, prepare berries and add honey.

Combine whipped cream and flavoring.

While roll is still warm, place a piece of wax paper on a cold cookie sheet and sprinkle the paper lightly with flour. Invert warm SPONGE ROLL on the wax paper and carefully peel off the parchment paper.

Strawberry Cream Roll

Spread the cake with half the whipped cream, cover with berries, then start rolling the cake. This can be done easily by gently lifting the end of the wax paper. When roll is complete, lift carefully to serving plate and top with remaining whipped cream. Drizzle the RASPBERRY SAUCE over the cream.

When ready to serve, slice and place on individual dessert plates.

Yield: 8 to 10 slices

This recipe may also be used to make a Blackberry Roll, using frozen, unsweetened blackberries or fresh berries in season.

1 SPONGE ROLL (see Index)
2 cups sliced fresh strawberries (or frozen: unsweetened, thawed, and drained)
1 teaspoon honey
1½ cups heavy cream, whipped
1 teaspoon vanilla, Kirsch or Framboise
½ cup RASPBERRY SAUCE (see Index)

Dessert Cakes and Small Cakes

Preheat oven to 350° F. and grease a
12 x 8-inch baking pan.

½ cup butter or oil
⅔ cup warmed honey
2 eggs
1 teaspoon vanilla
¼ cup buttermilk or yogurt
½ teaspoon soda
¼ teaspoon salt
1¾ cups whole wheat pastry flour
1½ cups diced, raw apples (unpeeled)
½ cup chopped pecans or walnuts

Cream butter or oil and honey together,
then add eggs and beat until smooth.
Add vanilla.

Combine buttermilk or yogurt with
soda and salt. Add to creamed mixture,
then add flour and mix well.

Add apples and nuts. Bake in prepared
pan for 35 minutes in preheated oven.

Yield: 24 2-inch squares

Golden Apple Squares

Preheat oven to 375° F. and grease 12
muffin tins.

1 egg
½ cup carob powder, sifted
½ cup softened butter
1½ cups whole wheat pastry flour
½ cup sour cream, yogurt,
or buttermilk
1 teaspoon soda
½ cup warmed honey
½ cup hot water

Put ingredients into bowl in order given.
Do not mix until last item has been
added, then beat well. Fill muffin tins
two-thirds full and bake in preheated
oven for 20 to 25 minutes.

If desired, frost with PEANUT BUTTER
ICING (see Index) or WHITE FROST-
ING (see Index).

Yield: 12 cupcakes

Carob Cupcakes

Dessert Cakes and
Small Cakes

Frosted Cream Squares

Preheat oven to 400° F. and grease an 8 x 8-inch baking pan.

Mix together butter, honey, and water. Allow to cool. Add molasses and eggs and mix well. Combine flour, cinnamon, ginger, soda, and salt. Add to first mixture gradually.

Spread dough evenly in prepared pan, and bake in preheated oven about 25 minutes.

When cool, frost with WHITE FROSTING (see Index) or LEMON ICING (see Index) and cut into 2-inch squares.

Yield: 16 squares

½ cup butter
¼ cup warmed honey
⅓ cup boiling water
½ cup light molasses
2 eggs, beaten
1¾ cups whole wheat pastry flour
½ teaspoon cinnamon
½ teaspoon ginger
½ teaspoon soda
¼ teaspoon salt

Hermits

Preheat oven to 350° F. and grease a 7 x 14-inch pan.

Mix raisins, currants, nuts, and flour.

Cream butter, add honey, molasses, eggs, sour cream or yogurt, and salt. Beat well.

Mix flour, soda, cream of tartar, and spices. Beat well, then stir in the floured fruit and nuts. Spread in the prepared pan and bake in preheated oven about 15 minutes, or until top is firm.

While still warm, cut into squares or bars.

Yield: 36 hermits

For thinner hermits, use an 11 x 14-inch pan.

¼ cup raisins, chopped
¼ cup currants
¼ cup chopped nuts
¼ cup whole wheat flour
4 tablespoons butter, softened
¼ cup warmed honey
⅓ cup molasses
2 eggs, well beaten
¼ cup sour cream or yogurt
½ teaspoon salt
1½ cups whole wheat flour
1 teaspoon soda
½ teaspoon cream of tartar
1 teaspoon cinnamon
½ teaspoon ground cloves
¼ teaspoon nutmeg
¼ teaspoon mace (optional)

Dessert Cakes and Small Cakes

138

2 eggs
⅓ cup oil or melted butter
½ cup warmed honey
¼ cup buttermilk
1½ tablespoons grated lemon peel
1½ cups whole wheat pastry flour
1 teaspoon salt
¾ teaspoon soda
½ cup chopped nuts
2 tablespoons honey
2 tablespoons lemon juice
2 tablespoons grated lemon peel

Preheat oven to 350° F. Butter a baking pan approximately 8 x 12 x 1 inches.

Beat eggs in a large bowl. Add oil or cooled, melted butter, honey, buttermilk, and lemon peel. Mix until thoroughly combined.

Stir together flour, salt, and soda, making sure there are no lumps in the soda. Add to the egg mixture and beat well. Stir in chopped nuts.

Bake in prepared pan for 20 to 25 minutes. Cool 5 minutes, then pour a mixture of remaining honey, lemon juice, and peel over top. Cut into squares and serve warm or at room temperature.

Yield: 15 squares

Lemon-Nut Squares

Brownies are a favorite with young and old alike. We make these with peanut butter and chopped fruit, not only for nutrition but also to keep them moist. They carry well in the lunch box and they can be frozen.

Peanut Butter Brownies

Preheat oven to 350° F. and oil a 9 x 9-inch baking pan.

In a medium-size bowl, combine all ingredients in the order given. Mix well. Spread batter evenly in the prepared pan. Bake in preheated oven for 20 to 25 minutes, or just until surface is firm to the touch.

Remove from the oven, cool slightly, and cut into 16 squares.

Yield: 16 brownies

¼ cup oil or melted butter
¾ cup peanut butter
⅔ cup honey
2 eggs, unbeaten
¼ teaspoon salt
½ cup pitted prunes, chopped
½ cup chopped figs (optional)
¼ cup chopped peanuts
⅓ cup whole wheat pastry flour

Georgia Pecan Brownies

Preheat oven to 325° F. and butter a 7 x 11-inch shallow baking pan.

Beat egg whites stiff, then add honey very gradually, continuing to beat until mixture is stiff and smooth. Carefully beat in maple syrup.

Mix nuts, crumbs, and salt. Fold gently into egg whites.

Spread into baking pan and bake in preheated oven for about 25 minutes. Cool completely in the pan, then cut into rectangles and serve.

Yield: 20 brownies

2 egg whites
⅓ cup warmed honey
1 tablespoon maple syrup (optional)
1 cup chopped pecans
1 cup fine, dry whole-grain bread crumbs
pinch of salt

Dessert Cakes and Small Cakes

Funny Cake

1 9-inch BASIC PRESSED PIE CRUST (see Index), prepared in advance but not baked
3 tablespoons BASIC CAROB SYRUP (see Index)
¼ cup warmed honey
¼ cup molasses
½ cup water
2 eggs
⅔ cup honey
½ cup buttermilk
2 tablespoons melted butter
1¾ cup whole wheat pastry flour
1 teaspoon soda

Preheat oven to 375° F.

In small saucepan, mix carob syrup, honey, molasses, and water. Place over low heat and stir until well blended. Cool.

In a mixing bowl, beat eggs. Add honey, buttermilk, and butter. Combine flour and soda, add to batter.

Pour cooled carob mixture into pie shell and drop batter by heaping tablespoonfuls on top.

Bake in preheated oven for about 40 minutes.

Yield: 1 9-inch pie

This unusual pie-like breakfast cake rates with SHOO-FLY PIE in popularity in some areas.

Combine molasses, water, and soda in a small saucepan; bring to boiling, stirring well. Set aside to cool.

Preheat oven to 400° F.

Mix flour and seasonings, then add butter and honey. Toss gently with fingers until mixture is crumb consistency. Chill.

Shoo-Fly Pie

Spread about one-fourth of the crumbs over the pastry in the pan. Pour cooled molasses mixture over this layer of crumbs. Set aside 2 tablespoonfuls of crumbs, then put remaining crumbs over the molasses mixture, spreading evenly. Bake for 25 minutes in preheated oven, then remove and top with the reserved crumbs. Return to oven and bake about 20 minutes longer. Cool before serving.

Yield: 1 9-inch pie

SHOO-FLY PIE is a traditional breakfast cake in the Pennsylvania Dutch area, but, since childhood, it has been a favorite of mine any time of day. My mother had a good recipe and our family really enjoyed it, but the best one I have ever found and used came to me from Fred Waring. I have given it to many friends through the years, but now, for the first time, I have adapted it for natural ingredients. The texture will be different—the flavor is excellent.

1 9-inch BASIC ROLLED PIE CRUST (see Index), prepared in advance but not baked
¾ cup molasses
¾ cup boiling water
1 teaspoon soda
1⅓ cups whole wheat pastry flour
½ teaspoon cinnamon
¼ teaspoon ginger
⅛ teaspoon ground cloves
¼ teaspoon salt
5 tablespoons butter, cut into small cubes
¼ cup warmed honey

Crumb Cake

Preheat oven to 375° F. and grease an 8 × 8-inch pan.

Sift together flour and salt. Add butter and crumb well with a fork, then add honey. Take out 1 cup of crumbs and, to the remaining crumbs, add eggs and honey. Dissolve soda in buttermilk. Stir into first mixture.

Pour batter into prepared pan, top with reserved crumbs, and bake in preheated oven for about 30 minutes.

Yield: 8 servings

This old-fashioned breakfast cake is sometimes called "*Krum Kuchen*" and is often baked in a pie shell, similar to Funny Cake and Shoo-Fly Pie. Try it both ways—you may have a preference.

2 cups whole wheat pastry flour
½ teaspoon salt
½ cup butter
2 tablespoons honey
2 eggs, well beaten
½ cup honey
1 teaspoon soda
½ cup buttermilk

Dough

½ cup scalded buttermilk
2 tablespoons butter or oil
¼ cup water
2 tablespoons honey
1 teaspoon salt
1 package dry yeast
1 egg
2¼ cups whole wheat flour

Filling

⅓ cup warmed honey
⅓ cup chopped nuts
½ teaspoon cinnamon
2 tablespoons grated orange peel
1 tablespoon orange juice

Combine buttermilk, butter or oil, water, honey, and salt. Allow mixture to cool to lukewarm, then add yeast and mix well. Blend in egg, then cover and allow to set in a warm place for about 10 minutes. Add flour and mix until dough is well blended and soft. Roll out on well-floured board forming a 14-inch square.

Combine honey, nuts, cinnamon, orange peel, juice, and milk powder. Spread filling evenly over dough. Roll as for jelly roll, cut into 1-inch slices, and arrange in layers in well-greased, 8-inch ring mold. Cover with damp cloth and let rise in warm place until light, about 45 minutes.

Preheat oven to 350° F.

Bake ring in preheated oven for about 40 minutes.

Remove from pan immediately and baste with any syrup remaining in the pan.

Yield: 6 to 8 servings

Coffee Ring Deluxe

Combine milk, butter or oil, honey, salt, and water. Allow to cool to lukewarm. Add yeast and mix well. Cover and allow to set in a warm place for about 10 minutes. Blend in egg, lemon peel, raisins, nuts and apricots. Add flour and mix until dough is well blended and soft.

Apricot Braid

Divide dough into 5 equal parts and shape each into an 18-inch strip. Place 3 strips on greased baking sheet and form into braid. Seal ends together. Twist the 2 remaining strips together and place on top of braid. Seal ends. Cover with damp cloth and let rise in warm place until double in bulk, about 1 hour.

Preheat oven to 350° F.

Bake braid in preheated oven for 45 minutes.

Yield: 1 large braid

This braid is very versatile; it is delicious fresh from the oven, makes tasty sandwiches for the lunch box, and is excellent toasted.

1 cup scalded milk
¼ cup butter or oil
3 tablespoons honey
1 teaspoon salt
¼ cup water
1 package dry yeast
1 egg
1 teaspoon grated lemon peel
½ cup chopped raisins
¼ cup chopped nuts
½ cup finely cut, uncooked, dried apricots
4 cups whole wheat flour

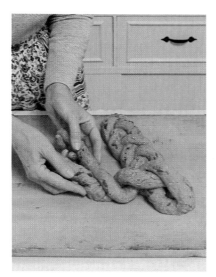

Combine milk, butter, honey, and salt. Cool to lukewarm by adding water. Add yeast and mix well. Blend in egg, then cover and allow to set in a warm place for about 10 minutes. Add flour and mix until dough is well blended and soft. Roll into 14 x 12-inch rectangle.

Simmer until thick prune pulp, juice, cinnamon, lemon juice, honey, and salt. Cool. Spread evenly on rolled dough. Roll as for jelly roll and place on greased baking sheet. Twist dough to form ring and join ends. With scissors, slash deep gashes about 1 inch apart. Turn each piece on its side, cut edge up.

Swedish Tea Ring

Cover with cloth and let rise in warm place until light, about 45 minutes.

Preheat oven to 350° F.

Bake ring in preheated oven for 30 minutes.

Glaze
1 tablespoon honey
¼ teaspoon vanilla
2 tablespoons milk powder

Combine honey, vanilla, and milk powder. Drizzle over the tea ring while still warm.

Yield: 1 large ring

Dough
½ cup scalded milk
2 tablespoons butter
2 tablespoons honey
1 teaspoon salt
½ cup water
1 package dry yeast
1 egg
3 cups whole wheat flour

Filling
1 cup prune pulp
¼ cup prune juice
¼ teaspoon cinnamon
1 tablespoon lemon juice
2 tablespoons honey
⅛ teaspoon salt

Breakfast Cakes
and Buns

Sour Cream Coffee Cake

Preheat oven to 350° F. and grease a 9 x 9-inch cake pan.

Cream butter, add honey and eggs, and beat well. Add flour, soda, sour cream, and vanilla. Mix thoroughly.

In a small bowl, combine honey, cinnamon, flour, and nuts.

Pour one-half the cake batter into prepared pan. Cover with half the honey-cinnamon mixture, then add remaining batter. Top with remaining honey-cinnamon mixture.

Bake in preheated oven for about 45 minutes.

Yield: 9 servings

½ cup butter
½ cup warmed honey
2 eggs
1⅓ cups whole wheat pastry flour
1 teaspoon soda
1 cup sour cream
1 teaspoon vanilla
2 tablespoons honey
2 teaspoons cinnamon
2 tablespoons whole wheat flour
¾ cup broken nuts

Honey Twirls

Combine milk, butter, honey, and salt. Cool to lukewarm by adding water. Add yeast, mix well, then blend in egg. Cover and set in a warm place for about 10 minutes. Add flour, and mix until dough is well blended and soft. Roll into an 18-inch square.

Combine butter, honey, and cinnamon. Spread on rolled dough. Roll as for jelly roll and cut into 1-inch slices. Arrange in well-greased 11 x 7-inch baking pan. Cover with damp cloth and let rise in warm place until double in bulk, about 1 hour.

Preheat oven to 350° F.

Mix butter and honey and drizzle over buns.

Bake in preheated oven for 35 minutes.

Yield: 18 twirls

Dough
½ cup scalded milk
2 tablespoons butter
1 tablespoon honey
1 teaspoon salt
½ cup water
1 package dry yeast
1 egg
3 cups whole wheat flour

Filling
1 tablespoon melted butter
2 tablespoons honey
½ teaspoon cinnamon

Glaze
1 tablespoon melted butter
2 tablespoons honey

Breakfast Cakes and Buns

150

Combine milk, butter or oil, honey, and salt. Cool to lukewarm by adding water. Add yeast, then egg and mix well. Cover and allow to set in a warm place for about 10 minutes. Add flour and mix until dough is well blended and soft.

Dough
½ cup scalded milk
3 tablespoons butter or oil
3 tablespoons honey
1 teaspoon salt
½ cup water
1 package dry yeast
1 egg
3 cups whole wheat flour

Filling
¼ cup melted butter
5 tablespoons honey
1½ teaspoons cinnamon
¾ cup chopped pecans

Roll out dough on well-floured board to form an 18 x 12-inch rectangle.

Mix butter, honey, cinnamon, and nuts and spread one-half of mixture evenly over the rolled dough. Roll as for a jelly roll, then cut into 1-inch slices.

Grease 18 muffin tins and divide remaining filling to cover the bottom of each tin.

Place rolls, cut side down, in the tins. Cover with cloth and let rise in warm place about 1 hour, until light.

Preheat oven to 375° F.

Bake in preheated oven for about 25 minutes.

Yield: 18 medium rolls

Sweet Rolls

Combine milk, butter or oil, honey, and salt. Cool to lukewarm by adding water. Stir in yeast, then beat in egg, cover and allow to set in a warm place for 10 to 15 minutes. Add flour and work until dough is well blended and soft. Shape into 12 buns.

Combine bread crumbs, honey, and cinnamon.

Fruity Buns

Dip each bun first in egg white, then in crumb mixture; place on greased cookie sheet, cover with cloth, and let rise in warm place until light (about 45 minutes).

Preheat oven to 375° F.

Press deep indentation in center of each bun. Place about 1 teaspoonful of fruit into each indentation. Bake in preheated oven for 25 minutes.

Yield: 12 large buns

Dough
½ cup scalded milk
¼ cup butter or oil
1 tablespoon honey
1 teaspoon salt
½ cup cold water
1 package dry yeast
1 egg
3 cups whole wheat flour

Topping
½ cup whole-grain bread crumbs
2 tablespoons honey
¼ teaspoon cinnamon
1 egg white, slightly beaten
⅓ cup chopped, cooked fruit (apricots, prunes, raisins, etc.)

Combine milk, butter, honey, and salt. Stir well and cool to lukewarm. Dissolve yeast in potato water and add to first mixture. Add potatoes and egg, then work in flour. Place in greased bowl, cover, and let rise about 1 hour, until light.

Baked Doughnuts

Place on floured board and knead for 5 to 8 minutes. Roll to ½-inch thickness and cut into circles, using 3-inch doughnut cutter. Place on buttered cookie sheets, and let rise again for about 45 minutes.

Preheat oven to 425° F.

Bake doughnuts about 12 minutes, until lightly browned. Remove from oven and brush immediately with butter and dust with COCONUT SUGAR.

Yield: 1½ dozen doughnuts

½ cup milk, scalded
⅓ cup butter
½ cup warmed honey
½ teaspoon salt
1 teaspoon dry yeast
2 tablespoons warm potato water
½ cup mashed potatoes
1 egg, well beaten
2½ cups whole wheat flour
softened butter and COCONUT
     SUGAR for dusting (see Index)

Cinnamon Date Fluffs

Soften yeast in lukewarm water. Add butter, honey, and salt. Blend in egg, then add flour and mix until dough is well blended and soft. Place in oiled bowl, cover with cloth and allow to rise for 1 hour in a warm place.

Roll dough on well-floured board to ¼-inch-thick rectangle and fit on greased baking sheet.

Mix nuts, dates, lemon peel, cinnamon, and honey. Spread mixture evenly over dough. Cut into 1½-inch squares.

Cover with a damp cloth and let rise in warm place until double in size (about 25 minutes).

Preheat oven to 400° F.

Bake in preheated oven for 15 minutes.

Yield: 3½ dozen cakes

Dough
1 package dry yeast
1 cup lukewarm water
3 tablespoons melted butter
1 tablespoon honey
1 teaspoon salt
1 egg
3 cups whole wheat flour

Topping
½ cup finely chopped walnuts
½ cup finely chopped dates
1 tablespoon grated lemon peel
1 teaspoon cinnamon
2 tablespoons honey

Buttermilk Oatmeal Muffins

Soak oats in buttermilk for at least ½ hour.

Preheat oven to 425° F.

Beat egg into oat mixture. Add honey and combine thoroughly.

Stir together flour, salt, and soda, making sure there are no lumps in the soda. Stir into first mixture, then add oil or cooled melted butter and mix only until ingredients are combined.

Bake in buttered muffin tins for 15 to 20 minutes or until browned.

Serve hot or at room temperature.

Yield: 1 dozen muffins

For less-sweet muffins, reduce the amount of honey to 2 tablespoons.

1 cup rolled oats
1 cup buttermilk
1 egg, unbeaten
¼ cup warmed honey
1 cup whole wheat pastry flour
½ teaspoon salt
1 teaspoon soda
⅓ cup oil or melted butter

Preheat oven to 375° F. and grease 3 dozen miniature (or 1 dozen full-size) muffin tins.

Mix cornmeal, flour, soda, and salt.

1 cup cornmeal
2 cups whole wheat pastry flour
1 teaspoon soda
1 teaspoon salt
2 eggs
2 tablespoons honey
1⅓ cups buttermilk
1½ tablespoons melted butter
1 teaspoon sesame seeds

In another bowl, beat eggs, add honey and buttermilk. Stir into cornmeal mixture, then add melted butter.

Cornmeal Muffins

Place about 2 teaspoonfuls of batter in each muffin cup, filling about ⅔ full.

Sprinkle with sesame seeds and bake in preheated oven for 25 minutes.

Yield: 3 dozen miniature or 1 dozen full-size muffins

This batter may be baked in cornstick pans. Baked that way, the yield would be about 18.

Soften yeast in warm water. Add butter, honey, and salt. Blend in egg. Add flour and mix until dough is well blended and soft.

Dough
1 package dry yeast
½ cup lukewarm water
2 tablespoons melted butter
1 tablespoon honey
1 teaspoon salt
1 egg
2 cups whole wheat flour

Topping
¼ cup honey
2 teaspoons lemon juice
2 tablespoons grated lemon peel

Grease 2 dozen 2-inch muffin tins and fill ½ full.

Lemon Tea Drops (muffins)

Combine honey, lemon juice, and lemon peel. Sprinkle over tea drops, allowing about one teaspoonful for each.

Cover with damp cloth and let rise in warm place until light (about 45 minutes).

Preheat oven to 375° F.

Bake in preheated oven for 20 to 25 minutes.

Yield: 2 dozen muffins.

Breakfast Cakes and Buns

157

Preheat oven to 425° F.

In a mixing bowl, combine flour, salt, and soda. With pastry blender, or fork, or fingertips, work in butter. Add honey and raisins or currants. Mix well.

Beat egg, add buttermilk, sour cream, or yogurt, then add to dough. Gather dough into ball, place on lightly floured board and knead about ½ minute. Pat or roll into an oblong ¾ inch thick. Cut into diamonds by making diagonal cuts with a sharp knife.

English Tea Scones

Place scones on the ungreased baking sheet about 1 inch apart and bake in preheated oven for about 15 minutes.

Yield: 12 to 16 scones

Scones are sometimes baked on a griddle similar to English muffins, but these are baked in the oven. To serve, split scones while still hot and spread with butter.

2 cups whole wheat pastry flour
½ teaspoon salt
¾ teaspoon soda
4 tablespoons butter
2 teaspoons honey
½ cup raisins or currants
1 egg
½ cup buttermilk, sour cream, or yogurt

Breakfast Cakes and Buns

Preheat oven to 375° F. and grease 18 muffin tins.

In a mixer bowl, combine butter or oil, eggs, bananas, and honey. Mix yogurt and soda and add to butter mixture. Cream well.

Stir together flour and salt. Add to creamed mixture, mixing until just blended. Stir in oats.

Fill muffin pans ⅔ full of batter. Bake in preheated oven for 18 to 20 minutes. Remove from pans and cool on wire rack.

Yield: 1½ dozen muffins

½ cup softened butter, or oil
2 eggs
1 cup mashed bananas (3 or 4 medium-size bananas)
½ cup warmed honey
¼ cup yogurt
1 teaspoon soda
1½ cups whole wheat pastry flour
¾ teaspoon salt
1 cup rolled oats

Oatmeal Banana Cakes (muffins)

Preheat oven to 400° F. and grease 1 dozen muffin tins.

In a large bowl, stir bran and milk together. Add butter or oil, egg, and syrup and mix well. Mix flour, soda, and salt together and add to the mixture. Stir well.

Spoon into prepared tins and bake in preheated oven for 15 minutes.

Yield: 1 dozen muffins

1 cup bran
¾ cup buttermilk
2 tablespoons melted butter, or oil
1 egg, beaten
⅓ cup maple syrup
1 cup whole wheat pastry flour
½ teaspoon soda
1 teaspoon salt

Maple Bran Muffins

Breakfast Cakes and Buns

Preheat oven to 450° F. and grease 1 dozen muffin tins.

Maple Corn Muffins

Combine milk, sour cream, maple syrup, and eggs. Blend well.

Mix flour, cornmeal, soda, and salt and add to the first mixture.

Spoon batter into prepared muffin tins, filling about ⅔ full and bake in preheated oven for about 15 minutes.

Yield: 1 dozen muffins

¾ cup milk
¼ cup sour cream
⅓ cup maple syrup
2 eggs
1 cup whole wheat pastry flour
¾ cup cornmeal
½ teaspoon soda
½ teaspoon salt

Prune Muffins

Preheat oven to 400° F.

Mix shortening and honey. Add egg. Mix dry ingredients and add to the batter alternately with milk. Fold in prunes. Pour into greased muffin tins and bake in preheated oven for about 25 minutes.

Yield: 1½ dozen

¼ cup butter or oil
¼ cup warmed honey
1 egg, beaten
1½ cups whole wheat flour
½ teaspoon salt
1 teaspoon soda
¾ cup buttermilk or yogurt
¾ cup stewed prunes, pitted and chopped

Breakfast Cakes and Buns

Top and sides	1 9-inch layer cake	¾ cup
Top and sides	2 9-inch layer cakes	1½ cups
Top and sides	3 9-inch layer cakes	2¼ cups
Top and sides	9½ x 5½ x 3-inch loaf	1 to 1½ cups
Top	16 x 5 x 4-inch loaf	2 to 2½ cups
Top	16 large cupcakes	1 to 1½ cups
Top	24 small cupcakes	1 to 1½ cups
For filling	10 x 15-inch roll	2 cups

Icing Requirements

Coconut-Pecan Frosting

1 cup light cream, milk, or
half-and-half
½ cup warmed honey
3 egg yolks, lightly beaten
½ cup butter
1 teaspoon vanilla
1⅓ cups grated, unsweetened coconut
1 cup chopped pecans

Combine milk, honey, egg yolks, butter, and vanilla in a saucepan. Stir over low heat until thickened, about 12 minutes. Remove from heat and beat until cool and thick enough to spread. Stir in coconut and nuts.

Yield: about 2¼ cups

Icings and
Cake Fillings

161

French
Butter Cream
Frosting

Put coffee, carob syrup, and honey into blender container. Cover and blend at medium speed for 2 or 3 minutes. Add egg yolks one at a time, then butter and brandy. Continue to process until smooth. Chill until mixture is spreading consistency.

Yield: about 2 cups

2 tablespoons strong, hot coffee
½ cup BASIC CAROB SYRUP
   (see Index)
2 tablespoons honey
4 egg yolks
½ cup soft butter
2 tablespoons brandy or rum

French
Coffee Icing

Beat butter until soft. Add salt. Dissolve coffee in boiling water. Add to butter. Gradually beat in honey, continuing to beat for 2 minutes. Add brandy. Let stand for 5 minutes. Beat again for 2 minutes.

Yield: 2 cups icing

This icing is delicious but must be used promptly—do not store overnight.

1 cup butter
¼ teaspoon salt
2 tablespoons powdered instant coffee
4 tablespoons boiling water
1 cup warmed honey
1 teaspoon brandy

Icings and
Cake Fillings

¼ cup warmed honey
2 tablespoons lemon juice
⅛ teaspoon cream of tartar
dash of salt
1 egg white
1 teaspoon grated lemon peel

In the top of a double boiler, mix honey, lemon juice, cream of tartar, salt, and egg white. Beat several minutes, then place over boiling water and beat until stiff enough to stand in peaks. This will take 5 to 8 minutes.

Remove from the heat and beat until thick enough to spread. Fold in lemon peel.

Yield: 1½ cups

This is a soft icing and the cake should be used the day it is iced or the icing might soak into the cake.

Lemon Icing

½ cup BASIC CAROB SYRUP
(see Index)
4 tablespoons honey
2 tablespoons powdered instant coffee
1 cup sour cream

In a small saucepan, combine carob syrup and honey. Simmer over low heat, stirring constantly, for 6 minutes. Remove from heat, stir in coffee, and allow to cool.

Add sour cream and stir until well mixed.

Yield: about 1¼ cups

This icing keeps well; it can be used immediately or stored, covered, in the refrigerator.

Mocha Frosting

Icings and
Cake Fillings

Peanut Butter Icing

Beat peanut butter until light and smooth. Gradually add honey and beat until well mixed. Fold in whipped cream.

Yield: about 2 cups

1 cup peanut butter
⅓ to ½ cup warmed honey
¼ cup heavy cream, whipped

Seven-Minute Frosting

Put the unbeaten egg whites, honey, and salt into the top of a double boiler over hot water. Beat with a hand beater (or an electric beater on low speed) while you bring the water to a boil. Continue to beat for 7 minutes or until the mixture forms soft mounds. Remove from the heat, add the vanilla slowly, and continue beating until frosting is stiff enough to hold its shape.

Yield: about 3 cups

3 egg whites
⅔ cup honey
pinch of salt
1 teaspoon vanilla

Icings and
Cake Fillings

1 cup COCONUT SUGAR (see Index)
2 tablespoons butter, softened
4 tablespoons warm milk or cream
½ teaspoon vanilla
2 tablespoons maple syrup or honey

Blend ingredients thoroughly and spread on top of cooled cake.

Yield: 1½ cups

White Frosting

½ cup butter
½ cup warmed honey
grated peel of 2 lemons (about 4 tablespoons)
juice of 3 lemons (about ½ cup)
6 eggs, lightly beaten
⅛ teaspoon salt

In the top of a double boiler, combine all ingredients. Mix well. Set over boiling water and cook (stirring constantly with a wooden spoon) for 15 to 20 minutes, or until mixture is thick and smooth.

Cool and store in a jar in refrigerator.

Yield: about 2½ cups

LEMON CURD is a popular English lemon butter which can be used in many ways: as a spread for toast at teatime, a filling for meringues and cakes, filling for sponge roll, or as a dessert pudding (garnished with whipped cream).

Lemon Curd

Icings and
Cake Fillings

CHAPTER V

COOKIES

COOKIES

Natural cookies are ideal sweets for everyone! Generally, they are easy to handle, carry well in lunch boxes, and can be made in a wide range of sizes, shapes, and flavors. Nutritious extras such as whole wheat flour, rolled oats, powdered milk, yogurt, raisins, seeds, nuts, honey, and molasses make them especially beneficial to the health of growing children.

The cookies in this book are all easy to make. I've abandoned the rolled cookies which, with our soft honey batters, are hard to handle and take too much time. I prefer the very easy drop cookies, refrigerator cookies, and bar cookies.

All kinds of cookies are successful with all-natural ingredients—thick or thin, crisp or chewy. *Whole wheat pastry flour yields a cookie dough which spreads out during baking to produce thin, delicate cookies. Whole wheat flour makes a firmer cookie which holds its shape while baking.*

The amount of flour used makes an important difference, too. Because flours vary in behavior, you may want to bake a sample batch of a cookie using a minimum amount of flour. If you find it hard to handle, add just a little more flour in succeeding batches until you get the desired thickness. Do not add too much or you will sacrifice flavor for appearance.

Butter and oil can be used interchangeably in most of these recipes. If basic flavor is important, use butter; if the cookie is flavored with spices or other reasonably distinct flavoring, oil may be used.

Most dough handles well if it has been chilled. It is easy to make up several batches of dough and keep them in the refrigerator or freezer until you want to bake them. It saves energy, too. Our recipes are for small batches so that you can enjoy a variety of types and flavors.

Honey makes a softer dough than sugar would, but that is no problem. Bake the cookies until the edges are just starting to turn brown, cool slightly (usually one to three minutes is long enough), then, with a spatula large enough to fit under the *complete* cookie (very important), move to a wire rack to cool. When the cookie is completely cooled, if the texture is the way you want it to be, store immediately between layers of plastic wrap in a tightly covered can or jar. If the cookies are too soft and sticky for your taste, allow them to dry out at room temperature for several hours, then store in airtight containers.

If you plan to keep the cookies for longer than a week, store them in the refrigerator.

The very delicate, crisp, wafer-type cookie does not travel well, so don't select that kind for lunch boxes.

Select heavy cookie sheets—cookies bake better on heavy ones. Be sure the sheets are small enough, in relation to your oven, so the heat can circulate around them.

Parchment paper is a great boon to cookie baking. Simply cut a piece to fit your cookie sheet, and arrange the cookies on the paper. After they are baked, slide the whole sheet onto a rack to cool. You can then cool the cookie sheet slightly, place another sheet of paper on it, and fill immediately. As the cookies cool, it is easy to remove them from the paper, wipe the paper with a paper towel, and reuse it.

If you don't use parchment, very light greasing of the sheet is all that is necessary. Rub the sheet lightly with butter, vegetable oil, or liquid lecithin. Usually, one coating is enough for a whole batch of cookies.

As a general rule on timing, cookies should be baked until they are delicately browned with a dry, glossy surface and firm edges. For drop cookies this usually takes 12 to 15 minutes. For bar cookies, if the top of the dough springs back when you press it, baking time is completed; this is usually 18 to 20 minutes.

Cookies tend to improve in flavor after a few days' storage in an airtight container. Because flavors mingle, do not store more than one kind of cookie in the same tin.

When a recipe calls for nuts, use any kind you and your family enjoy. Sometimes, for a change in flavor and for added nutrition, you might want to add sunflower seeds, sesame seeds, or wheat germ, either in addition to the nuts, or in place of them.

Drop Cookies

For drop cookies, usually the dough is quite thin and a level teaspoon is the correct amount for one cookie. I use a round measuring spoon which makes cookies the right shape. If the dough does not drop readily from the spoon, push it onto the sheet with another spoon or with your finger. Leave space between cookies for them to spread—usually two or three inches is sufficient. The cookies will flatten and spread during baking.

Refrigerator Cookies

Refrigerator cookies are sometimes called sliced cookies, because the dough is chilled or frozen until firm enough to cut into thin slices and bake. One reason this type of cookie is so popular is its ease of preparation.

Shape dough into firm rolls 1½ or 2 inches in diameter, wrap in wax paper or pack tightly into a square pan. When ready to bake, slice into rounds, squares, or oblongs from ⅛ to ½ inch thick. Bake as directed.

Bar Cookies

Bar cookies are the type baked in a pan, then cut into small bars or squares, usually while they are warm. The cookies can be stored in the baking pan, covered, or transferred to airtight tins.

½ cup butter
½ cup warmed honey
1 egg
1 tablespoon buttermilk
1 teaspoon vanilla
2 cups whole wheat pastry flour
½ teaspoon soda

Cream butter, honey, egg, buttermilk, and vanilla. Mix flour and soda and add to creamed mixture, combining thoroughly. Chill dough several hours.

Preheat oven to 350° F.

Drop dough by the slightly rounded teaspoonful about 2 inches apart, onto buttered baking sheet. Flatten each cookie by pressing with a flat-bottomed glass covered with a damp cloth.

Apricot Sandwich Cookies

Bake 8 to 10 minutes.

Spread apricot filling on half the cookies and cover with another cookie. Use about 1 teaspoon filling for each sandwich.

Apricot Filling
¾ cup diced, dried apricots
⅓ cup honey
½ cup water

Cook apricots, honey, and water in heavy saucepan over low heat for 30 minutes. Cool slightly, then process in blender until smooth. If necessary, add a teaspoon or two more water during blending process so that a spreadable consistency results.

Yield: 25 to 30 sandwiches

Cookies

½ cup warmed honey
¼ cup softened butter
¼ cup oil
1 egg
3 tablespoons brandy
2 to 2⅓ cups whole wheat flour
¾ teaspoon soda
¼ teaspoon salt
½ cup raisins
½ cup currants
½ cup chopped hickory nuts (or chopped English walnuts or pecans)

Preheat oven to 350° F.

Combine and beat well the honey, butter, oil, egg, and brandy. Stir together the flour, soda, and salt and add to first mixture, mixing thoroughly. Stir in the raisins, currants, and nuts.

Drop by the level tablespoonful onto buttered baking sheet. Bake 12 to 15 minutes.

Yield: about 3 dozen cookies

Brandy Drops

Preheat oven to 350° F.

Beat together oil, syrup, and yogurt. Combine flour, soda, and cinnamon. Fold into the first mixture and blend well.

Place a sheet of parchment paper on a cookie sheet. Drop dough by the level teaspoonful onto paper, about 2½ inches apart. Bake in preheated oven for 10 to 12 minutes. Allow to set for about 3 minutes, then transfer from paper to wire rack to cool.

⅓ cup oil
⅓ cup maple syrup
⅓ cup yogurt
½ cup whole wheat pastry flour
1 teaspoon soda
1 teaspoon cinnamon

Yield: 4 dozen 2-inch round cookies

Cinnamon Crisps

This cookie is thin and delicate but not hard to handle. Although we make it with oil, it is rich and tasty. If, after baking, the cookies are too moist for storing, spread them on a sheet of wax paper and let them "dry out" for several hours or overnight. A thin, crisp wafer will result and can be stored for several weeks in an airtight container.

Cookies

Preheat oven to 350° F.

Put oats into blender, one cup at a time, set at chop and process a few minutes until a coarse flour results. Set aside.

Carob-Coconut Clusters

Combine honey, egg, vanilla, salt, butter, and carob. Mix well, then add oat flour and beat thoroughly. Stir in the coconut.

Drop by the rounded teaspoonful onto parchment-lined baking sheet. Bake 12 to 15 minutes. Remove from baking sheet and cool on rack.

Yield: 4 dozen clusters

Baked cookies will still look shiny and wet. Cooled clusters remain moist and chewy.

2 cups rolled oats
1 cup warmed honey
1 beaten egg
1 teaspoon vanilla
¾ teaspoon salt
½ cup melted butter
3 tablespoons carob powder, sifted
2 cups grated, unsweetened coconut

Preheat oven to 350° F.

Carob-Nut Drops

Combine and beat thoroughly all ingredients but the flour and nuts. Add these and mix well.

Drop by the rounded teaspoonful onto buttered baking sheet and bake 10 to 12 minutes.

Yield: 3 to 3½ dozen cookies

⅔ cup softened butter
½ cup warmed honey
¾ teaspoon salt
1½ teaspoons vanilla
¼ cup carob powder, sifted
2 eggs
1 cup whole wheat flour
1 cup chopped pecans, English walnuts, or black walnuts

Cookies

Preheat oven to 325° F. and grease 2 large cookie sheets.

½ cup warmed honey
½ cup oil
2 eggs
3 tablespoons BASIC CAROB SYRUP
(see Index)
pinch of salt
½ teaspoon vanilla
1 cup whole wheat flour
¼ cup chopped sunflower seeds
¼ cup sesame seeds
2 tablespoons wheat germ

Mix honey, oil, eggs, carob syrup, salt, and vanilla. Stir in flour and mix well.

Drop by the teaspoonful onto greased cookie sheet, leaving about 2 inches between. Mix seeds and wheat germ and sprinkle over each cookie.

Bake in preheated oven 12 to 15 minutes. Cool on rack and store in an airtight container.

Yield: 4 dozen

Carob Wafers

Preheat oven to 350° F.

Cream butter, then add maple syrup and cream until smooth. Add eggs and mix thoroughly. Stir in lemon juice and peel. Add flour and salt and mix well. Stir in currants.

⅓ cup butter
¼ cup maple syrup
2 eggs
1 teaspoon lemon juice
½ teaspoon grated lemon peel
¾ cup whole wheat pastry flour
dash of salt
¼ cup currants

Place a sheet of parchment paper on a cookie sheet and drop batter by the level teaspoonful about 3 inches apart on the paper. Bake in preheated oven for 12 to 15 minutes. Cool on wire rack and store in sealed container.

Yield: 4 dozen cookies

This batter will be very thin—the cakes taste much better that way. Bake a few as a sample so you will know how to handle them. If you are tempted to add more flour, be very careful not to add too much or the flavor will be lost.

Currant Cakes
(An old-fashioned Christmas drop cookie)

Cookies

Beat egg with oil, honey, milk powder, and soda dissolved in buttermilk. Stir in salt and vanilla. Add flour and mix thoroughly. Chill for several hours.

Preheat oven to 325° F. and grease large cookie sheet.

Fruit-Filled Cookies

Drop dough by the teaspoonful onto prepared baking sheet. With a small coffee spoon, make a well in the center of each cookie and fill with about ¼ teaspoon fruit glaze.

Bake in preheated oven for 12 to 15 minutes. Cool on wire rack and store in airtight container.

Yield: 30 cookies

1 egg
⅓ cup oil
⅓ cup honey
2 tablespoons dry milk powder
½ teaspoon soda
2 tablespoons buttermilk
⅛ teaspoon salt
½ teaspoon vanilla
1 cup whole wheat pastry flour
¼ cup APRICOT GLAZE (see Index) or
       RASPBERRY GLAZE (see Index)

Cookies

Joe Froggers
(giant gingersnaps)

In a large bowl, combine water, rum, soda, molasses, oil, and honey. Mix flour, salt, and spices and add to the batter. Mix thoroughly.

Chill the dough.

When ready to bake, preheat oven to 375° F. and grease two cookie sheets.

Drop five mounds of dough onto each cookie sheet, leaving 3 or 4 inches between each mound. With the floured bottom of a glass, press each mound into a 4-inch circle about ¼ inch thick. Bake in preheated oven for about 10 minutes.

Yield: 10 4-inch cookies

2 tablespoons hot water
3 tablespoons rum
½ teaspoon soda
¼ cup dark molasses
¼ cup oil
½ cup warmed honey
2 cups whole wheat pastry flour
½ teaspoon salt
1 teaspoon ground ginger
⅛ teaspoon ground cloves
⅛ teaspoon ground nutmeg
dash of allspice

Cookies

Joe Frogger was the name given to these giant rum-flavored gingersnaps two centuries ago by sailors who took them along on long voyages.

For an interesting and delicious teatime dainty, bake this dough in wafers about 2 inches in diameter and about ⅛ inch thick. Then put together sandwich-fashion with cottage or ricotta cheese between the wafers.

Preheat oven to 325° F.

Cream butter, honey, egg, salt, and vanilla until light and fluffy. Add flour and beat thoroughly with a wooden spoon.

Ice Cream Wafers

Drop by the teaspoonful onto ungreased baking sheet. Place nut on each.

Bake 8 to 10 minutes.

Yield: 3½ to 4 dozen wafers

These wafers are very rich in butter and quite crumbly, so handle carefully.

½ cup softened butter
⅓ cup warmed honey
1 egg
½ teaspoon salt
¾ teaspoon vanilla
1 cup whole wheat pastry flour
48 walnut or pecan halves

Preheat oven to 325° F.

Cream together egg yolks and honey or maple syrup until very smooth and thick. Add lemon peel. Combine flour, starch, and almonds and add to first mixture. Beat well. Fold in egg whites. Drop by the rounded teaspoonful onto parchment-lined cookie sheet, about 2 inches apart, and bake for about 18 minutes. Cool on wire rack and store in cookie tin.

Lemon Cookies

Yield: 32 to 40 cookies

2 egg yolks
2 tablespoons honey or maple syrup
grated peel of 1 lemon
¼ cup sifted whole wheat pastry flour
2 tablespoons potato starch
1 teaspoon ground almonds
2 egg whites, beaten stiff

Cookies

2 egg yolks
⅓ cup oil
⅓ cup maple syrup
½ teaspoon soda
1 tablespoon sour cream
⅛ teaspoon salt
½ teaspoon vanilla
2 tablespoons dry milk powder
1 cup whole wheat pastry flour
½ cup chopped walnuts

Beat egg yolks, then add oil, maple syrup, soda mixed with sour cream, salt, vanilla, and dry milk powder. Mix well.

Stir in flour, mix thoroughly, and chill.

Preheat oven to 325°F., and grease cookie sheet.

Drop dough by the teaspoonful 'onto prepared baking sheet, top with nuts, and bake in preheated oven for 12 to 15 minutes. Cool on wire rack and store in airtight container.

Yield: 30 cookies

Maple Walnut Drops

Preheat oven to 350° F., and butter and flour a cookie sheet.

Cream butter until light, then add honey and mix well. Beat in egg whites, one at a time, and mix thoroughly.

Sift together flour and salt, and gradually add to first mixture. Stir in vanilla and lemon peel.

⅔ cup butter, softened
⅓ cup honey
2 egg whites
⅔ cup whole wheat pastry flour
¼ teaspoon salt
1 teaspoon vanilla
½ teaspoon grated lemon peel

With a small spoon, drop dough onto prepared sheet, forming strips about ¾ inch wide and 3 inches long. Space strips at least 2 inches apart to allow batter to spread during baking.

Bake in preheated oven for 10 minutes or until lightly browned. Remove immediately to wire rack to cool. Store in airtight container.

Yield: 4 dozen

Cat's Tongues

Cookies

181

Preheat oven to 325° F. and butter an 8 x 12-inch baking pan.

Thoroughly mix the ingredients in Part I and spread batter evenly into prepared baking pan. Bake for 20 minutes.

Rich Molasses-Pecan Squares

Cream butter, honey, molasses, egg, vanilla, and yogurt until light. Stir together flour, salt, and soda. Add ¾ cup pecans, then mix with creamed mixture, combining thoroughly.

Pour over partly baked bottom layer, spreading evenly, and sprinkle with ½ cup pecans.

Return to oven and bake about 25 minutes. Cool thoroughly before cutting into squares.

Yield: 40 squares

Part I
½ cup softened butter
¼ cup warmed honey
1 teaspoon vanilla
⅛ teaspoon salt
1⅓ cups whole wheat pastry flour

Part II
¼ cup softened butter
⅓ cup honey
3 tablespoons unsulphured molasses
1 egg, unbeaten
1 teaspoon vanilla
3 tablespoons yogurt
¾ cup whole wheat pastry flour
¼ teaspoon salt
½ teaspoon soda
¾ cup finely chopped pecans
½ cup finely chopped pecans
     for topping

Cookies

Preheat oven to 350° F.

Combine the butter, honey, salt, vanilla, cinnamon, and egg and beat thoroughly. Add the walnuts.

Stir together the flour, soda, and oats and add to the butter mixture, combining thoroughly.

Oat and Nut Macaroons

Drop dough by the rounded teaspoonful onto parchment-lined baking sheet, about 1½ inches apart. Bake about 12 minutes or until golden. Cool a few minutes before removing from baking sheet.

½ cup softened butter
½ cup warmed honey
½ (scant) teaspoon salt
½ teaspoon vanilla
¼ teaspoon cinnamon
1 unbeaten egg
½ cup finely chopped walnuts
⅔ cup whole wheat pastry flour
½ teaspoon soda
1½ cups rolled oats

Yield: about 3½ dozen macaroons

These spread during baking, and are quite rich, thin, and fragile. Handle delicately.

Preheat oven to 350° F.

Add salt to egg whites, and beat until stiff.

Oatmeal Macaroons

Combine maple syrup and oats and mix well. Add coconut. Fold in egg whites.

Drop by the teaspoonful onto parchment-lined baking sheet and bake for about 12 minutes.

¼ teaspoon salt
2 egg whites
⅓ cup maple syrup
1 cup rolled oats
½ cup grated, unsweetened coconut

Yield: 20 to 24 macaroons

These are very sweet and difficult to store because of their stickiness.

Cookies

Preheat oven to 350°F.

Put oats into blender, set at "chop," and process a few minutes, until they become a coarse flour (or put through food grinder, using fine blade).

In a medium-size bowl, cream butter, then add honey and mix well. Add egg and stir until mixture is smooth. Add vanilla and salt, then stir in oatmeal flour.

1 cup rolled oats
½ cup soft butter
½ cup warmed honey
1 egg, lightly beaten
1 teaspoon vanilla
½ teaspoon salt

Oatmeal Lace Cookies

Drop by the half-teaspoonful onto greased cookie sheet, about three inches apart, because they will spread while baking.

Bake for 12 minutes in the preheated oven. Remove cookies from sheet while they are still hot—allow to stand for only 1 minute. Cool on wire rack and store in sealed container.

Cool cookie sheet completely before filling with second batch of cookies.

Yield: about 4 dozen cookies

These cookies are very thin, very rich and hard to handle, but if care is taken, they are so good—you'll agree they're worth the effort.

Cookies

Combine butter, honey, egg, and orange peel. Mix well. Add orange juice and dry ingredients, combining thoroughly. Let dough stand for 15 minutes.

Orange Cookies

Preheat oven to 350° F.

Drop by the teaspoonful 2 inches apart onto ungreased baking sheet. Dough spreads during baking.

Bake 8 to 10 minutes. Store in airtight container.

Yield: 3½ to 4 dozen 2-inch cookies

These are delicately flavored and not overly sweet. Very nice with tea.

½ cup butter
½ cup warmed honey
1 egg
3 teaspoons grated orange peel
⅓ cup orange juice
¾ teaspoon soda
¼ teaspoon salt
2 to 2¼ cups whole wheat pastry flour

Combine butter, peanut butter, honey, salt, vanilla, and egg. Beat thoroughly.

Stir together flour and soda. Add to first mixture and blend. Add peanuts and mix.

Peanut Butter Cookies

Chill dough several hours or overnight.

Preheat oven to 325° F.

Drop by the level tablespoonful onto buttered baking sheet.

Bake 10 to 15 minutes or until lightly browned. Let stand a few minutes on baking sheet before removing to rack to cool.

Yield: 5 dozen cookies

½ cup softened butter
½ cup peanut butter
⅔ cup warmed honey
¼ teaspoon salt
½ teaspoon vanilla
1 egg
1½ cups whole wheat flour
¾ teaspoon soda
1 cup chopped, salted peanuts

Cookies

Preheat oven to 375° F.

1 cup butter
¾ cup warmed honey
1 teaspoon salt
½ teaspoon cinnamon
½ teaspoon cloves
2 eggs
2 tablespoons buttermilk
2 to 2½ cups whole wheat flour
¾ teaspoon soda
2 cups rolled oats
1 cup chopped nuts
1 cup chopped, seeded raisins

Combine and beat thoroughly butter, honey, salt, spices, eggs, and buttermilk.

Stir together flour and soda and add to first mixture. Add oats, nuts, and raisins and mix thoroughly.

Drop by the level tablespoonful onto buttered baking sheets.

Bake for 10 to 12 minutes.

Yield: 5 dozen cookies

Rob Roy Cookies

Mix all ingredients thoroughly. Form into roll about 1½ inches in diameter and chill in the refrigerator or freeze overnight.

When ready to bake, preheat oven to 350° F.

½ cup butter
⅔ cup warmed honey
2 eggs
2 tablespoons sour cream
1 teaspoon soda
½ teaspoon cream of tartar
2 teaspoons finely ground star anise
3 cups whole wheat pastry flour

Line cookie sheets with parchment paper. Cut dough into rounds $^3/_{16}$ inch thick and place several inches apart on the parchment. (Cookies will rise and spread while baking.) Bake in preheated oven for 12 to 15 minutes.

Remove from oven and lift from paper. Cool on rack and store in airtight container.

Yield: 50 cookies

Anise Cookies

Cookies

Cream butter, honey, and vanilla until light. Add remaining ingredients and mix well.

Chill until firm, several hours or overnight.

Preheat oven to 350° F.

Filbert Crescents

Shape small pieces of chilled dough into tiny rolls. Twist into crescents and place on ungreased baking sheets.

Bake about 12 minutes. Let crescents stand for a few minutes before removing from baking sheet.

Yield: 6 dozen crescents

These cookies are very fragile while they are still warm from the oven and are likely to crumble if removed too soon from the baking sheet. Handle with care!

1 cup butter, softened
2 tablespoons honey
1 teaspoon vanilla
2 cups whole wheat pastry flour
1 cup ground filberts

Cookies

½ cup butter
½ cup unsulphured molasses
3 tablespoons honey
1 unbeaten egg
3 to 3⅓ cups whole wheat pastry flour
½ teaspoon salt
½ teaspoon soda
1 teaspoon ginger
½ teaspoon cinnamon
¼ teaspoon nutmeg
¼ teaspoon ground cloves
2 tablespoons brandy

Mix butter, molasses, and honey in saucepan. Bring to boil over low heat and boil 2 minutes. Cool to lukewarm, then add the egg and mix.

Stir together flour, salt, soda, and spices and add to molasses mixture, combining thoroughly. Stir in the brandy.

Pack dough firmly in 8 x 8-inch buttered pan lined with wax paper. Freeze dough overnight. (Chilling in refrigerator does not make dough firm enough to slice easily.)

Preheat oven to 350° F.

Slice cookies of desired length ⅛ inch thick. Place on buttered baking sheets. Store remaining dough in freezer until ready to use.

Bake in preheated oven 10 to 15 minutes.

Yield: about 4 dozen cookies

Molasses-Brandy Cookies

Cookies

Combine and beat thoroughly, all ingredients but flour, soda, and pecans. Stir together flour and soda and add to first mixture. Add chopped pecans. Chill dough several hours.

Preheat oven to 350° F.

Party Molasses Snaps

Measure out level tablespoonfuls of dough, form into balls, and place on buttered baking sheet. Lightly press pecan half in center of each cookie.

Bake 12 minutes. Let cookies cool a few minutes on baking sheet before removing to rack.

Yield: 3 dozen cookies

These cookies are very spicy. For a milder flavor, decrease the amount of ginger to ½ to ¾ teaspoon.

½ cup softened butter
¼ cup warmed honey
½ cup molasses
½ teaspoon salt
1 teaspoon ginger
½ teaspoon cinnamon
¼ teaspoon ground cloves
¼ teaspoon nutmeg
1 tablespoon grated orange peel
1 teaspoon fresh orange juice
2⅔ cups whole wheat flour
1 teaspoon soda
½ cup chopped pecans
36 pecan halves

Preheat oven to 350° F.

Cream butter, honey, and vanilla until light. Add remaining ingredients and mix well.

Nusles

Roll pieces of dough in palm of hand to form small balls, ¾ to 1 inch in diameter. Place on ungreased baking sheet.

Bake for 15 to 20 minutes or until delicately browned. Let the cookies stand a few minutes before removing from baking sheet.

Yield: about 6 dozen *nusles*

1 cup softened butter
2 tablespoons honey
1 teaspoon vanilla
2 cups whole wheat pastry flour
2 cups finely chopped nuts (English walnuts, black walnuts, pecans, or hickory nuts)

Cookies

Combine and beat thoroughly the butter, honey, salt, egg, vanilla, and orange peel.

Stir together the flours and soda; add to butter mixture and blend. Add pecans and mix thoroughly. Chill.

½ cup butter
½ cup warmed honey
¾ teaspoon salt
1 egg
½ teaspoon vanilla
2 teaspoons grated orange peel
1 cup whole wheat flour
1 cup whole wheat pastry flour
½ teaspoon soda
¾ cup ground pecans

Orange-Pecan Cookies

Preheat oven to 375° F.

Press chilled dough very firmly together into a roll 1½ to 2 inches in diameter. Cut ¼-inch slices and place on buttered baking sheets. Wrap remaining dough in double thickness of wax paper, twisting ends tightly, and refrigerate until needed for baking.

Bake 8 to 10 minutes.

Yield: 4 to 4½ dozen cookies

Preheat oven to 325° F.

Cream butter, oil, honey, and maple syrup until smooth. Stir in flour and salt; add vanilla and pecans. Mix well.

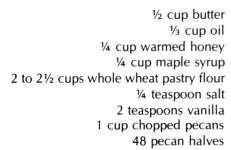

½ cup butter
⅓ cup oil
¼ cup warmed honey
¼ cup maple syrup
2 to 2½ cups whole wheat pastry flour
¼ teaspoon salt
2 teaspoons vanilla
1 cup chopped pecans
48 pecan halves

Pecan Cookies

Form dough into 1-inch balls, place on ungreased baking sheet, and press pecan half lightly into center of each, flattening cookie slightly in the process.

Bake 15 to 20 minutes until light brown.

Yield: 4 dozen cookies

Storing a few days in an airtight container or freezing improves the flavor of these cookies.

Cookies

½ cup butter
½ cup warmed honey or maple syrup
1 egg
¼ cup sour cream
½ teaspoon soda
2 to 2¼ cups whole wheat pastry flour
cinnamon

Cream butter, add honey, then egg, and beat well.

Combine sour cream and soda. Add to mixture.

Sour Cream Sandies

Add flour and mix well. Shape into a roll about 1½ inches in diameter, roll in wax paper, and freeze for several hours or overnight.

When ready to bake, preheat oven to 350° F.

Place a sheet of parchment paper on a cookie sheet. Slice the dough as thin as possible and place on paper about 1½ inches apart. Cover a flat-bottomed glass with a damp cloth and press each cookie flat. This is easy to do and will make them very thin. Sprinkle cinnamon over the top of each cookie and bake in preheated oven for 12 minutes.

Yield: 56 cookies

Cookies

½ cup butter
½ cup oil
½ cup warmed honey
2 egg yolks
1¾ cups whole wheat flour
¼ teaspoon salt

Frosting
½ cup BASIC CAROB SYRUP
(see Index)
2 tablespoons honey
2 tablespoons butter

Mix butter, oil, and honey. Then add egg yolks and beat until smooth.

Preheat oven to 350° F. and grease an 11 x 14-inch baking pan.

Stir in flour and salt.

Pat evenly into prepared pan to about ¼-inch thickness.

Bake in preheated oven for about 20 minutes or until firm.

Combine carob syrup, honey, and butter. Place over low heat and beat until smooth.

Remove baking pan from oven and while dough is still hot, spread the frosting evenly over the top. Cut into squares or bars. Cool.

Yield: 80 to 100 bars

Carob-Frosted Cookies

Cookies

Scottish Shortbread Cookies

Beat butter until soft and creamy. Add honey and continue beating. Add vanilla.

Combine flour, salt, and soda. Stir into the butter-honey mixture. Mix thoroughly. Chill the dough for several hours.

Preheat oven to 350° F. and grease a cookie sheet.

When ready to bake, sprinkle flour lightly over the greased sheet. Rub flour on your hands and press the dough gently onto the sheet in the form of a rectangle about 8 x 10 inches, ¼ inch thick. Cut dough into 1¼-inch squares and prick each one with a fork.

Bake in preheated oven for 15 to 20 minutes or until lightly browned.

Yield: 40 square shortbreads

½ cup butter
¼ cup warmed honey
½ teaspoon vanilla
1 cup whole wheat pastry flour
⅛ teaspoon salt
⅛ teaspoon soda

Walnut Bars

Preheat oven to 325° F. and grease a 7 x 11-inch baking pan.

In a medium-size bowl, beat egg with honey and vanilla. Combine flour, soda, and salt and add to the first mixture. Mix well.

Spread the batter in prepared pan, sprinkle nuts over the top, and bake in preheated oven for about 25 minutes.

Cut into squares or bars while still warm.

Yield: about 40 bars

1 egg
½ cup warmed honey
½ teaspoon vanilla
¾ cup whole wheat flour
½ teaspoon soda
pinch of salt
¾ cup chopped walnuts

Cookies

Preheat oven to 325° F.

Mix the ingredients of Part I, and spread batter into a well-buttered 8 × 12-inch baking pan.

Bake for 20 minutes.

Make a batter of the ingredients in Part II, except for the nuts and coconut, beating well. Add the nuts and mix.

Pour batter over the partly baked bottom layer and sprinkle the coconut on top.

Bake about 25 minutes until slightly brown.

Cut into bars while warm but not hot. Cool in pan. Serve warm or cold.

Yield: 32 squares

Coconut Dreams

Part I
½ cup softened butter
¼ cup warmed honey
1 teaspoon vanilla
1⅓ cup whole wheat pastry flour
⅛ teaspoon salt

Part II
1 egg
¼ cup yogurt or buttermilk
⅛ teaspoon salt
½ cup warmed honey
3 tablespoons light molasses
1 teaspoon vanilla
3 tablespoons whole wheat pastry flour
½ teaspoon soda
1 cup chopped nuts
1 cup grated, unsweetened coconut

Preheat oven to 325° F.

Thoroughly mix ingredients in order given.

Place a sheet of parchment paper on a cookie sheet. Sprinkle paper with about ½ teaspoon flour. With your fingers, press dough into a square (on the paper) about 7 x 9 inches, ⅓ inch thick. Cut into small squares (1 to 1¼ inch).

Bake in preheated oven for 15 minutes. Cool, then transfer to cookie tin, cover, and store at room temperature.

Yield: 36 squares

Moravian Scotch Cakes

⅓ cup oil
2 tablespoons maple syrup
½ teaspoon caraway seeds
½ cup whole wheat flour
½ cup whole wheat pastry flour

Cookies

Peanut Butter Bars

Preheat oven to 350° F. and butter a cookie sheet or 11 x 14-inch pan.

Mix the first nine ingredients into a batter and spread on cookie sheet or in baking pan. Bake in preheated oven for 20 to 25 minutes, until lightly browned.

While dough is baking, in a small bowl mix carob syrup, honey, and peanut butter. Beat or stir until smooth.

Remove sheet or pan from oven and spread immediately with carob mixture.

Cool and cut into bars.

Yield: about 80 bars

½ cup butter, softened
½ cup warmed honey
1 egg
⅓ cup peanut butter
½ teaspoon soda
¼ teaspoon salt
½ teaspoon vanilla
1 cup whole wheat pastry flour
1 cup rolled oats
6 tablespoons BASIC CAROB SYRUP (see Index)
3 tablespoons warmed honey
½ cup peanut butter

Cookies

CHAPTER VI

PIES

PIES

Pies are probably the most popular American dessert and the crust is often the deciding factor between success and failure. Although pie is not the easiest dessert to prepare, with some practice, some patience, and some valuable tricks just about anyone can do it and do it well.

Good pie pastry is light, crisp, and flaky—tender enough to break easily but not so tender it crumbles when cut. Undercrusts should never be soggy, but they should not be so tough that they resist the fork.

These high standards may be achieved by combining high-quality ingredients in the proper proportions, by careful handling of the dough, and by watchful baking.

Pie Crusts

Flour, shortening, and water are the basic ingredients of pastry. In special instances others may be added—spices, ground nuts, grated orange or lemon rind, for example. Fruit juice, or cottage or ricotta cheese are sometimes specified in place of part or all of the water. Grated cheese is used occasionally to replace some of the shortening, especially in fruit pies.

I offer a choice of pie crust recipes that cover a wide range, for all tastes and skills. Most of them are made with whole wheat pastry flour, which is ground from soft wheat and is very fine, producing a tender pastry. One of the recipes, HALF AND HALF PIE CRUST, calls for half unbleached white flour for those whose families are unaccustomed to the darker color and the richer flavor of whole wheat. Rolled oats is used sometimes for extra nutrition and flavor.

For a softer, more tender pie crust use butter rather than oil. In some crusts, I use all butter; in some, a combination of butter and oil. They can be used interchangeably if you use just about one-sixth less oil than you would butter.

Use ice water in making pie crust to insure a flakier crust. Always add water gradually in small quantities, and add only as much as is necessary to hold the dough together. This is tricky. If you use too little water the dough will be crumbly and will fall apart when rolled; use too much water and the dough will be sticky and hard to roll, and the finished pastry will be tough. So when you select the crust recipe which appeals to you, assemble the ingredients and mix the crust very carefully, following the directions exactly. Handle the dough tenderly and as little as possible—if you are preparing a rolled crust, every stroke of the rolling pin toughens it, so go easy! Be careful, too, to use as little flour as possible to coat the rolling pin and board.

Some beginners have difficulty rolling a crust evenly, and if you are one of these use a pressed crust which is very easy to handle. (All the crusts suggested in this book can be pressed.) When you have pressed the crust into place with your fingers, use the bottom of a flat cup or glass to smooth dough and set it firmly into the pie pan.

Be prepared for the fact that no pressed crust will be as thin or flaky as a rolled one. Also you should know that whole-grain flours are coarse and make coarse crusts. When a fine, flaky crust is necessary use the HALF AND HALF PIE CRUST (see Index).

When making a baked pastry shell for a pie that takes a cooked filling, prick the crust with a fork before baking, to prevent buckling while it is in the oven. Bake 12 to 15 minutes in a 425° F. oven.

Fruit Pies

Apple pie is a national favorite; probably that is why there are many different types of apple pie. Some of the recipes included here are a bit unusual, but do try them because they're worth adding to your specialties. For baking of any kind, the best apples are Winesap, Jonathan, or Northern Spy. There is valuable nutrition in the skins and they add to the color of the dish, so try to get apples that have tender skins and have not been sprayed with insecticides, so you don't have to peel them. Squeeze the juice of half a lemon over the apples for a special flavor. For a deluxe apple topping, I mix one cup of whipped cream with one-half cup of cottage cheese.

Apricots (fresh, dried, or frozen) make delicious pies; grapes are excellent too, but they take a lot of time in preparation; ground-cherries are unusual and very tasty; raisins, currants, pears, and rhubarb add variety to your baking.

Custard Pies

Custard pies differ from fruit pies in that they are prepared with beaten eggs which, when baked, form a custard to complement the fruit. This type of pie tends to become soggy. To prevent this, cool the pie quickly, as soon as it comes from the oven, by placing it on an inverted colander so the air will circulate easily under it. Also, custard pies should not be stored for any length of time—use them the same day they are baked for best flavor and texture.

Cream Pies

Cream pies are very attractive (they suggest party fare to me) yet they are surprisingly easy to prepare. They are always placed in a prebaked shell—this is their first "plus," because the shell will not become soggy. Cream pie fillings can be thickened with egg yolks, cornstarch, or gelatin, so they are virtually foolproof and will always set up very well. The filling can be heaped luxuriously high since there is no danger of its cooking over. Decorate with whipped cream, sour cream, or any colorful fruit or garnish.

For fun sometime, put bits and pieces of peanut brittle through a food chopper, then mix them with whipped cream and serve in a baked pie shell.

Meringue

You can find as many ways to prepare meringue as there are uses for it. However, when you make meringue with honey there are pitfalls, so be careful to follow recipe directions to the letter.

When a meringue has been prepared for a pie topping, be sure to spread it over the filling while the filling is still warm. A cold filling can cause meringue to "weep." Spread the meringue to the very edge of the pie for a good seal. It should be about an inch thick and spread in peaks, never flat, to permit the oven heat to touch more of the surface.

In spreading the meringue on the pie, use a knife or spatula which has been dipped in cold water. This permits the meringue to slip off the knife more easily.

Do not bake the meringue too long. At 425° F. bake 6 minutes; at 400° F. bake 8 minutes; at 350° F. bake about 12 to 15 minutes. Serve the pie as soon as possible after the meringue has been baked.

ITALIAN MERINGUE (see Index) is considered trouble-free. It is easy to make and can be used in many ways: as a topping for cream pie filling, as a delicious cake frosting, or for individual meringue shells. It is drier and crisper than the usual meringue.

When cutting any meringue-topped pie, remember to butter the cutting knife to prevent tearing the meringue.

NATURALLY
DELICIOUS
DESSERTS
AND
SNACKS

¾ cup rolled oats
¾ cup whole wheat pastry flour
¼ cup coconut
⅓ cup oil
2 tablespoons ice water

Place oats in bowl of blender and blend into coarse flour. Transfer to mixing bowl, add flour and coconut. Mix well. Blend in oil, then ice water.

Preheat oven to 425° F.

Press dough into greased 9-inch pie pan to about ⅛-inch thickness and bake in preheated oven for 12 to 15 minutes.

Yield: 1 9-inch pie crust

Basic Pressed Pie Crust

½ cup ricotta cheese
⅓ cup butter
1¼ cup whole wheat pastry flour

Add cheese and butter to the flour and toss together gently to form dough. Chill.

When ready to use, press into a greased 9-inch pie pan.

Yield: 1 9-inch pie crust

Rich Pie Crust

Pies

Measure flour into a medium-size bowl. Add butter and cut into flour with a fork or pastry cutter. Add oil slowly and continue to cut or mix until dough looks crumbly. Slowly add ice water and mix until you can gather the dough into a ball.

Place dough on a piece of floured wax paper, either on flat counter top or wooden board. Flatten the dough with your hand, sprinkle a little flour over it, cover with another piece of wax paper and roll out to form a circle about 12 inches in diameter, ⅛ to ¼ inch thick.

Basic Rolled Pie Crust

Remove top piece of wax paper, invert greased 9-inch pie pan over dough, turn pan, dough, and remaining piece of wax paper right side up, remove wax paper and fit dough into pan. Flute edges or simply trim away excess dough with a knife.

1¼ cups whole wheat pastry flour
3 tablespoons butter
3 tablespoons oil
2 tablespoons ice water

If recipe calls for a baked crust, prick dough with fork and bake for 12 to 15 minutes at 425° F.

Yield: 1 9-inch pie crust

1½ cups whole wheat pastry flour
½ cup finely grated sharp
cheddar cheese
¼ teaspoon salt
⅓ cup oil
1 tablespoon melted butter
2 tablespoons ice water

Stir together flour, cheese, and salt. Blend in oil and butter until crumbly. Sprinkle in ice water a little at a time. Form dough into a ball, wrap and chill at least one hour.

On lightly floured board, roll out dough to ⅛-inch thickness. Fit into greased 9-inch pie pan and flute edges.

Yield: 1 9-inch pie crust

Cheddar Cheese Pie Crust

Mix nuts and honey in a greased 9-inch pie pan. Press the mixture evenly against the bottom and sides of the pan.

1½ cups ground hazelnuts
3 tablespoons honey

Fill with filling of your choice and chill.

Yield: 1 9-inch pie

This crust is especially good filled with fruit chiffon, lemon, cream, or custard filling.

Hazelnut Pie Crust

Pies

Crumb Pie Crust

Combine crumbs, honey, butter, and oil. Mix thoroughly. Reserve ½ cup crumbs for topping. Press the remaining portion of the crumbs into a greased 9-inch pie pan, spreading evenly against the bottom and sides of the pan.

Chill for 20 minutes or bake immediately at 325° F. for about 10 minutes. Cool. Add filling, top with reserved crumbs, and chill again before serving.

Yield: 1 9-inch pie

2 cups fine natural cookie crumbs
1 tablespoon honey
3 tablespoons melted butter
3 tablespoons oil

Sour Cream Pie Crust

Combine flour and salt. Cut in butter, leaving the mixture in coarse lumps. Add sour cream a little at a time so that no more is added than is necessary to hold the dough together.

Chill for 30 minutes or more. Roll out to ¼-inch thickness and place in greased 9-inch pie pan.

Yield: 1 9-inch pie crust

1¼ cups whole wheat pastry flour
¼ teaspoon salt
¼ cup butter
5 to 6 tablespoons cold sour cream (approximate quantity)

Pies

1¼ cups whole wheat pastry flour
¼ teaspoon salt
¼ teaspoon soda
⅓ cup butter
1 egg
1 tablespoon lemon juice
1 tablespoon water

Combine flour, salt, and soda. Cut in butter until pieces are about the size of peas. Beat egg with lemon juice and water. Add slowly to flour mixture. Handle gently and do not overmix.

Roll out dough, fit into greased 9-inch pie pan, and flute edges.

When ready to use, bake at 425° F. for 15 minutes.

Yield: 1 9-inch pie crust

Foolproof Pie Crust

⅔ cup whole wheat pastry flour
⅔ cup unbleached white floor
3 tablespoons butter
3 tablespoons oil
2 tablespoons ice water

Measure flour into a medium-size bowl. Add butter and cut into flour with a fork or pastry cutter. Add oil and mix until dough looks crumbly. Add ice water a little at a time (using only enough to hold dough together) and mix until you can gather the dough into a ball.

Roll dough, between pieces of wax paper, into a circle about 12 inches in diameter and about ⅛ to ¼ inch thick. Fit into greased 9-inch pie pan and flute or trim edges.

Yield: 1 9-inch pie crust

Half and Half Pie Crust

Pies

In a large skillet, combine cider and honey. Bring to a boil, stirring to dissolve honey. Add apples, raisins, lemon juice, and rind. Simmer, uncovered, for 5 to 8 minutes, stirring occasionally.

In a small bowl, mix cornstarch, cinnamon, and cider. Stir until smooth, then add to apple mixture. Stir and cook until thick, about 5 minutes. Cool.

Preheat oven to 425° F.

Apple-Cider Foldovers

Divide pastry into 6 parts. On a floured board, roll each part into a 5-inch circle. Moisten edge of each circle, brush with butter, and spread one-half of each circle with several tablespoonfuls of apple filling. Fold over. Press edges together firmly. Make 3 gashes in center of folded edge for steam to escape.

Bake on ungreased cookie sheet in preheated oven for about 30 minutes. Serve warm, topped with dollop of sour cream, if desired.

Yield: 6 foldovers

1 recipe HALF AND HALF PIE CRUST (see Index) mixed in advance but not rolled
¾ cup cider
3 tablespoons warmed honey
3 cups apples, pared and cut into large dice
¼ cup seedless raisins
1 tablespoon lemon juice
1 teaspoon grated lemon rind
2 teaspoons cornstarch
¼ teaspoon cinnamon
2 tablespoons cider
2 tablespoons softened butter
½ to 1 cup sour cream (optional)

Pies

Shenandoah Apple Pie

(with Cheddar Cheese)

Preheat oven to 350° F.

Combine apples, honey, butter, flour, and spices. Put one-half of the apple mixture in bottom of crust. Top with a layer of cheese, then the rest of the apples and the remaining cheese.

Bake in preheated oven for 45 minutes or until apples are tender.

Yield: 1 9-inch pie

When baking a fruit pie which might cook over, it is wise to grease the pie pan and coat it with a light dusting of flour. The pie will not stick to the pan and will be easier to serve.

1 9-inch BASIC ROLLED PIE CRUST (see Index) prepared in advance but not baked
4 cups sliced apples
⅓ cup honey
1 tablespoon melted butter
2 tablespoons whole wheat flour
½ teaspoon nutmeg
½ teaspoon cinnamon
1 cup grated sharp cheddar cheese

Pies

Preheat over to 425° F.

Arrange half the apples over the pastry. Combine honey, cinnamon, nutmeg, and salt. Sprinkle half the mixture over the apples. Repeat layer of apples, then honey mixture.

Bake in preheated oven for 10 minutes, then reduce heat to 375° F. and bake 30 minutes longer, or until apples are tender. Remove from the oven and top with sour cream. Serve hot or cold.

Yield: 1 9-inch pie

Sour Cream Apple Pie

1 9-inch BASIC ROLLED PIE CRUST (see Index), prepared in advance but not baked
5 medium-size tart apples, pared, cored, and sliced
⅓ to ½ cup warmed honey
½ teaspoon cinnamon
dash of nutmeg
¼ teaspoon salt
¾ cup sour cream

Preheat oven to 450° F.

Arrange cooked, drained apricots in pie shell. In a small bowl, beat eggs, add honey, salt, lemon juice, fruit liquid, and nutmeg. Pour mixture over apricots.

Blend flour, cinnamon, and butter into crumbs. Add honey. Sprinkle over filling in pie shell and bake in preheated oven for 10 minutes. Reduce heat to 350° F. and bake 20 to 30 minutes longer, or until set in center.

Yield: 1 9-inch pie

If using fresh apricots for this pie, cook only 3 to 5 minutes; frozen, about 7 minutes; and dried, about 15 minutes. Drain and reserve the liquid.

Apricot Crumb Pie

1 9-inch SOUR CREAM PIE CRUST (see Index) prepared in advance but not baked

Filling:
2¾ cups cooked fresh, frozen (unsweetened), or dried apricots
2 eggs
3 tablespoons warmed honey
⅛ teaspoon salt
1 tablespoon lemon juice
½ cup cooking liquid from apricots (or orange juice)
dash of nutmeg

Crumbs:
¼ cup whole wheat flour
½ teaspoon cinnamon
2 tablespoons soft butter
1 tablespoon honey

Pies

1 9-inch CHEDDAR CHEESE PIE
CRUST (see Index), baked
2 pounds Concord grapes (about
4 cups after preparation)
2 tablespoons warmed honey
2 tablespoons cornstarch
½ cup orange juice
2 tablespoons grated lemon rind
1 cup chopped walnuts

Wash grapes, stem, and remove skins.
Cook pulp about 10 minutes, then put
through strainer to remove seeds, pressing to get all the pulp. Put skins through
food chopper, using medium blade for
coarse chopping.

Mix skins, pulp, and honey. Combine
cornstarch and orange juice, add to
mixture. Cook over medium heat for 5
minutes, then add lemon peel and cook
until thick.

Spoon mixture into baked pie shell and
top with walnuts. Cool.

Yield: 1 9-inch pie

Grape-Nut Pie

Ground-Cherry Pie

1 9-inch BASIC ROLLED PIE CRUST
(see Index), prepared in
advance but not baked
2½ cups husked ground-cherries
2 eggs
⅛ teaspoon salt
⅓ cup warmed honey
1 tablespoon whole wheat pastry flour
1 cup milk
1 teaspoon vanilla

Preheat oven to 425° F.

Put ground-cherries into unbaked pie
shell.

Beat eggs, add salt, honey, flour, milk,
and vanilla. Pour over cherries and
bake in preheated oven for 10 minutes,
then reduce heat to 350° F. and bake
for about 30 minutes longer, until a
knife inserted in center comes out
clean.

Serve plain or with whipped cream.

Yield: 1 9-inch pie

The ground-cherry is a luscious,
golden, little fruit which grows wild on
a low, bushy plant. It can be found in
the Mississippi Valley and in some
areas of Pennsylvania. It is first cousin
to the Japanese lantern.

Pies

Preheat oven to 450° F.

In a heavy saucepan, combine fruit and orange juice. Place over medium heat and cook slowly for 15 minutes. Turn off heat and allow fruit to steep, covered, for another 15 minutes.

Raisin (or Currant) Pie

Combine egg, honey, lemon juice and rind, salt, and flour. Mix well and add to fruit mixture in saucepan. Cook slowly for about 10 minutes until thick and smooth. Cool.

1 9-inch BASIC ROLLED PIE CRUST (see Index) prepared in advance but not baked
1¼ cup raisins or dried currants
2 cups orange juice
1 egg, well beaten
¼ cup warmed honey (less, if using raisins)
juice of 1 lemon
1 tablespoon grated lemon rind
¼ teaspoon salt
4 tablespoons whole wheat flour

Pour filling into pastry-lined pie pan and bake in preheated oven for 10 minutes, then reduce heat to 350° F. and bake another 25 minutes.

Yield: 1 9-inch pie

If you like a tart, piquant flavor, use currants for this pie; using raisins yields a much sweeter pie.

The traditional raisin pie is made with strips of dough, latticed across the top of the pie. For this, you will need an additional one-fourth recipe of dough.

Pies

Preheat oven to 400° F.

1 9-inch CHEDDAR CHEESE PIE
CRUST (see Index), prepared
in advance but not baked
4 cups MEATLESS MINCEMEAT
(see below)
grated peel of 1 lemon
juice of 1 lemon

Combine mincemeat, lemon peel, and
juice. Spoon into pastry-lined pie pan.
Bake on lowest rack of preheated oven
about 40 minutes, or until edges of
crust are golden brown.

Serve warm.

Yield: 1 9-inch pie

Mincemeat
Pie

1 cup raisins
3 tart apples, cored but not peeled
½ orange
¼ lemon
½ cup cider
⅓ cup warmed honey
½ teaspoon salt
½ teaspoon cinnamon
½ teaspoon nutmeg
½ teaspoon ground cloves

Using the coarse blade of a food chopper, put through the raisins, apples,
orange, and lemon.

Place in a saucepan, add cider and
cook slowly for 8 to 10 minutes. Add
remaining ingredients and simmer 15
minutes longer. Cool.

Yield: about 3½ to 4 cups (enough for
1 9-inch pie)

Meatless
Mincemeat

Pies

Preheat oven to 450° F.

Divide pie dough into 6 equal portions and roll each one into a 5-inch circle about ¼ inch thick. Fit dough over the backs of 6 muffin tins, fitting tightly around the tins by pressing with your fingers. Prick the dough with a fork. Bake in preheated oven for 12 to 15 minutes, or until very lightly browned. Cool and remove carefully from tins.

In the top of a double boiler, mix egg yolks, milk, and honey. Place over hot water and cook for about 5 to 8 minutes or until custard is thick, stirring constantly.

Fruit Tarts

Beat egg white with salt and almond extract. Fold into custard. Cool.

Spoon about 2 tablespoonfuls of custard into each tart shell. Cover with prepared fruit. Chill.

Just before serving, spoon 1 tablespoonful RASPBERRY GLAZE or RED CURRANT GLAZE over fruit and, if desired, decorate with whipped cream.

Yield: 6 fruit tarts

Individual tart pans may be used if you prefer a more shallow tart. The muffin tin system yields a deeper, more attractive tart.

1 recipe HALF AND HALF PIE CRUST (see Index) prepared in advance but not rolled
2 egg yolks, lightly beaten
½ cup milk
3 tablespoons warmed honey
1 egg white
a few grains of salt
2 drops of almond extract (no more)
2 cups fresh fruit or berries, washed and drained on paper towels
1 cup RED CURRANT GLAZE or RASPBERRY GLAZE (see Index)
¼ cup heavy cream, whipped (optional)

Pies

Preheat oven to 325° F.

Mix cheese, honey, eggs, and vanilla. Pour into prepared pie shell and bake in preheated oven for 25 minutes.

Cheese Pie

Combine sour cream, honey, and vanilla.

Increase oven heat to 425° F.

Spread sour cream mixture on top of custard and bake another 5 minutes. Cool.

Yield: 1 9-inch pie

1 9-inch CRUMB PIE CRUST (see Index) prepared in advance but not baked
1 pound ricotta cheese
⅓ cup warmed honey
4 eggs, lightly beaten
½ teaspoon vanilla
½ pint sour cream
1 tablespoon warmed honey
½ teaspoon vanilla

Preheat oven to 375° F.

Mix eggs, honey, and butter.

Add oats and coconut and pour into prepared pie shell. Bake in preheated oven about 45 minutes. Serve warm.

Oatmeal Pie

Yield: 1 9-inch pie

OATMEAL PIE may also be served cold, but it is especially good slightly warm.

1 9-inch BASIC ROLLED PIE CRUST (see Index) prepared in advance but not baked
3 eggs, well beaten
⅓ cup warmed honey
⅓ cup melted butter
1 cup rolled oats
½ cup unsweetened coconut

Pies

1 9-inch BASIC ROLLED PIE CRUST
(see Index), prepared in
advance but not baked
¼ cup butter
3 eggs
½ cup warmed honey
2 tablespoons milk
1 teaspoon vanilla
1 tablespoon whole wheat flour
1 cup pecan halves

Pecan Pie

Preheat oven to 350° F.

Cream butter until light. Beat in eggs, honey, and milk. Add vanilla and flour and mix thoroughly. Put pecans into pie shell, pour custard over all and bake in preheated oven for 30 to 40 minutes or until knife inserted in center comes out clean. Serve warm or cold.

Yield: 1 9-inch pie

1 9-inch BASIC ROLLED PIE CRUST
(see Index), prepared in
advance but not baked
3 cups fresh rhubarb, cut into ½-inch
pieces (or 3 cups frozen, thawed)
boiling water
3 egg yolks, beaten
⅔ cup warmed honey
3 tablespoons whole wheat pastry flour
pinch of salt
3 egg whites, beaten stiff
1 tablespoon butter

Rhubarb Custard Pie

Place rhubarb in a deep bowl which has a tight-fitting lid. Cover with boiling water, cover with lid, and allow to stand for about 20 minutes. (If you wish, you can prepare the crust at this time.)

Preheat oven to 425° F.

Drain water from rhubarb, add beaten egg yolks, honey, flour, and salt. Mix well, then carefully fold in beaten egg whites. Spoon into pastry shell and dot surface with butter.

Bake at 425° F. for 10 minutes, then reduce temperature to 350° F., and bake 30 minutes longer.

Yield: 1 9-inch pie

Pies

Preheat oven to 400° F.

Combine sour cream, egg, vanilla, and nutmeg. Add flour, salt, and honey. Beat to a smooth, thin batter.

Pear Custard Pie

Arrange sliced pears in pie shell, then pour batter over the fruit. Bake in preheated oven for 15 minutes, then reduce heat to 350° F. and bake for 30 minutes longer. Remove from oven and top with crumbs made of:

⅓ cup whole wheat flour
1 tablespoon butter
1 tablespoon honey
1 teaspoon cinnamon

Increase oven heat to 400° F. and return pie to brown for 10 or 15 minutes.

Yield: 1 9-inch pie

1 9-inch HALF AND HALF PIE CRUST
    (see Index), prepared in
    advance but not baked
1 cup sour cream
1 egg
1 teaspoon vanilla
¼ teaspoon nutmeg
2 tablespoons whole wheat flour
⅛ teaspoon salt
⅓ cup warmed honey
2 cups sliced fresh pears (about 8 pears)

Pies

Pour 1½ cups milk into the top of a double boiler. Combine the other ½ cup milk with cornstarch and add to the milk in double boiler. Add honey and salt and cook over boiling water, stirring constantly, until well thickened. Blend a small amount of the hot milk mixture into beaten egg yolks, then pour back into remaining hot milk mixture, stirring well. Cook 1 minute longer. Remove from heat and add butter and vanilla. Cool.

Banana Cream Pie

Peel and slice bananas and place in pie shell. (The bottom should be well covered with about 3 layers of banana.) Cover immediately with cooled custard.

Top with whipped cream.

Yield: 1 9-inch pie

Bananas discolor very fast; be sure to slice them at the very last moment, using a stainless steel knife.

1 9-inch BASIC ROLLED PIE CRUST (see Index), prepared and baked in advance
2 cups milk
5 tablespoons cornstarch
¼ cup warmed honey
¼ teaspoon salt
2 egg yolks, lightly beaten
1 tablespoon butter
½ teaspoon vanilla
3 or 4 ripe bananas (depending on size)
½ pint heavy cream, whipped

Pies

Mix ½ cup milk with coconut. Heat remaining milk in heavy saucepan.

Mix egg yolks, honey, butter, and vanilla.

Stir in flour and salt. Mix thoroughly.

1 9-inch BASIC ROLLED PIE CRUST (see Index), prepared and baked in advance
2 cups milk
1 cup unsweetened coconut
3 egg yolks
¼ cup warmed honey
2 tablespoons soft butter
2 teaspoons vanilla
¼ cup whole wheat flour
½ teaspoon salt
¼ cup toasted coconut for garnish

Pour about ½ cup of hot milk into egg yolk mixture. Stir well, then pour into hot mixture in saucepan. Cook over medium heat until thick and smooth, stirring constantly. Remove from heat and add the coconut-milk mixture. Stir until well blended.

Pour into baked pie shell and cool. Top with toasted coconut and chill until ready to serve.

Yield: 1 9-inch pie

Fresh coconut may be used for the filling in this pie. It is not necessary to soak the coconut in milk; simply omit that step, and use only 1¾ cups milk for the custard. For the garnish, use dried coconut—it is easier to toast.

Coconut Cream Pie

Pies

Scald milk in top of double boiler, then add egg yolks and honey slowly, stirring briskly. Dissolve cornstarch in water and add to mixture. Place over boiling water and cook for about 20 minutes, stirring occasionally.

Remove from heat and take out 1 cup of custard. To this add carob syrup and rum. Set aside to cool.

Soak gelatin in cold water. When softened, add to hot custard mixture remaining in the double boiler. Stir until gelatin is dissolved, then set aside to cool.

Black Bottom Pie

Pour carob-rum mixture into cooled pie shell and chill.

Beat egg whites with cream of tartar until foamy. Add honey slowly and beat until stiff and shiny. Add vanilla, then fold into plain custard mixture.

When carob layer is cooled and partly set, pour the plain vanilla custard on top of the carob layer in the pie shell. Chill.

When ready to serve, remove the side of the springform pan and place pie on crystal cake stand or plate.

Decorate with whipped cream, if desired.

Yield: 8 servings

Crust:
2 cups natural cookie crumbs
1 teaspoon ground ginger
1 tablespoon warmed honey
3 tablespoons melted butter

Preheat oven to 425° F.

Combine crumbs, ginger, honey, and butter. Press into a 9-inch springform pan covering the bottom and building the sides to about 1¼-inch height. Bake in preheated oven for 10 minutes. Allow to cool.

Filling:
2 cups milk
4 egg yolks, well beaten
¼ cup warmed honey
1½ tablespoons cornstarch
1½ tablespoons water
5 tablespoons BASIC CAROB SYRUP (see Index)
3 tablespoons rum
1 tablespoon gelatin
2 tablespoons cold water
4 egg whites
¼ teaspoon cream of tartar
2 teaspoons warmed honey
½ teaspoon vanilla
1 pint heavy cream, whipped (optional)

Pies

Golden Chiffon Pie

Soak gelatin in cold water.

In a saucepan, beat egg yolks, add honey and salt. Stir in gelatin and cook over low heat, stirring constantly, till mixture thickens. Remove from heat and blend in peanut butter. Add sour cream.

Beat egg whites until stiff. Fold into mixture. Pour into pie shell and chill until firm.

Serve topped with whipped cream.

Yield: 1 9-inch pie

1 9-inch CRUMB PIE CRUST (see Index), prepared and baked in advance
1 envelope unflavored gelatin
⅔ cup cold water
3 egg yolks
5 tablespoons warmed honey
¼ teaspoon salt
⅔ cup peanut butter
1 cup sour cream
3 egg whites
½ cup heavy cream, whipped

Lemon Chiffon Pie

Soak gelatin in cold water.

In the top of double boiler, beat egg yolks, add honey, lemon juice, lemon rind, and salt. Place over hot water and cook until thickened, stirring constantly. Cool.

Fold in stiffly beaten egg whites and spoon into baked shell. Serve topped with whipped cream and chopped nuts.

Yield: 1 9-inch pie

1 9-inch CRUMB PIE CRUST (see Index), prepared and baked in advance
1 envelope unflavored gelatin
¼ cup cold water
4 egg yolks, beaten
½ cup warmed honey
½ cup lemon juice
1 teaspoon grated lemon rind
½ teaspoon salt
4 egg whites, beaten stiff
½ cup whipped cream
¼ cup chopped nuts

Pies

☐ Be sure egg whites are at room temperature—the volume will be greater and the beating is easier.

☐ Use a clean, dry bowl, large enough to allow plenty of air to reach the mass. You can beat whites by hand with a whisk or hand beater, or with an electric beater. Start beating slowly, then increase to medium speed.

☐ Add a pinch of salt and beat until whites are foamy.

☐ Gradually beat in the honey (warmed), a small amount at a time, until the honey is completely incorporated into the whites and the whole mixture is smooth, fine, and stiff.

☐ Be sure to use the right proportions, too; one teaspoon of honey for each egg white should be plenty, unless the recipe specifies otherwise.

☐ When the meringue is ready—smooth, shiny, and stiff—it will have a very fine texture and will look somewhat like marshmallow.

Standard Procedure for Meringue

Pineapple Meringue Pie

In a saucepan, combine pineapple, cornstarch, honey, lemon juice, and butter. Cook, stirring frequently, until thick. Pour a little of the pineapple mixture over the yolks, mix well, then stir into the hot mixture in the saucepan. Cook over low heat, stirring constantly for one minute longer, until yolks have thickened. Cool.

Preheat oven to 325° F.

Pour custard into baked pie shell.

Beat egg whites and salt until frothy. Gradually add honey, continuing to beat until meringue is stiff, smooth, and shiny. Spread meringue over pineapple custard and bake in preheated oven for 15 to 20 minutes until meringue is browned slightly. Cool.

Yield: 1 9-inch pie

1 9-inch SOUR CREAM PIE CRUST (see Index), prepared and baked in advance
2 cups crushed pineapple, drained
1 tablespoon cornstarch
2 tablespoons warmed honey
1 teaspoon lemon juice
1 tablespoon butter
2 egg yolks, beaten lightly
3 egg whites
⅛ teaspoon salt
2 teaspoons warmed honey

Pies

1 9-inch CRUMB PIE CRUST
(see Index), prepared and
baked in advance
4 cups milk, divided
2 tablespoons butter
⅓ to ½ cup warmed honey
4 tablespoons carob syrup
7 tablespoons cornstarch
4 egg yolks, slightly beaten
2 tablespoons rum
½ teaspoon salt
¼ cup heavy cream, whipped,
or 1 cup sour cream or yogurt
1 tablespoon BASIC CAROB SAUCE
(see Index)

In a heavy-bottom saucepan, over low heat, combine ¾ cup milk, butter, honey, and carob syrup. Blend cornstarch with ½ cup milk to make a thin paste. Add remaining milk, stir until well combined, then add to the hot carob mixture, cooking until thickened (about 15 minutes), stirring constantly.

Stir a few tablespoons of the hot mixture into the egg yolks and mix well. Then add mixture to the hot pudding in the saucepan. Cook, stirring, for about 1 minute longer. Remove from heat, add rum, and spoon into baked pie shell. Chill until firm.

Pile whipped cream, sour cream, or yogurt onto top of the pie. Drizzle carob sauce over topping for an attractive effect.

Yield: 1 9-inch pie

Rum Carob Cream Pie

In a saucepan, combine milk, honey, and cornstarch. Bring to a boil over low heat, stirring constantly.

Pour a little of the hot mixture over egg yolks, then return to the milk mixture in the saucepan and cook slowly until thick, continuing to stir. Remove from heat and add butter and vanilla.

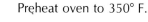

Peanut Butter Surprise Pie

Preheat oven to 350° F.

Combine peanut butter and honey and spread over bottom of baked pie shell.

Beat egg whites until frothy, then slowly add honey, a few drops at a time, and beat until stiff, smooth, and shiny (see Standard Procedure for Meringue, page 229).

Pour custard over peanut butter mixture in pie shell. Cover with meringue and bake in preheated oven about 10 minutes until lightly browned.

Chill thoroughly before serving.

Yield: 1 9-inch pie

1 9-inch BASIC ROLLED PIE CRUST (see Index), prepared and baked in advance
2½ cups milk
¼ cup warmed honey
¼ cup cornstarch
4 egg yolks, beaten
2 tablespoons butter
1 teaspoon vanilla
¾ cup peanut butter
¼ cup warmed honey
4 egg whites
2 teaspoons warmed honey

Pies

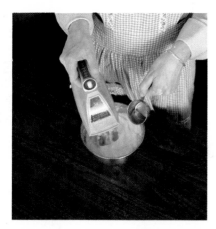

In the top of a double boiler, scald milk. Add vanilla and honey. Combine flour and salt. Blend in a little of the hot milk, then stir mixture into remaining milk. Place over hot water and cook until thick.

Raspberry Cream Pie

Beat together the egg yolks and whole egg. Gradually stir in about 1 cup of the milk mixture. Return to the rest of the milk mixture in the double boiler and continue to cook, stirring constantly, until thick. Cool.

Fold whipped cream into cooled egg mixture. Turn into baked pie shell. Cover with raspberries. Carefully spoon glaze over berries. Chill.

Yield: 1 9-inch pie

1 9-inch BASIC ROLLED PIE CRUST (see Index), prepared and baked in advance
2 cups milk
1 teaspoon vanilla
¼ cup warmed honey
⅓ cup whole wheat flour
¼ teaspoon salt
4 egg yolks
1 whole egg
¼ cup heavy cream, whipped
1 pint fresh raspberries, or 2 10-ounce packages frozen, drained
½ cup RED CURRANT GLAZE (see Index)

Pies

Individual
Italian
Meringues

In a round-bottom mixer bowl, beat egg whites at low speed for 1 minute. Add salt and cream of tartar. Gradually increase speed to high and beat until whites form stiff peaks. Lower speed and beat for 10 to 15 minutes while you prepare syrup.

Preheat oven to 350° F.

In a small, heavy saucepan, combine honey and water, place over low heat and bring to a boil. Cover and allow to boil for 2 minutes, watching carefully so it won't boil over. Uncover and boil without stirring until syrup forms a soft ball when tested in cold water (about 10 minutes). Remove from heat and slowly drizzle the hot syrup into the egg whites, beating continually for about 5 minutes, or until mixture is cool. Beat in vanilla.

Line a baking sheet with parchment paper and drop meringues by spoonfuls forming four large or six medium-size meringues. Bake in preheated oven for 18 minutes. Remove from paper and cool on a wire rack.

Fill with fruit filling or with custard, garnished with fruit.

Yield: 4 or 6 individual meringues

This recipe may be used also for meringue topping for cream pie filling or for cake frosting.

3 egg whites
pinch of salt
¼ teaspoon cream of tartar
⅓ cup warmed honey
¼ cup water
1 to 2 teaspoons vanilla

CHAPTER VII

SAUCES AND GLAZES

SAUCES AND GLAZES

Sauces are the cook's secret weapon when it is necessary to develop flavor, provide moisture, add richness, give color, or add to the appearance of foods. Some desserts require a particular sauce to complete the blending of flavor and texture that makes for perfection, and when this is so for a recipe in this book, you will be directed to the special sauce required. Often you can concoct a delicious dessert out of leftover cake or pudding just by adding an interesting sauce.

A dessert sauce should complement the dessert, adding zest or flavor if necessary, but the sauce must never mask the dessert. A light sauce for a rich dessert, and a rich sauce for a plain one is the general rule. Hard sauce is served with steamed puddings, gingerbread, and mincemeat pie. Fruit sauces are served with cake, bread pudding, and some steamed puddings.

The thickening agent for cooked sauces may be whole egg or egg yolk, flour, cornstarch, or arrowroot flour. Fruit sauces are quite often thickened with cornstarch, which keeps them clear. The liquid used in cooked sauces may be milk, cream, or fruit juices.

When liquor or flavorings are added to cooked sauce, they should be added after the sauce has been removed from the heat or just before serving. This prevents dissipation of the flavoring essences which might occur during cooking. Serve these sauces hot with desserts which are served hot, and well chilled with cold desserts.

One cup of sauce usually serves six to eight, but of course this is a matter of individual taste. If the sauce is served on the side, you will probably need more than if you arrange the individual servings yourself.

Most sauces can be made in advance and stored in a covered jar in the refrigerator. If jars are not completely filled, turn them upside down—their contents will stay fresh for a much longer time.

I have suggested and given recipes for many different sauces, but don't hesitate to concoct some of your own from any leftover fruit or natural fruit juice you might have. For example: grape juice sauce makes a pleasant change when served over puddings or custards; blackberry sauce makes a delicious topping for rice pudding; plum or peach glaze adds to the appearance and flavor of cornstarch pudding; add broken pecans or sliced Brazil nuts to maple syrup to make a delicious sauce for baked or steamed puddings.

Like sauces, glazes may be made from any kind of fruit. However, glazes are thickened in a different way. A glaze is made by adding honey to the fruit and cooking it the same as you cook jam, but not as long. It will become thick, sweet, and brilliant in color. Its purpose is to enhance flavor and appearance of a dessert, adding color naturally.

The cooking process of glazes makes them almost as durable as jams so they keep very well for a long time if stored in a sealed container in the refrigerator.

NATURALLY
DELICIOUS
DESSERTS
AND
SNACKS

¾ cup diced, dried apricots, soaked overnight
⅓ cup honey
1½ cups water or soaking juice from apricots

Cook apricots, honey, and water in heavy saucepan, over low heat, for about 30 minutes. Cool slightly, then process in blender until smooth. If necessary, add water or any fruit juice to obtain the right consistency.

Cool completely, put into sealed container, and store in refrigerator.

Yield: about 2 cups sauce

Apricot Sauce

1 cup light cream
1 cup milk
¼ cup honey
2 eggs, well beaten
1 tablespoon lemon juice
1 cup sieved avocado

In a heavy-bottom saucepan, heat cream, milk, and honey. Slowly stir in eggs, and continue to stir over very low heat until sauce is thick and smooth. Remove from heat and allow to cool slightly.

Combine lemon juice and avocado. Add to sauce, and stir until well blended. Cool completely, then chill until ready to serve.

Yield: about 2½ cups sauce

This attractive, light green sauce is delicious served over ice cream, fresh fruit, plain custard, or cake.

Avocado Sauce

Sauces and Glazes

Banana Fluff

Mash bananas, add lemon juice and honey, and mix until smooth. Fold in whipped cream. Serve immediately.

Yield: about 2 cups

This sauce is excellent on gingerbread, carob *crepes*, or any kind of fritter.

3 ripe bananas
1½ tablespoons lemon juice
½ to 1 tablespoon honey
⅓ cup heavy cream, whipped

Blueberry Sauce

Place blueberries in the bowl of a blender. Add lemon juice and peel. Blend at medium speed until berries are chopped but not pureed. Place in small saucepan and add honey. Stir over low heat until just below boiling. Mix cornstarch, salt, and water, and add to berries. Cook slowly, about 7 minutes, until thick, dark, and smooth. Cool. Place in jar and store in refrigerator.

Yield: about 2¼ cups

2 cups blueberries, fresh or frozen, unsweetened
1 teaspoon lemon juice
1 teaspoon grated lemon peel
2 to 3 tablespoons honey
2 teaspoons cornstarch
dash of salt
¼ cup water

Sauces
and Glazes

¾ cup honey
¼ cup water
4 tablespoons butter
½ cup finely chopped nuts (pecans, walnuts, almonds)

In a small saucepan, boil honey and water together over low heat, until mixture forms a soft ball when dropped in cold water (234° F.). Remove from heat and add butter and nuts. Place in covered jar and store in refrigerator.

Yield: about 2 cups

Butterscotch Sauce

2 tablespoons butter
⅓ cup honey
½ cup BASIC CAROB SYRUP (see Index)
1 egg
1 teaspoon vanilla

Mix all ingredients and cook over low heat until thick and smooth. Cool and store in refrigerator.

Yield: about 1 cup

Carob Sauce

Sauces and Glazes

Custard Sauce

In a heavy, medium-size saucepan, combine ½ cup of the milk with the cornstarch. Stir with a whisk until the cornstarch is dissolved. Add the remaining milk and the honey, and cook over low heat until the sauce thickens and comes to a boil, stirring constantly.

In a small bowl, beat the egg yolks lightly. Stir a few tablespoons of the hot sauce into the egg yolks, then add to the rest of the sauce. Bring to a boil again and boil for 1 minute, continuing to stir. Remove the pan from the heat and add the vanilla.

Yield: 3 cups

3 cups milk
4 teaspoons cornstarch
1 tablespoon honey
3 egg yolks
½ teaspoon vanilla

Foamy Sauce for Puddings, Fritters, and Crepes

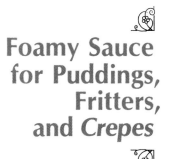

In medium-size bowl, cream butter, and beat in remaining ingredients gradually. Beat until very light and smooth. Place bowl in pan of hot water and stir about 2 minutes or until sauce is frothy and foamy.

Serve immediately.

Yield: about 1½ cups

1 cup butter
¾ cup honey
⅓ cup sherry
2 egg whites
¼ cup boiling water

Sauces and Glazes

Put cherries in container of blender and process at medium speed until chopped but not pureed, (or chop in food chopper, using medium blade).

Place chopped cherries in small saucepan; add honey. Stir over low heat until just below boiling. Mix cornstarch, salt, and water, and add to cherries. Cook slowly until thick and smooth. Cool. Place in jar, cover, and store in refrigerator.

Yield: about 2 cups

Sour cherries are not always available, but they make the best sauce. If you have plenty of freezer space, make the sauce in quantity when cherries are in season and freeze in small containers, ready for use.

Any kind of cherries may be used for sauce: sweet, Oxheart, or Bing, but if you substitute sweet cherries be sure to use less sweetening or none at all, according to your taste.

2 cups fresh sour cherries, pitted
3 tablespoons honey
2 teaspoons cornstarch
dash of salt
¼ cup water

Cherry Sauce

Sauces and Glazes

Ginger Sauce

Scrape and dice ginger root into ⅛-inch cubes or slices. Place in saucepan, add water, cover, and cook slowly for about ½ hour. Drain. Put 1 cup of the liquid back into the saucepan, add the honey and the diced ginger root. Boil, covered, for about 10 minutes, or until mixture becomes syrupy.

Combine cornstarch and water and add slowly to the ginger syrup. Cook until thick and smooth. Cool.

Store in tightly closed jar in refrigerator.

Yield: 1½ cups

GINGER SAUCE is very powerful! But it is tasty and adds an exotic flavor if used sparingly over vanilla ice cream or plain pudding or custard.

1 cup ginger root, soaked overnight
3 cups water
1 cup honey
1 tablespoon cornstarch
1 tablespoon water

Honey Brandy Sauce

In a small, heavy saucepan, combine honey, water, and salt. Bring to a boil and cook for 3 or 4 minutes. Dissolve cornstarch in water, and add slowly to the honey mixture. Cook over very low heat, stirring constantly until the mixture thickens. Remove from heat, add butter, stirring until it is blended into the sauce. Add the brandy and stir well to combine.

Serve warm over ice cream, pudding, or fruit.

Yield: about 1 cup sauce

Care must be taken in cooking this sauce. Use very low heat and watch carefully to prevent scorching.

⅔ cup honey
½ cup water
pinch of salt
4 teaspoons cornstarch
4 tablespoons water
4 teaspoons butter
6 tablespoons brandy

Sauces and Glazes

Lemon Custard Sauce

2 cups water
¼ cup lemon juice
½ teaspoon salt
⅓ cup honey
¼ cup cornstarch
2 teaspoons grated lemon peel
1 egg, well beaten

Combine all ingredients except egg in saucepan and cook over low heat, stirring constantly until mixture becomes thick and transparent.

Add a little of the hot mixture to the egg. Mix well, then return to hot mixture. Cook about 2 minutes longer, stirring constantly.

Yield: about 2 cups

Lingonberry Sauce

2 cups lingonberries
⅓ cup honey
¼ cup water

Wash berries, pick over, and drain.

In a saucepan, combine berries, honey, and water. Bring to a boil and simmer about 10 minutes.

Serve hot or cold.

Yield: about 2 cups

Lingonberries are wild cranberries which grow widely in Norway, Sweden, and Newfoundland. In the United States, they are found wherever temperatures are cold enough to permit freezing of the roots of the plants. They are found in the White Mountains and Rocky Mountains, as well as the bogs in northern Wisconsin and Minnesota.

Sauces
and Glazes

Maple Syrup Pudding Sauce

In a saucepan, boil syrup and water for 7 to 10 minutes, (228° F.).

In a medium-size bowl, beat egg whites until stiff. Add syrup gradually, beating constantly with electric or hand beater. When well blended and light, add lemon juice carefully, then fold in whipped cream. Use immediately or sauce will separate.

Yield: about 2 cups

¾ cup maple syrup
¼ cup water
2 egg whites
1 teaspoon lemon juice
½ cup heavy cream, whipped

Sour Cream Orange Sauce

Cream butter, add honey, and beat until mixture is very light and fluffy. Add sour cream, orange peel, and juice. Mix thoroughly and chill.

Serve with cake or puddings.

Yield: about 1½ cups

3 tablespoons butter
⅓ cup honey
1 cup sour cream
1 teaspoon grated orange peel
3 tablespoons orange juice

Sauces and Glazes

2 cups fresh raspberries, or
2 10-ounce packages, frozen
3 tablespoons honey
2 teaspoons cornstarch
¼ cup water

In a small saucepan, combine berries and honey. Stir over low heat until just below boiling. Mix cornstarch and water and add to berry-honey mixture. Cook slowly until thick and smooth (5 to 7 minutes).

Strain sauce through coarse sieve, cool, place in covered container, and store in refrigerator.

Yield: about 2 cups

Raspberry Sauce

6 tablespoons light cream
3 tablespoons light rum
½ cup soft butter
⅓ cup honey
½ cup golden raisins

Put cream, rum, and butter into the container of a blender, cover, and process at medium speed until smooth. (At this point the mixture will look slightly curdled or separated, but don't be concerned, just continue.)

Add honey, then process again until smooth. Add raisins and process just until raisins are chopped fine, not pureed.

Yield: about 2 cups

This sauce is excellent over vanilla ice cream or pudding. It can also be used as the base in making RUM-RAISIN ICE CREAM (see Index).

Rum-Raisin Sauce

Sauces
and Glazes

Strawberry Foam

Cream butter thoroughly, and add honey slowly. Fold in egg white, then strawberries. Serve immediately.

Yield: about 1¾ cups sauce

Red or black raspberries or mulberries (hulled) may be used in place of strawberries. Adjust amount of honey according to sweetness of berry used.

⅓ cup butter
½ cup honey
1 egg white, beaten stiff
2 cups fresh strawberries, mashed

Whipped Dry Milk

Mix milk powder, water, and lemon juice. Whip until light. Add honey gradually, then vanilla, and beat until well blended and fluffy.

Yield: 2 to 3 cups

A light, fluffy topping, which can be used in place of whipped cream. It is especially recommended for its high protein and low fat content.

½ cup dry milk powder
½ cup water
1 tablespoon lemon juice
2 tablespoons honey
½ teaspoon vanilla

Sauces and Glazes

2 cups pitted and chopped, fresh
apricots (or frozen,
unsweetened, chopped)
1 thin slice lemon with peel, chopped
⅓ cup honey

In a medium-size saucepan, combine apricots, lemon, and honey. Heat slowly over low heat until honey is dissolved and fruit becomes juicy. Put mixture into the container of a blender and blend at medium speed until completely pureed. Return to saucepan and cook slowly for 5 to 8 minutes, stirring so glaze will not scorch.

Cool, place in covered container or jar, and store in refrigerator.

Yield: 1¾ cups

Apricot Glaze

1 cup finely chopped, fresh pineapple
1 tablespoon honey

In a small saucepan, over low heat, cook pineapple with honey for 12 to 15 minutes, or until slightly thickened and syrupy.

Pour into jar, cover tightly, and store in refrigerator until ready to use. Glaze will keep for several weeks.

Yield: about 1 cup

Pineapple Glaze

Sauces and Glazes

Raspberry Glaze

Boil honey and water together slowly for about 12 minutes. Add berries and cook another minute. Cool.

Chill before serving, or store in jar in refrigerator until ready to use.

Yield: about 2 cups

½ cup honey
½ cup water
2 cups crushed raspberries

Red Currant Glaze

Wash currants and put into a saucepan. With a fork, crush the berries against the side of the pan. Add just enough water to keep the fruit from scorching. Cover and place over low heat, and cook for about 5 minutes. Strain through a dampened cheesecloth jelly bag. Do not squeeze or press the bag.

When all juice is extracted, pour juice into a flat-bottom saucepan. Add honey and boil over medium heat for about 8 minutes. Pour into a jar, cover tightly, and refrigerate.

When ready to use, place in a small saucepan over low heat. Add Kirsch and stir until well blended. This should take about 3 minutes. Use as recipe directs.

Yield: about 1 cup

2 cups red currants
1 to 2 tablespoons water
⅓ cup honey
1 teaspoon Kirsch

Sauces and Glazes

In a small saucepan, mix carob and water. Bring to a boil over very low heat, stirring constantly. Cook for 5 to 8 minutes or until the syrup is completely smooth. Cool and store, covered, in the refrigerator.

Yield: about 1½ cups

1 cup carob powder
1 cup water

Basic Carob Syrup

This basic syrup is used in our natural recipes in place of bitter or unsweetened chocolate. If you wish to convert one of your own recipes which calls for melted, semisweet chocolate, use the above recipe, adding ¼ cup honey and (if you wish) 2 tablespoons butter. The same preparation procedure is recommended.

Place coconut in the container of a blender or in a coffee mill, and process at medium speed until coconut is very fine. Store in sealed jar and use in place of powdered sugar to dust doughnuts, cookies, small cakes, or buns.

1 cup unsweetened, dried coconut

Coconut Sugar

Yield: 1 cup

Sauces and Glazes

CHAPTER VIII

CANDY AND CONFECTIONS

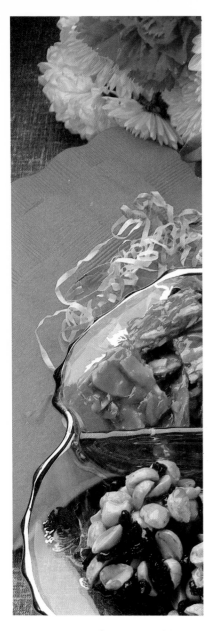

CANDY AND CONFECTIONS

Homemade candy is usually made just for fun. However, some cooks make it to keep the family from buying less wholesome candies at the supermarket. Whatever your reason, you will want to make good candy and, though it might lack the look of professional perfection, it will have an appeal all its own. If you follow the fundamental techniques of candy-making, your achievement may surprise you!

The basic types of candy fall into two categories: crystalline, like the fudges and fondants; and noncrystalline, like the taffies and brittles. The first type is almost impossible to make with natural ingredients (substituting honey for sugar). The honey never loses its stickiness and the texture is far from ideal. Maple syrup is better than honey as a substitute for sugar, but that, too, produces a candy which lacks something in texture.

The noncrystalline candies, on the other hand, are very easy to make and are delicious. I've included recipes that use either honey or maple syrup and provide a wide choice of flavors.

Candy cooks best in cool, dry weather; in warm, sticky weather it tends to become "grainy." So, if at all possible, pick an appropriate day to do your candy making. If you must cook candy on a rainy day, cook it at 2° F. higher temperature than that called for in the recipe.

Select a pan which is large enough so the candy will not boil over, and butter it for an inch or two down from the top. A two-quart smooth, heavy utensil is good. Always use a wooden spoon (it helps to prevent crystallizing). Cooking time depends on the thickness of the pan—if you use a thin pan, you will need to remove it from the heat sooner.

Timing is the most important factor in candy-making. Some people have learned to judge "doneness" by color and consistency. That takes experience! If you are a beginner, cook to the recommended stage in the recipe, testing either with a candy thermometer or the cold water method described below.

Candy thermometers are not expensive and would be a wise investment if you cook candy frequently.

In the candy recipes in this book, I give both the cold water test stages and the desired reading on the candy thermometer. These should help you determine cooking time. Success, of course, also depends on your own excellent cooking sense, and fine natural ingredients.

Confections
Confections are those delightful little tidbits which are not a candy and not quite a cake or cookie! They're nice to have around the house for that tiny something to munch on between meals—especially after school. Some are particularly good served with coffee as a dessert, or as a party refreshment.

Many confections are made from dried fruits and nuts which means that, in addition to being delicious, they are an excellent "pick-up" because they are high in protein. In fact, confections are a wonderful means of adding some of those nutrition "extras" to the diet.

Confections are very easy to make and are fun because you can let your imagination run wild in creating many different combinations of flavors (and using a lot of little leftovers from last week's baking).

Since most of these dainty confections are not cooked and, of course, have no preservatives, it is wise to store them in the refrigerator. There they will keep well for weeks.

Be sure to include the children when you plan to prepare some of these goodies. Youngsters seem to have a knack for the finger work necessary for shaping, rolling, and pressing the mixture into shape. They have good ideas too, and they might suggest some interesting flavor combinations which the whole family will enjoy.

NATURALLY
DELICIOUS
DESSERTS
AND
SNACKS

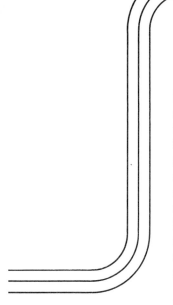

Basic Procedure for Testing Candy

If you use a thermometer, never put it directly into the boiling syrup. Either heat it first in water brought slowly to the boiling point, or stand the thermometer in the mixture before you start cooking and leave it there. The bulb must be completely covered with syrup, yet must not touch the bottom of the pan. When candy reaches the required temperature, remove the thermometer and put it where it may cool gradually, before you wash it.

To make the cold water test, when the candy is nearly ready, remove the pan from the heat so the cooking will stop. Fill a cup or small bowl with cold water. Drop about a half-teaspoonful of the syrup into the cold water and shape it with your fingers into a ball. Test for degree of hardness according to these stages:

Soft Ball (234° F. to 238° F.) The ball of candy flattens out somewhat.

Medium-Soft Ball (238° F. to 240° F.) The ball of candy just barely holds its shape.

Firm Ball (244° F. to 250° F.) The ball of candy is firm but not hard.

Hard Ball (265° F.) The ball of candy is very firm and hard.

Hard Crack (270° F. to 310° F.) The syrup separates into threads when poured into the cup. The ball of candy is brittle when you tap it against the side of the cup.

Butter an 8 x 8-inch shallow pan.

Melt butter in heavy frying pan; stir in honey. Add almonds. Cook over medium heat, stirring constantly until mixture turns golden brown (about 7 minutes).

⅓ cup butter
¼ cup honey
¾ cup slivered almonds

Spread mixture in prepared pan, working quickly, while still very hot. With buttered, sharp knife, cut into squares immediately. Cool.

Chill in refrigerator and store in covered container.

Yield: about 36 pieces

Almond Crunch Candy

Butter an 8 x 8-inch shallow pan.

Place sesame seeds in heavy skillet and stir over moderate heat until slightly brown. Pour into bowl and set aside.

In the same skillet, melt butter and stir in honey. Cook over medium heat for about 3 minutes. Add sesame seeds and continue to cook, stirring constantly but not vigorously, until mixture turns golden brown, about 2 to 4 minutes.

1 cup sesame seeds
⅓ cup butter
¼ cup honey

Spread mixture in prepared pan while still hot. With buttered knife, cut into squares immediately. Cool.

Yield: about 36 squares

Benne is wild sesame, but the candy is just as good made from cultivated sesame seeds.

Benne Brittle

Candy and Confections

Cashew Brittle

In an iron skillet, boil the honey and water until it forms a soft ball when dropped into cold water or reaches 234° F. (see Basic Procedure for Testing Candy on page 262). Add nuts and continue to boil until golden brown, about 10 to 12 minutes, stirring continuously.

Remove from heat and add butter, vanilla, and soda. Mix well, then pour onto a greased cookie sheet. When cool, break into pieces.

Yield: about 1 pound

¾ cup honey
¼ cup water
1 cup raw cashews
1 tablespoon butter
½ teaspoon vanilla
1 teaspoon soda

Coconut-Molasses Chews

Combine molasses, vinegar, honey, and butter in a saucepan. Cook over low heat, stirring occasionally until the mixture forms a soft ball when dropped into cold water or reaches 234° F. (see Basic Procedure for Testing Candy on page 262). Remove from heat and add coconut, vanilla, and salt.

Drop by teaspoonful onto a greased cookie sheet. Cool and store in refrigerator.

Yield: 3 dozen chews

¼ cup molasses
1 tablespoon white vinegar
¾ cup honey
2 tablespoons butter
2 cups grated, unsweetened coconut
1 teaspoon vanilla
dash of salt

Candy and
Confections

1⅓ cups honey
½ cup butter
2 cups light cream

Combine honey, butter, and 1 cup of cream in a saucepan. Bring to a boil, stirring frequently, and cook until mixture begins to darken and thicken. Add remaining cup of cream and continue to cook until mixture forms a fairly firm ball when dropped into cold water or reaches 244° F. (see Basic Procedure for Testing Candy on page 262).

Pour into buttered 8 x 8-inch pan. When cool, cut into 1-inch squares and wrap individually.

Yield: 64 squares

Cream Caramels

¼ cup molasses
1 teaspoon cider vinegar
½ cup honey
3 tablespoons butter
2 cups peanut halves
1 cup dried currants

In a saucepan, combine molasses, vinegar, and honey, and cook over low heat until mixture forms a firm ball when dropped in cold water, or reaches 250° F. (see Basic Procedure for Testing Candy on page 262). Stir occasionally.

Remove from heat and add butter, then nuts and currants.

Drop by the teaspoonful onto a buttered baking sheet.

Yield: about 40 clusters

Currant-Peanut Clusters

Candy and Confections

Date Candy Loaf

Cook honey and milk until mixture forms a soft ball when dropped into cold water or reaches 234° F.

Add dates and nuts and cook until mixture forms a firm ball or reaches 244° F. (see Basic Procedure for Testing Candy on page 262). Remove from heat, add vanilla and butter. Stir vigorously until stiff. Form into two 2-inch rolls and roll in a wet cloth. Cool and store in an airtight container, dampening cloth when necessary. Slice as needed.

Yield: about 25 slices

½ cup honey
1 cup milk
1 cup chopped dates
1 cup chopped nuts
1 teaspoon vanilla
1 tablespoon butter

Divinity

In a saucepan, cook honey, water, and vinegar until mixture forms a firm ball when dropped into cold water, or reaches 244° F. (see Basic Procedure for Testing Candy on page 262).

While the mixture is cooking, beat the egg white until stiff but not dry. When syrup is the correct consistency, pour it very slowly into egg white, beating continually until creamy, light, and firm. Add chopped nuts and vanilla.

Drop by the teaspoonful on buttered wax paper or spread in a buttered 8 x 8-inch pan. When partly cooled, cut into squares. Press a pecan half into center of each piece.

Yield: 30 pieces

¾ cup honey
¼ cup water
1 teaspoon vinegar
1 egg white
½ cup chopped pecans
½ teaspoon vanilla
30 pecan halves

Candy and
Confections

266

In a saucepan, mix honey, vinegar, and molasses. Boil until mixture forms a hard ball when dropped into cold water or reaches 270° F. (see Basic Procedure for Testing Candy on page 262). Stir in the soda and butter. Mix well.

¼ cup honey
¼ cup white vinegar
2 cups molasses
1 teaspoon soda
1 tablespoon butter

Pour onto large buttered platter or cookie sheet. When cool enough to handle with buttered fingers, pull until taffy is light and shiny. Place the long pieces of pulled candy on buttered dish and cut into pieces. Wrap each piece separately to prevent sticking.

Yield: 3 dozen 1-inch pieces

Molasses Taffy

Put syrup, milk, cream, and salt into a saucepan and cook briskly for 15 minutes. Remove from heat, add peanut butter, and beat until creamy. Pour into a buttered 8 x 8-inch pan and cool to room temperature. Cut into squares.

1 cup maple syrup
¾ cup milk
¼ cup light cream
2 tablespoons dry milk powder
½ teaspoon salt
2 tablespoons soft peanut butter

Yield: 16 squares of fudge

Be sure to beat the fudge until very smooth and creamy.

Maple-Peanut Butter Fudge

Candy and
Confections

Maple-Glazed Nuts

In an iron skillet, stir together syrup, cinnamon, butter, and salt. Cook and stir over medium heat until mixture becomes brown and starts to thicken. Add vanilla, then nuts and toss until the nuts are covered evenly with glaze.

Cool on wax paper.

Yield: 2 cups

½ cup maple syrup
1 teaspoon cinnamon
1 tablespoon butter
¼ teaspoon salt
1½ teaspoons vanilla
2 cups walnuts

Candy and Confections

Pralines

In a saucepan, mix honey, buttermilk, soda, and salt. Cook over high heat for 5 minutes. Add butter and continue to cook, frequently stirring until mixture forms a soft ball when dropped into cold water or reaches 234° F. (see Basic Procedure for Testing Candy on page 262). Remove from heat and cool for 5 minutes. Beat with electric beater until creamy. Add nuts. Immediately drop by the tablespoonful onto buttered wax paper.

For storing, wrap each praline in plastic wrap.

Yield: 1 dozen pralines

½ cup honey
½ cup buttermilk
½ teaspoon soda
dash of salt
1 tablespoon butter
¾ cup pecan pieces

Candy and
Confections

English Toffee

Butter a shallow 8 x 8-inch pan. Sprinkle nuts evenly on bottom.

In a saucepan, melt butter over medium heat. Gradually add honey, stirring occasionally to prevent burning. Cook 4 to 7 minutes until mixture turns golden brown. Pour over nuts in pan and cool slightly. With a knife, mark into 1-inch squares. Cool completely and break into pieces along lines.

Yield: about ¾ pound candy

½ cup finely chopped nuts (peanuts, cashews, pecans, or almonds)
½ cup butter
½ cup honey

Candy and
Confections

Bakeless Carob Confections

In a heavy saucepan, combine honey, carob, buttermilk, butter, and salt, and boil for one minute. Remove from heat and add peanut butter, blending thoroughly. Add oats and 1½ cups coconut, stirring well. Cool to a workable temperature.

Form dough into balls about 1 inch in diameter. Roll balls in ¾ cup coconut and place on wax paper. Chill before serving.

Store in refrigerator.

Yield: About 5 dozen 1-inch confections.

These are quite sweet and rich, a bit messy to form into balls but worth the effort.

1 scant cup honey
¼ cup carob powder
⅓ cup buttermilk
½ cup butter
pinch of salt
½ cup peanut butter
3 cups rolled oats
1½ cups grated, unsweetened coconut
¾ cup grated coconut for rolling

Fruit-Nut Bonbons

Put all ingredients except cinnamon into food chopper and grind together. Mix thoroughly with your hands, then shape into small balls (about the size of walnuts). Dust lightly with cinnamon. Store in refrigerator.

Yield: about 30 balls

1 cup dried currants
½ cup figs
½ cup pitted dates
½ cup walnuts
½ cup sunflower seeds
cinnamon

Candy and
Confections

274

¾ cup milk
3 tablespoons carob powder, sifted
¼ cup butter
1 cup honey
1 teaspoon vanilla
½ teaspoon lemon juice
½ cup nuts, or sunflower or sesame seeds (or combination)

Combine milk, carob, and butter. Bring to a boil, stirring constantly, until smooth and thick. Add honey, stirring until dissolved. Cook without stirring until a small amount of the mixture forms a soft ball when dropped into cold water or reaches 234° F. (see Basic Procedure for Testing Candy on page 262). Cool to lukewarm. Add vanilla and lemon and beat until thick. Add nuts or seeds. Cool to room temperature and form into balls about the size of hickory nuts.

Yield: 20 to 24 balls

Carob Fudge Balls
(or chews)

¾ cup honey
½ cup carob powder
½ cup milk
1 teaspoon vanilla
¼ teaspoon salt
½ cup butter
3 cups rolled oats

In a saucepan, combine honey, carob, milk, vanilla, salt, and butter. Boil for 5 to 6 minutes, stirring constantly.

Remove from heat. Add oats and mix well.

Drop by teaspoon onto wax paper and let cool.

No baking—this is a quickie.

Yield: 42

Carob Wisps

Candy and Confections

275

Carob Balls

In a small saucepan, mix carob, honey, and coffee. Place over low heat until well blended, stirring constantly (about 5 minutes). Remove from heat. Add butter, milk powder, and almond paste or extract. Work together into a smooth paste. Shape into small balls. Chill. When firm, roll in mixture of cinnamon and carob. Store in refrigerator.

Yield: 1 dozen balls

3 tablespoons carob powder, sifted
2 tablespoons honey
1 tablespoon powdered instant coffee
1 tablespoon butter
½ cup dry milk powder
⅓ cup almond paste or 1 teaspoon
    almond extract
1 teaspoon cinnamon
1 teaspoon carob powder, sifted

Blender Almond Paste

In the bowl of an electric blender, combine orange juice, first cup of almonds and honey. Blend at medium speed until nuts are very fine. Add second cup of nuts and blend again until nuts are very fine.

Store in refrigerator.

Yield: about 2 cups

½ cup orange juice
1 cup blanched almonds
½ cup warmed honey
1 (additional) cup blanched almonds

Candy and Confections

Recipe for ALMOND CRUNCH CANDY (top of photo), page 263; recipe for CURRANT-PEANUT CLUSTERS (bottom of photo), page 265; CAROB BALLS (right center), this page.

Chew-Chews

Preheat oven to 350° F. and grease a 9 x 13-inch jelly roll pan.

Combine butter, honey, and molasses and mix well. Add egg whites and beat until fluffy. Combine flour, soda, and salt and stir into the first mixture. Blend in coconut.

Spread evenly in prepared pan and bake in preheated oven for 30 minutes. Cool for 5 minutes, then cut into 1½-inch squares.

Yield: 35 squares

⅓ cup softened butter
½ cup honey
¾ cup molasses
4 egg whites
1¾ cups whole wheat flour
¼ teaspoon soda
¼ teaspoon salt
1 cup unsweetened coconut

Kindergarten Patties

Mix all ingredients in a large bowl. Rub hands generously with oil, then shape dough into patties about 1½ inches in diameter and ¼ inch thick. Place on cookie sheet, and allow to stand for 30 minutes.

Yield: 30 patties

Since there is no baking necessary, this confection is one which children love to make—and eat!

1 cup dry milk powder
1 cup rolled oats
½ cup peanut butter
¼ cup honey
½ cup BASIC CAROB SYRUP
   (see Index)
¼ cup boiling water

Candy and
Confections

278

2 cups finely chopped, pitted dates
¼ cup honey
½ cup water
½ teaspoon vanilla
1 cup finely chopped English
walnuts or pecans
1½ cups grated, unsweetened coconut

In heavy saucepan, cook dates, honey, and water over low heat, stirring constantly until thick, about 5 minutes. Remove from heat, add vanilla, nuts, and coconut.

When mixture has cooled to workable temperature, form into 1-inch balls. Place on wax paper.

Store in refrigerator, serve at room temperature. May be frozen.

Yield: about 40 confections

Coco-Date-Nut Confections

2 cups chopped dates
½ cup butter
½ cup honey
1 egg, beaten
1 teaspoon vanilla
2 cups chopped sunflower seeds
¼ cup coconut for rolling

Mix dates, butter, honey, egg, and vanilla in a saucepan. Bring to a rolling boil and boil 1 minute. Cool. Add seeds.

Form into 1-inch balls and roll in coconut. Store in refrigerator.

Yield: 40 1-inch balls

Date Balls

Candy and
Confections

Soak figs in boiling water for about 10 minutes. Drain and dry on paper towels. Remove ends and put through food chopper, along with nuts, using medium blade. Mix figs and nuts and pat into an 8 x 8-inch square on a buttered pan or sheet.

Fig-Nut Confection

In a small saucepan, mix carob syrup, milk powder, honey, and butter. Stir over low heat for about 5 minutes, until well blended. Spread one-half of carob mixture over fig-nut square. Chill, turn square over, and spread remaining carob mixture over the other side. Cut into small squares.

Yield: about 24 pieces

1 cup dried figs
1 cup nuts (English walnuts, pecans, or almonds)
⅓ cup BASIC CAROB SYRUP (see Index)
¼ cup dry milk powder
1 teaspoon honey
1 tablespoon butter

Mix honey, peanut butter, and milk powder. Work into smooth paste and roll into small balls. Chill.

Peanut Butter Balls

In a saucepan, mix carob syrup, milk powder, honey, and butter. Place over low heat and stir until well blended. Remove from heat.

Dip peanut butter balls into hot carob mixture, drop onto buttered wax paper, and chill. Store in refrigerator.

Yield: about 20 balls

½ cup warmed honey
1 cup peanut butter
¼ cup dry milk powder
½ cup BASIC CAROB SYRUP (see Index)
¼ cup dry milk powder
1 teaspoon honey
2 tablespoons butter

Candy and Confections

Butter an 8 × 8-inch pan.

Grind together raisins and nuts. Mix with honey, and press into prepared pan. Cover with wax paper, then place a weight on top, and allow to stand for 24 hours.

Cut into bars, then dip into ground nuts. Store in covered container in the refrigerator.

Yield: 36 bars

2 cups raisins
1 cup mixed nuts
¼ cup honey
⅓ cup mixed nuts, ground fine

Honey-Nut Bars

Wash apricots, cover with boiling water, and allow to stand for 5 minutes.

Drain apricots, then combine with coconut and put through food chopper, using medium blade. Add orange and lemon peel and orange juice. Mix until well blended.

Shape into 1-inch balls, allow to stand at room temperature for about 2 hours, then roll in coconut if desired. Place in covered container, and store in refrigerator.

Yield: 2 dozen balls

1½ cups dried apricots
1½ cups unsweetened coconut
1 teaspoon grated orange peel
1 teaspoon grated lemon peel
2 tablespoons orange juice
¼ cup coconut for rolling (optional)

Coconut-Apricot Confection

Candy and Confections

Haystacks

Preheat oven to 350° F.

Beat egg well. Add honey, vanilla, yogurt, and butter, mixing thoroughly. Stir in flour, then add the coconut and work it in well with wooden spoon.

Dip the small end of an egg cup in cold water, then press about 1 tablespoonful of coconut mixture firmly into the cup, slip out onto parchment-lined baking sheet, and sprinkle with a little cinnamon. Continue until mixture is used.

Bake in preheated oven for 20 minutes or until light brown. Cool completely before serving.

Yield: 2 dozen haystacks

Haystacks are fragile and must be stored carefully to keep them from disintegrating.

1 egg
⅓ cup warmed honey
½ teaspoon vanilla
1 tablespoon yogurt
1 tablespoon melted butter
1 tablespoon whole wheat pastry flour
½ pound grated, unsweetened coconut

Candy and
Confections

CHAPTER IX

CRACKERS AND SNACKS

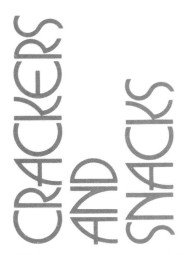

CRACKERS AND SNACKS

We have become a "snacking" society! Almost everywhere we go people are nibbling at something, mostly foods of the pick-up variety. Fast-food stands line all the highways, popcorn vendors are found in every movie theatre, and kitchen shelves and refrigerators are stacked with snack-type food.

Undoubtedly, the habit is here to stay, so let's make our snacking pay off in food value.

It's pleasant to nibble on bite-size tidbits while waiting for a meal; it's fun to munch while watching TV; it's refreshing to take a snack break along the road; and it's great to have a mid-morning or mid-afternoon bite to carry you through to mealtime. Supermarkets have shelf after shelf of items to fill this need (indeed, it has become big business) but if you read the labels you'll notice, from the ingredients, that the product will not fill the need for nutritional help at all.

You can solve the problem by learning to make your own snacks from basic, natural foods. Have them available for family and friends and know that you are getting nutrition without preservatives or too much salt.

Crackers

Tasty crackers are very simple to prepare. Start with any of a number of whole-grain flours, add your favorite herbs and seasonings, and top with a variety of seeds. Bind them with eggs, oil, milk, or buttermilk, and cut them into any shape your imagination dictates—you'll never want to go back to the supermarket variety.

Cooked grains add an extra dimension to crackers and snacks. Roll them right into the dough along with the herbs and seeds. Bake them a little longer than you would ordinarily, to be sure the crackers will be crisp and dry.

Homemade crackers store well. Keep them on hand in an airtight container and it will soon become as popular as the cookie jar.

Packables

Nutrition can be packed into a lunch box—our recipes for sturdy packables are proof of this. They can be served hot or cold and were created to put variety into everyday lunches. Put them to the test and you'll find that they satisfy the most demanding appetite. They'll win over white bread and cold cuts every time.

You don't have to carry these treats outside the home to enjoy them. You can serve them hot at lunch time or as a hardy after-school treat; at a buffet supper or a cocktail party.

Many interesting and delicious snacks can be prepared without a recipe. Have you ever tried fresh fruit at cocktail or teatime? Spread raw apple slices, banana chunks, or pineapple wedges with peanut butter or cottage cheese. Stuff dried apricots, prunes, dates, or figs with a mixture of grated carrots and crushed pineapple. Mix deviled raisins with nuts and seeds as a new treat.

NATURALLY
DELICIOUS
DESSERTS
AND
SNACKS

Preheat oven to 425° F.

In a small bowl, combine flour, cheese, onion salt, and celery seed. Add oil, working mixture with your fingers. Add water and buttermilk a little at a time until evenly mixed, and dough holds together and is workable.

2 cups whole wheat flour
1 cup grated, sharp Cheddar cheese
2 teaspoons onion salt
½ teaspoon celery seed
¾ cup oil
3 tablespoons water
2 or more tablespoons buttermilk

Crisp Cheese Wafers

Divide dough into thirds, and roll between wax paper to thickness of 1/8 to 3/16 inch. Cut into circles and other shapes with cookie cutters about 1½ inches in diameter. Place on ungreased baking sheet. Prick wafers with a fork. Bake in preheated oven about 7 minutes or until golden brown. Cool on wire rack. Store in airtight container.

Yield: Approximately 11 to 12 dozen wafers

Mix all ingredients, except water, until thoroughly combined. Add the water, a little at a time, and work into a rollable dough. Add a small amount of additional water if necessary. Refrigerate dough until firm.

¼ cup oil
1 cup whole wheat pastry flour
1 cup grated sharp cheese
seasoned salt to taste
¼ teaspoon sage
¼ teaspoon thyme
dash or two of cayenne
2 tablespoons cold water

Preheat oven to 350° F.

Cheese Snacks

Roll dough on a lightly floured board to the thickness of pie crust, and cut into circles 1½ inches in diameter. Place on ungreased baking sheet and prick each cracker with a fork.

Bake in preheated oven for about 15 minutes. Store in airtight container.

Yield: about 42 small crackers

Dough may be prepared in advance and refrigerated until ready to use.

Crackers and Snacks

289

Chili Corn Chips

Preheat oven to 350° F.

Combine buttermilk and oil. In mixing bowl, thoroughly stir together the dry ingredients. Add milk mixture and stir until dough forms a ball. Knead on floured board (adding a little more flour if necessary) about 5 minutes.

Divide dough in half. Roll each into a 12-inch square. Cut into 1-inch squares. Sprinkle with salt or paprika.

Bake on lightly greased baking sheet for 15 minutes or until slightly brown around edges. Cool slightly before removing from baking sheet, finish cooling on wire rack.

Store in loosely covered container.

Yield: 8 to 10 dozen small chips

½ cup buttermilk
3 tablespoons oil
½ cup yellow cornmeal
½ cup toasted cornmeal
½ cup whole wheat pastry flour
¾ teaspoon salt
¼ teaspoon soda
⅛ teaspoon cayenne
½ teaspoon chili powder, or more, to taste
salt or paprika

Crackers
and Snacks

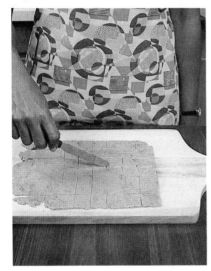

In a large bowl, stir together oats, flour, almonds, wheat germ, sesame seeds, honey, salt, oregano, thyme, and onion powder. With a fork, beat together eggs and oil. Stir into oat mixture.

Preheat oven to 400° F. and grease a 10 x 15-inch jelly roll pan.

Savory Granola Crackers

With a spatula, press dough evenly into prepared pan, and bake in preheated oven for 20 minutes or until golden. Cut into 1½-inch squares, then into triangles.

Remove to rack to cool. Store in airtight container.

Yield: about 70 crackers

These unusual crackers will keep several weeks at room temperature—several months in the refrigerator or freezer.

2 cups rolled oats
¾ cup whole wheat flour
½ cup slivered almonds
¼ cup wheat germ
¼ cup sesame seeds
1 tablespoon honey
½ teaspoon salt
½ teaspoon oregano
1 teaspoon thyme
½ teaspoon onion powder
3 eggs
¾ cup oil

Crackers
and Snacks

Preheat oven to 325° F.

Mix all ingredients as listed, except for buttermilk, and combine thoroughly. Add buttermilk to make a cookie-type dough. (A few tablespoons of additional buttermilk may be needed to make a workable dough). Divide dough in half. Roll out, one-half at a time, between wax paper to a thickness of 3/16 inch. Cut into squares or rectangles 1 to 1½ inch across. Prick each with a fork. Place on greased baking sheet.

Oat Crackers

3 cups whole wheat flour
2 cups rolled oats
¼ cup warmed honey
1 teaspoon salt
1/3 teaspoon soda
½ cup butter
¾ cup buttermilk, heated

Bake in preheated oven for about 25 minutes. Store in airtight container.

Yield: about 12 dozen crackers

Preheat oven to 425° F.

In small bowl, add poppy seeds to boiling water, let stand until cool. Sift together flour, salt, soda, and pepper. Add oil, honey, egg, onion, and poppy seed mixture to flour mixture. Stir until stiff dough forms. Knead lightly until dough is smooth. Shape into two balls.

Poppy Seed Crackers

1/3 cup poppy seeds
1/3 cup boiling water
2 cups whole wheat pastry flour
1½ teaspoons salt
½ teaspoon soda
1/3 teaspoon black pepper
1/3 cup oil
1 teaspoon honey
1 egg, slightly beaten
¼ cup minced onion

Roll dough ⅛ inch thick on lightly floured board. Cut with 1½-inch biscuit cutter. Place crackers on ungreased baking sheet. Prick each one with a fork. Bake in preheated oven 10 to 12 minutes or until lightly browned. Store in airtight container.

Yield: about 8 dozen crackers

Crackers and Snacks

293

Preheat oven to 375° F.

Combine flour, cheese, salt, and oil. Blend until crumbly. Add ice water a little at a time to form dough.

Sesame-Cheese Strips

Roll between two pieces of wax paper to a thickness of ⅛ inch. Remove top piece of wax paper. Invert greased, lightly floured cookie sheet over dough, turn the sheet, dough, and paper right side up, and remove paper.

Sprinkle sesame seeds over dough, and roll lightly with rolling pin to make seeds adhere. Cut into tiny strips 1 x ¼ inch. Bake in preheated oven for about 15 minutes.

Yield: ½ pound of strips

1¼ cups whole wheat pastry flour
¾ cup grated, sharp cheddar cheese
¼ teaspoon salt
1/3 cup oil
2 tablespoons ice water
2 tablespoons sesame seeds

Preheat griddle.

Place all ingredients in blender in order listed. Whirl just until smooth.

Cottage Cheese Pancakes

Bake batter, using ¼ cup for each pancake, on preheated, lightly oiled griddle or in heavy skillet. Turn once to brown both sides.

Yield: 7 5-inch pancakes

Children love these pancakes spread with honey or jam and rolled like a jelly roll; or omit cinnamon and fill with a meat spread and roll up in the same manner.

4 eggs
¼ cup whole wheat pastry flour
¾ cup cottage cheese
¼ teaspoon salt
¼ teaspoon cinnamon (optional)

Crackers
and Snacks

294

Combine milk, butter or oil, honey, salt, and water. Cool to lukewarm. Add yeast, then eggs, and mix well. Work in flour, and mix until dough is well blended and soft.

Dough
½ cup scalded milk
¼ cup butter or oil
1 teaspoon honey
1 teaspoon salt
¼ cup water
1 package dry yeast
2 eggs
3 cups whole wheat flour

Filling
2 tablespoons chopped onion
1 tablespoon oil
2 cups ground, cooked meat
(leftovers would be fine)
1 teaspoon salt
¼ teaspoon pepper
3 tablespoons prepared mustard

Roll dough on well-floured board to ⅛-inch thickness and cut into 12 5-inch rounds.

Brown onion in oil; add meat, salt, pepper, and mustard.

Place two tablespoons meat mixture on half of each round. Moisten edges, fold over, and seal edges together with a fork. Slash straight side of each foldover to allow steam to escape during cooking. Place on greased baking sheet.

Let rise in warm place until double in bulk, about 1 hour.

Preheat oven to 425° F.

Bake in preheated oven for about 12 minutes.

Yield: 1 dozen foldovers

Lunch Box Foldovers

Crackers and Snacks

To prepare dough

Dissolve yeast in warm water. Add milk, butter, salt, honey, and beaten egg, mixing well. Beat in the whole wheat flour and work in the pastry flour, first with a wooden spoon, then by hand, enough to form a soft dough. Knead dough 5 minutes on floured board, adding a little more flour as necessary to prevent sticking. Place dough in oiled bowl, and let rise in a warm place for an hour or an hour and a quarter.

Meanwhile, prepare filling

Heat butter in large, heavy skillet. Add garlic, onion, carrot, and cabbage, and cook over medium heat, covered, a few minutes until vegetables are tender. Remove from heat and cool. Blend in the cheese to distribute evenly, and stir in the meat and salt and other seasonings.

Preheat oven to 425° F.

Punch down dough, let it rest a few minutes, then roll it on a lightly floured board to a thickness of about ⅛ inch. Cut out 20 4-inch circles. On each of 10 of the circles heap several tablespoons of the filling to within ½-inch of the edge of the dough. Dampen edges of the pastry. Cover with the remaining 10 dough circles, and seal by pressing with the tines of a fork. Place on lightly buttered baking sheet, let rise 30 minutes, and bake in preheated oven about 12 minutes or until lightly browned.

Serve hot or cold. Refrigerate if not served immediately.

Yield: 10 pasties

Savory Meat and Vegetable-Filled Pasties

Dough

1 package dry yeast
¼ cup warm water
¼ cup milk
3 tablespoons melted butter, cooled to lukewarm
½ teaspoon salt, slightly rounded
1 tablespoon honey
1 beaten egg
1 cup whole wheat flour
1¼ to 1½ cups whole wheat pastry flour

Filling

2 tablespoons butter
1 clove garlic, finely chopped
½ cup finely chopped onion
1 cup grated raw carrot
1 cup grated raw cabbage
1 cup grated swiss cheese
¾ pound cooked ground beef, sauteed and drained of fat
¾ teaspoon salt
¼ teaspoon black pepper
¾ teaspoon basil
¼ teaspoon thyme
¼ teaspoon celery seed
2 to 3 teaspoons Worcestershire sauce

Crackers and Snacks

To prepare crust

Dissolve yeast and honey in water. Let stand a few minutes. Add salt and oil, then the flours gradually; mix with spoon, then by hand. Knead dough on floured board for 5 minutes; additional flour may be necessary to prevent dough from sticking.

Place dough in an oiled bowl, cover, and let rise in a warm place about an hour. Punch down dough and let it rest a few minutes. Roll out on a lightly floured board to a thickness of ¼ to ⅜ inch to fit an oiled baking sheet or jelly roll pan. Set in warm place to rise about 20 minutes.

Meanwhile, preheat oven to 400° F., and prepare filling.

To prepare filling

Heat butter in heavy skillet, and add onion, salt, and caraway seeds; stir, cover, and steam a few minutes or until onions are yellow, not brown, being careful they do not scorch. Sprinkle flour over onions, and stir until absorbed. Let mixture cool slightly.

In a blender, whirl cottage cheese, yogurt, and milk until satiny. Add to onions in skillet along with lightly beaten eggs. Cook slowly over very low heat, stirring constantly, for a minute or two until thick and well blended. Add sunflower seeds. Spread filling over dough, and allow to rise another 15 minutes.

Bake in preheated oven for 30 minutes or until dough is crisp and brown around the edges and filling has set. Cut into squares and serve hot or cold. Refrigerate if not served immediately.

Yield: 24 squares

Stuttgart Onion Tart

Crust

1 package dry yeast
1½ teaspoons honey
1 cup lukewarm water
1 teaspoon salt
2 tablespoons oil
2 cups whole wheat flour
1 cup whole wheat pastry flour

Filling

3 tablespoons butter
4 cups finely chopped onions
¾ teaspoon salt
1 teaspoon caraway seeds
1 tablespoon whole wheat pastry flour
¾ cup cottage cheese
2 tablespoons yogurt
2 tablespoons milk
2 eggs, lightly beaten
¼ cup sunflower seeds

Crackers and Snacks

In mixing bowl, dissolve yeast in warm water. Add honey, salt, olive oil, and 1¼ cup flour. Mix thoroughly. Add remaining flour, enough to form soft dough. Knead on floured board 5 minutes. Cover and let rise in warm place for 45 minutes.

Preheat oven to 375° F., and prepare filling while dough rises.

Crust

½ cup warm water
1½ teaspoons dry yeast
1 teaspoon honey
½ teaspoon salt
1 tablespoon olive oil
1¼ cup whole wheat pastry flour
additional ½ to ¾ cup whole wheat pastry flour

Filling

1 tablespoon olive oil
1 medium-size onion, very finely chopped
1 green pepper, very finely chopped
1 clove garlic, minced
2/3 cup tomato paste
1/3 to ½ cup water
1 tablespoon olive oil
¾ teaspoon salt
½ teaspoon each, basil and sage
¼ teaspoon oregano
⅛ teaspoon anise seed
⅛ teaspoon crushed red peppers (optional)
½ pound ground beef, sauteed and drained of fat
1 cup grated mozzarella cheese

Punch down dough and roll out to a thickness of 3/16 inch on a floured board. Cut into 18 circles about 2¾ inches in diameter. Turn up a tiny edge of dough around perimeter of each circle. Place on lightly oiled baking sheet.

To prepare filling

Heat first tablespoon of olive oil in heavy skillet. Saute onion, green pepper, and garlic until tender but not brown. Set aside.

In small saucepan, stir together tomato paste, water, second tablespoon of olive oil, salt, and other seasonings. Add cooked beef and sauteed vegetables, and simmer gently for 5 to 10 minutes, stirring occasionally. Mixture will be quite thick. Allow to cool to lukewarm.

Spoon filling onto the dough circles, dividing evenly; top with grated mozzarella. Add a slice of green or black olive or an anchovy in the center, if desired.

Bake in preheated oven for 15 minutes or until cheese is bubbly and slightly browned. Serve hot or cold. Store in refrigerator if not served immediately.

Yield: 18 baby pizzas

The baby pizzas are a favorite with children and do very nicely packed in lunches.

Baby Pizza

Preheat oven to 400° F.

Mix together flour and salt.

Mix together oil and water.

Add liquids to dry ingredients, and stir with fork until dough forms a ball. Divide into twelve small balls and press each ball of dough into one space of a miniature muffin tin, forming a little pastry shell. Build up a nice edge.

Fry bacon until crisp; drain and crumble. Place bits of crumbled bacon and grated cheese in each of the twelve miniature quiche shells.

Lightly beat together remaining ingredients and carefully spoon into shells. Sprinkle with nutmeg.

Bake in preheated oven for about 15 minutes.

Yield: 1 dozen bite-size *quiches*

Bite-Size Quiches

Crust
1½ cups whole wheat pastry flour
½ teaspoon salt
1/3 cup oil
about 4 tablespoons ice water

Filling
6 slices bacon, nitrite-free
about 1 ounce grated swiss cheese
1 egg
1/3 cup light cream
1 teaspoon chopped chives
dash of white pepper
⅛ teaspoon nutmeg
¼ teaspoon salt

Crackers
and Snacks

Spinach-Mushroom Omelet Appetizers

Heat butter in a large, heavy skillet. Add mushrooms, onion, and garlic and saute until tender. Remove from heat.

Lightly beat the eggs with the salt and other seasonings. Add the spinach and sauteed mushroom mixture, combining thoroughly.

Heat oil in a large, heavy skillet over low-medium heat. Pour in mixture and cook about 8 minutes or until bottom is golden but not brown, and omelet is no longer liquid in the center. Very carefully turn to cook the second side for several minutes until omelet is firm. Cut in wedges and serve hot or cold. (Cooling omelet slightly first makes cutting easier.)

Yield: 12 wedges

As many as 9 eggs may be used, if desired.

3 tablespoons butter
¾ pound fresh mushrooms, cleaned and cut into pieces
¾ cup chopped onion
1 clove garlic, very finely chopped
6 eggs
¾ teaspoon salt, slightly rounded
¾ teaspoon curry powder (optional)
⅛ teaspoon black pepper
2 teaspoons Worcestershire sauce
1 box frozen, chopped spinach, cooked and thoroughly drained
3 tablespoons oil

Crackers
and Snacks

½ cup butter
2¾ cups whole wheat pastry flour
3 eggs, well beaten
2 tablespoons light cream
½ teaspoon vanilla
¼ cup honey
½ teaspoon salt
1 egg white for glaze
1 tablespoon milk
¼ cup finely chopped almonds

Cut butter into flour as for pie crust. Combine eggs, cream, vanilla, honey, and salt. Add to flour and butter mixture and chill.

Preheat oven to 350° F.

Form into rolls about 8 inches long and as thick as a pencil. Twist into a pretzel shape. Beat egg white and add milk. Brush mixture over each pretzel and sprinkle with almonds.

Arrange on ungreased cookie sheets, and bake in preheated oven about 12 to 15 minutes.

Yield: 2½ dozen pretzels

Almond Pretzels

¼ teaspoon soda
½ cup buttermilk
2 cups whole wheat flour
½ teaspoon salt
3 tablespoons butter
1 tablespoon honey
coarse salt or seasoned salt for light dusting

Preheat oven to 425° F.

Dissolve soda in buttermilk.

Mix dry ingredients together, then cut in butter. Add honey and buttermilk-soda mixture. Form into ball.

Roll dough very thin (about ⅛ inch), cut into 2-inch squares, and sprinkle lightly with salt. Press gently with your fingers to make salt adhere.

Place on cookie sheet, and bake in preheated oven for 10 minutes, or until crisp. Store in airtight container.

Yield: 4 dozen squares

Whole Wheat Hardtack

Crackers and Snacks

Egg Bread

Preheat oven to 425° F.

Stir together cornmeal and salt. Dissolve soda in buttermilk and stir into mixture.

Beat eggs and combine with oil or melted butter, then blend thoroughly into batter. Stir well and spread ½ inch thick in 8 x 12-inch preheated greased pan.

Bake in preheated oven for 20 minutes. Sprinkle with grated cheese, and bake about 5 minutes more. Cool slightly and cut into squares. Serve warm or at room temperature. Store in refrigerator.

Yield: 24 squares

Variation: Use seasoned salt, ¼ teaspoon sage, ½ teaspoon thyme, and 1 teaspoon parsley flakes to make an herbed egg bread, if desired.

2 cups cornmeal
½ teaspoon salt
1 teaspoon soda
2 cups buttermilk
2 eggs
1/3 cup oil or melted butter
1 cup grated, sharp cheddar cheese

Crackers
and Snacks

Preheat oven to 450° F.

In a large bowl, stir together flour, soda, and salt. With two knives or pastry blender cut in butter until particles are fine. Stir in sesame seeds.

Add buttermilk to flour mixture and stir with fork just until mixed. Drop by the tablespoonful on greased baking sheet.

2 cups whole wheat pastry flour
1 teaspoon soda
½ teaspoon salt
½ cup butter
2 tablespoons sesame seeds
1 cup buttermilk

Bake in preheated oven about 12 to 14 minutes or until lightly browned.

Yield: 20 biscuits

Hot sesame biscuits make delicious small sandwiches—split, buttered, and put together with sliced strawberries, thin slices of cheese, or chopped chicken moistened with hot gravy.

For a man-size snack, double the size of these biscuits by using 2 tablespoons of dough for each biscuit. Then split and lightly butter them while they are still hot. Spread with honey and put together with a layer of ricotta cheese.

Sesame Drop Biscuits

Crackers and Snacks

Dissolve yeast in lukewarm water. Add 1 teaspoon honey.

In large bowl, mix oil or butter, 1½ tablespoons honey, salt, and boiling water. When lukewarm, add first beaten egg, then dissolved yeast. Gradually stir in whole wheat flour, mixing well, but do not knead. If dough is too soft and sticky, add a bit more flour. Put in refrigerator to chill until firm.

Preheat oven to 425° F.

Soft Bread Sticks

Divide dough into 12 equal parts. On floured board and in hands, roll into sticks about a foot in length. Place 1½ inches apart on greased baking sheet, and brush with beaten egg to which ½ teaspoon water has been added. Then sprinkle with seeds. Let rise about 30 minutes.

Bake for 15 minutes in preheated oven. Cool on wire rack or serve warm.

Yield: 1 dozen long or 2 dozen short sticks

For shorter sticks, divide dough into 24 parts.

1 package dry yeast
½ cup lukewarm water
1 teaspoon honey
½ cup oil or melted butter
1½ tablespoons honey
1 teaspoon salt
½ cup boiling water
1 egg, beaten
about 3½ cups whole wheat
    pastry flour
1 egg, beaten
½ teaspoon water
sesame, poppy, or caraway seeds

Crackers
and Snacks

Sunny Buckwheat Cornbread

Preheat oven to 350° F.

In mixing bowl, stir together thoroughly the flours, cornmeal, soda, and salt.

Combine liquid ingredients, beating lightly, and add to flour mixture, mixing only until blended. Stir in sunflower seeds.

Pour batter into oiled or buttered 8½ x 4½ x 2½-inch loaf pan.

Bake in preheated oven for 35 to 40 minutes or until bread tests done.

Cool a few minutes in pan, then remove to wire rack to cool completely.

Cut into slices, then strips, if desired.

Yield: 1 loaf

The buckwheat contributes to the unusual flavor of this bread. The loaf remains moist surprisingly long in an airtight container.

½ cup whole wheat pastry flour
½ cup buckwheat flour
½ cup cornmeal
1½ teaspoons soda
¾ teaspoon salt
2 eggs
½ cup yogurt
¾ cup milk
¼ cup oil
1½ tablespoons honey
¼ cup sunflower seeds

Crackers and Snacks

Combine scalded milk, butter, salt, and honey. Cool to lukewarm. Add yeast and mix well. Add flour and work until dough is well blended and soft.

Roll out on floured board to ½-inch thickness and cut into 3-inch circles.

1 cup scalded milk
¼ cup butter
1½ teaspoons salt
1 tablespoon honey
1 package dry yeast
2½ to 3 cups whole wheat flour
2 tablespoons cornmeal

Sprinkle cornmeal on baking sheet. Place muffins on sheet and dust tops with cornmeal. Let rise in warm place, for at least an hour, until muffins are light.

English Muffins

Bake on hot, ungreased griddle for about 5 minutes on each side. Cool.

Yield: about 10 muffins

Split the cooled muffins and toast to be served with butter and natural jam. Use unsplit muffins as base for excellent open sandwiches or teatime snacks.

Crackers and Snacks

In bowl combine yeast, warm water, and honey. Let yeast dissolve for a few minutes.

Mix flour and salt. Stir into the yeast mixture with the oil and enough water to form a firm dough. Knead 5 to 10 minutes. Cover bowl with a damp cloth and allow dough to rise in warm place for 1 hour.

Preheat oven to 450° F.

Grissini

Roll the dough on a lightly floured board into a rectangle about 8 x 18 inches and ¼ inch thick. Cut into 9 2-inch strips (8 inches long) and roll into sticks.

Place on a greased baking sheet, cover, and allow to stand for 30 minutes.

Brush with beaten egg and sprinkle with salt or seeds. Bake in preheated oven for 10 to 15 minutes or until brown and crisp. Cool on wire rack.

Yield: 9 sticks

1 teaspoon dry yeast
about ½ cup warm water
2 teaspoons honey
2 cups whole wheat flour
1 teaspoon seasoned salt
1 tablespoon olive oil
beaten egg for glaze
coarse salt, poppy seeds, caraway
seeds, or sesame seeds

Crackers
and Snacks

2½ cups whole wheat flour
1 cup buttermilk
1 teaspoon salt
1 teaspoon soda
¼ cup melted butter, or oil

Put 1½ cups of the flour into a bowl. Add remaining ingredients and stir to make a smooth dough. With spoon or hands, work in as much of the remaining flour as needed to make a stiff dough. Turn onto a well-floured board and knead a few seconds. Divide dough into 12 pieces.

Preheat oven to 350° F., and grease 4 large baking sheets.

Roll out each piece of dough separately into paper-thin circles about 7 inches in diameter. Place circles on the prepared baking sheets, and cut into wedges or leave in one large bread.

Bake in preheated oven for 10 to 15 minutes until browned, being careful not to let bread burn.

Remove from oven to wire rack to cool.

Roll out remaining pieces of dough and bake.

Store in airtight container at room temperature for not more than 24 hours.

Yield: about 12 7-inch flatbreads

The flatbreads are cracker-like and are excellent served with soup or soft cheese. Their raggedy edges, from rolling rather than cutting out in rounds, make them interesting to look at, too.

Knackbrod
(Norwegian flatbread)

Crackers
and Snacks

Soften yeast in water. Add butter or oil, honey, and salt. Mix well, then add egg. When well blended, add flour and mix until dough is soft.

Divide dough into 3 equal parts. Roll each part to a 5 x 16-inch rectangle about ⅛ inch thick.

Cocktail Twirl-Ups

Mix cheese, olives, and walnuts and spread over dough. Roll as for a jelly roll, starting with the 16-inch side.

Cut into ½-inch slices, and place on greased baking sheet. Flatten out slightly. Cover with cloth and let rise in warm place about 45 minutes, until light.

Preheat oven to 425° F.

Bake in preheated oven for 15 minutes.

Yield: 8 dozen twirl-ups

1 package dry yeast
½ cup lukewarm water
½ cup melted butter, or oil
1 teaspoon honey
1 teaspoon salt
1 egg
2¼ cups whole wheat flour
1 cup ricotta cheese
¼ cup chopped olives
¼ cup chopped walnuts

Crackers and Snacks

Preheat oven to 450° F.

Soften yeast in lukewarm water. Add butter or oil, honey, and salt. Mix well, then add egg. Stir in flour and mix until well blended and soft.

Divide dough into four parts and roll each part paper-thin on a well-floured board.

1 package dry yeast
1 cup lukewarm water
3 tablespoons melted butter, or oil
2 teaspoons honey
1 teaspoon salt
1 egg
3 cups whole wheat flour
¼ cup melted butter
¼ cup grated cheese
½ teaspoon celery salt
1 teaspoon dill seed

Mix butter, cheese, celery salt, and dill. Spread over each sheet, reserving 1 tablespoonful for topping, then fold each sheet of dough in half and roll again to paper-thinness.

Crispies

Prick with a fork and mark into 2 x 1½-inch wafers with the dull edge of a knife or with a pastry wheel.

Brush tops with the remaining seasoned butter mixture, and bake in preheated oven for 8 to 10 minutes, until golden brown.

Break bars apart, cool, and store in sealed container.

Yield: 15 dozen wafers

Crackers
and Snacks

Preheat oven to 350° F.

Combine all ingredients and form into patties about 2½ inches in diameter. Place on lightly greased baking sheet, and bake in preheated oven for 30 to 40 minutes.

Yield: 1 dozen large patties

For a cocktail snack which is tasty and different, make patties about 1 inch in diameter and ½ inch thick. Serve hot or cold. The recipe will yield about 3 dozen small patties.

Cornmeal-Bulgur Patties

2 cups cornmeal mush
1 cup cooked bulgur
½ cup chopped peanuts
¼ cup sesame seeds
vegetable salt to taste

Crackers and Snacks

Beat cheese with egg until thoroughly blended. Add grated onion and salt. Mix well.

Toast 20 to 24 1¾-inch rounds of whole-grain bread on one side. Heap cheese mixture on the untoasted side of the bread.

Ricotta Puffs

Broil for about one minute or until brown and puffy. Sprinkle with paprika. Serve hot.

Yield: at least 20 puffs

Variation: Use whole wheat raisin bread rounds. Omit onion from cheese mixture and add ½ teaspoon grated orange rind, ¼ teaspoon cinnamon, and 1 teaspoon honey. Sprinkle with cinnamon or very finely chopped nuts after broiling.

1 cup ricotta cheese
1 egg
½ teaspoon grated onion
⅛ teaspoon salt
¼ teaspoon paprika

Crackers
and Snacks

Cocktail Grapes

Slit grapes part way, without cutting through entirely. Remove seeds.

Combine remaining ingredients and mix well with a fork. Stuff grapes with filling and press together lightly.

Arrange on carefully washed grape or geranium leaves and serve at cocktail or snack time.

Yield: about 4 cups

½ pound large grapes
¾ cup thick yogurt
½ cup finely grated Roquefort cheese
1 teaspoon onion juice
½ teaspoon soy sauce

Crackers
and Snacks

Popcorn-Nut Munchies

Pour the oil into a large, heavy skillet with tight-fitting lid; sprinkle the popping corn into the oil. Cover skillet.

Heat slowly, shaking skillet gently as soon as corn begins to pop, and continuing until popping stops. Pour popped corn into large bowl.

Melt butter in small saucepan until it bubbles but does not brown. Add curry powder and stir.

Add nuts to popcorn in bowl, drizzle butter mixture over, sprinkle with salt, and toss until well coated.

Yield: 9 cups popcorn

3 tablespoons vegetable oil
½ cup popping corn
2 tablespoons butter
1 teaspoon curry powder
½ teaspoon salt
1 cup nuts (English walnuts, pecans, peanuts, cashews)

Seasoned Popcorn

Heat oil in heavy skillet. Add popped corn and seasonings and toss until well heated, about 5 to 7 minutes.

Serve at once or store in airtight container until ready to serve.

Yield: 3 cups

1 tablespoon oil
3 cups popped corn
½ teaspoon chopped chives
½ teaspoon dill weed
1 teaspoon grated Parmesan cheese
½ teaspoon celery salt

Crackers and Snacks

1 pound raisins
1 cup salad oil
salt
chili powder

In a saucepan, combine raisins and oil. Cook about 10 minutes or until raisins are plump. Drain on absorbent paper. Sprinkle with salt and chili powder.

Yield: 10 to 12 servings
2 cups

Deviled Raisins

1 teaspoon butter
1 teaspoon oil
1 cup sunflower seeds
1 teaspoon chopped chives
½ teaspoon celery salt

In a small skillet, heat butter and oil over low heat. Add sunflower seeds, chives, and salt, and toast for about 8 minutes. Shake or stir occasionally.

Yield: 1 cup

Savory Sunflower Seeds

Crackers and Snacks

Curried Pumpkin Seeds

In a saucepan, mix curry powder, water, garlic, and salt. When well blended, add 1 cup water and heat until liquid simmers.

Add pumpkin seeds and simmer for 5 minutes.

Preheat oven to 225° F.

Spread seeds on a cookie sheet, dot with butter, and sprinkle with salt. Toast in very slow oven until crisp, about 25 minutes.

Yield: 2 cups

¼ cup curry powder
¼ cup warm water
1 clove garlic, finely minced
1 teaspoon salt
1 cup water
2 cups plain, hulled pumpkin seeds
1 teaspoon butter
dash of salt

Crackers
and Snacks

Recipes for other snacks (clockwise): SAVORY SUNFLOWER SEEDS, page 321; DEVILED RAISINS, page 321; POPCORN-NUT MUNCHIES, page 320.

CHAPTER X

DESSERT CREPES, FONDUES, AND FRITTERS

Dessert Crepes, Fondues, and Fritters

Borrowed from our friends across the sea, *crepes* and fondues are currently very popular in America. Fritters have been familiar to us for a much longer time. Used as desserts, *crepes*, fondues, and fritters can provide a very interesting change from the ordinary, more typical fare.

Crepes

Almost every European country has its own type of dessert pancake. The names are different; the ingredients and manner of serving are similar.

One of the best known and most versatile is the one indigenous to France—the tissue-thin pancake called "*crepe.*" *Crepes* are very easy to make and are convenient because they can be made ahead for reheating at the last moment.

Dessert *crepes* can be very glamorous, and the variations are limitless in number. Fruit fillings are especially tasty and can be made with any of the fruit sauce recipes given in this book. Bake the basic *crepes* and fill with about two tablespoons of fruit sauce.

No matter what the filling, the result is elegant! *Crepes* may be served at most any time of day or night. For that festive touch, flambe with any fruit liqueur or cognac.

Fondues

Fondue is a term used to describe many different dishes. We are particularly interested in two: baked fondue, which is a souffle prepared with bread or cake crumbs; and the Swiss fondue, which is a special kind of cheese sauce originally from Switzerland.

The basic baked fondue is a batter lightened with egg whites and flavored with chopped fresh fruit. It should be baked slowly in a dish attractive enough to be taken to the table. Use your imagination in selecting fruits for the fondue, but avoid dried fruits which tend to make the fondue heavy.

The well-known Swiss fondue is usually made to be dipped with cubes of bread. I've created a dipped dessert fondue in which pieces or fingers of fruit are dipped into this superb cheese sauce. The range of fruits which can be used is very wide, including apple, pear, pineapple, and cherries with their stems.

Skillet-Baked Fruit Fritters

The batter for fritters is a little thicker and heavier than that for *crepes*. Usually, fewer eggs are used and more flour. Instead of deep-frying the fritters, which is the customary way of preparing them, I bake them in oil in a heavy skillet.

The basic recipe is written for apple fritters. It may be used also for pears, pineapple, peaches, apricots, and bananas. Berries or cherries may be stirred into the batter and dropped by the tablespoon into the skillet.

Maple syrup is delicious with any of the fruit fritters, or try dusting them with COCONUT SUGAR (see Index) mixed with cinnamon.

In a mixing bowl, beat eggs, add honey or maple syrup, brandy, vanilla, butter, and milk. Beat with electric beater at low speed until well mixed. Add flour and salt, and continue to beat until batter is the consistency of light cream. Allow batter to stand for an hour or two.

Basic Crepes

3 eggs
1 teaspoon honey or maple syrup
2 tablespoons brandy
1 teaspoon vanilla
2 tablespoons melted butter
2/3 cup milk
1/3 cup whole wheat pastry flour
⅛ teaspoon salt

When ready to bake, heat a 6-inch *crepe* pan or small skillet and oil it. Pour in about 1½ tablespoons of the batter, and tip the pan to spread the batter over the entire surface. Cook *crepe* until it shakes loose from the bottom of the pan. Turn and brown lightly on reverse side.

Yield: 14 to 16 *crepes*

Crepes may be kept for several days in the refrigerator or for four weeks in the freezer.

Peel and split 4 bananas lengthwise.

Prepare 8 BASIC *CREPES* (see above)
and set aside
4 bananas
2 tablespoons butter
1 cup RASPBERRY SAUCE (see Index)
¼ cup brandy

Banana Crepes

In a skillet, heat butter, and put the banana halves in for about 3 minutes, or long enough to coat with butter. Turn and coat other side. With slotted spoon, remove bananas from pan. Spread out the *crepes* on a board or large plate. Roll a banana half in each. Place in skillet, chafing dish, or casserole. Spoon 2 tablespoons sauce over each *crepe*. Heat brandy, pour over *crepes*, and ignite.

Yield: 4 servings

Dessert Crepes,
Fondues,
and Fritters

329

Carob *Crepes*

In the container of a blender, combine flour, carob, salt, eggs, honey, oil, and milk. Blend at medium speed until smooth. Chill for 45 minutes.

When ready to bake, heat a 6-inch *crepe* pan or small skillet and oil it lightly. Pour in about 1½ tablespoons of the batter, and tip the pan quickly to spread the batter over the entire surface of the pan. Cook for about 1 minute or until the edges brown and pull away from the sides of the pan, then turn and cook the other side for about ½ minute.

Beat cream until it starts to thicken, then add coffee, and continue to beat until cream is stiff.

Put a heaping tablespoon of cream mixture on each *crepe* and roll. Top with carob sauce.

Yield: 12 *crepes,* 6 servings

6 tablespoons whole wheat pastry flour
3 tablespoons carob powder
¼ teaspoon salt
3 whole eggs
4 teaspoons honey
¼ cup oil
1/3 cup milk
oil for baking *crepes*
2 cups heavy cream
2 tablespoons powdered instant coffee
2 cups BASIC CAROB SAUCE
    (see Index)

Dessert Crepes,
Fondues,
and Fritters

Carob-Filled Crepes

As you bake the *crepes,* spoon about 1 tablespoon carob sauce over each one; stack until you have 14 or 16 *crepes.* Keep warm. When all are baked and stacked, cover top and sides with remaining sauce. Cut into wedges and top with whipped cream, seasoned with brandy.

Garnish each serving with chopped nuts.

Yield: 8 servings

1 recipe BASIC *CREPES* (see Index)
2 cups BASIC CAROB SAUCE
(see Index)
2 cups heavy cream, whipped
2 tablespoons brandy
½ cup chopped nuts

Cheese Crepes

In the bowl of an electric blender, combine cheeses and blend until smooth. Transfer to mixing bowl and add egg yolk, honey, lemon peel, pecans, and dates. Mix thoroughly.

Spoon 1 heaping tablespoon of filling onto center of each *crepe.* Fold over bottom, both sides, and top.

Melt butter in skillet, and lightly brown *crepes* on both sides. Serve warm, topped with yogurt and CHERRY SAUCE (if desired).

Yield: 12 *crepes*
or 6 servings

1 cup cottage cheese
1 cup ricotta cheese
1 egg yolk
1 teaspoon honey
1 teaspoon grated lemon peel
¼ cup chopped pecans
½ cup chopped dates
12 *crepes,* prepared in advance
2 tablespoons butter
¾ cup yogurt
¾ cup CHERRY SAUCE (see Index),
(optional)

Dessert Crepes,
Fondues,
and Fritters

Preheat oven to 325° F. and butter a 1-quart casserole.

Cream butter until soft, add honey gradually, and beat until light and fluffy. Add egg yolks one at a time, beating well after each addition. Add crumbs and chopped peaches.

Beat egg whites until foamy, then add salt and beat until stiff but not dry. Fold into yolk-fruit mixture, then add almond flavoring.

1/3 cup butter
¼ cup warmed honey
3 egg yolks
1 cup cookie or cake crumbs
1 cup finely chopped fresh peaches
3 egg whites
¼ teaspoon salt
¼ teaspoon almond flavoring

Pour into the prepared casserole, and bake in preheated oven for about 30 minutes, or until lightly browned.

Serve immediately, directly from the baking dish.

Yield: 4 or 5 servings

This recipe may be used for any fresh fruit fondue—simply substitute 1 cup of your favorite fruit (or a combination) for the peaches. Fresh pineapple is delicious, also strawberries, raspberries, pears, and apricots.

Baked Peach Fondue

Dessert *Crepes,*
Fondues,
and Fritters

Dipped Fruit Fondue

In a chafing dish or heavy saucepan over low heat, pour the wine and heat to the boiling point. Add cheese and bring to a boil, stirring until cheese is melted. Combine arrowroot and water and add to the cheese mixture. Stir until thick and smooth. Add nutmeg if desired.

Arrange fruit on serving platter to be speared on long forks and dipped into the cheese sauce by each guest.

Yield: 4 or 5 servings

For the authentic Swiss touch, add 2 tablespoons Kirsch to the cheese sauce just before serving.

1 cup dry white wine
½ pound grated swiss cheese
½ pound grated cheddar cheese
1 tablespoon arrowroot flour
1 tablespoon water
dash of nutmeg (optional)
1 cup each of fresh sliced or cubed
    apple, pineapple, pear, banana,
    and melon

Dessert Crepes,
Fondues,
and Fritters

Beat egg yolks with honey until smooth and light. Add yogurt and stir until smooth.

Sift together flour, nutmeg, salt, and soda. Add to egg mixture. Stir in melted butter, then fold in egg whites.

Apple Fritters

In a heavy iron skillet, put enough oil to measure about ¼ inch deep. Heat to 370° F. or until oil starts to smoke (medium-high). Dip apple rings into batter, then bake in hot oil until golden brown on both sides. Keep fritters warm until all apples and batter have been used.

Serve hot with a small pitcher of maple syrup on the side.

Yield: about 2 dozen fritters

Fresh peaches, pears, pineapple, or bananas may be substituted for apples in this recipe.

2 egg yolks
½ cup warmed honey
1 cup yogurt
2 cups whole wheat pastry flour
½ teaspoon nutmeg
½ teaspoon salt
½ teaspoon soda
1 tablespoon melted butter
2 egg whites, beaten stiff
4 tart apples, cored and sliced
　　　¼ inch thick
about ½ cup oil for baking
1 cup maple syrup

In a mixing bowl, beat eggs. Add flour and salt. Mix well, then add honey and milk, making a smooth, thin batter. Pour into a pitcher (or large measuring glass which has a pouring spout) and allow to stand for 30 minutes.

Peel and slice apples very thin; drizzle honey over them and toss until apple slices are coated.

Apple Pancake

In a skillet (about 8 inches in diameter), over medium heat, melt about a table-spoon butter and tilt the pan to coat sides. Pour ¼ cup batter into pan and tilt pan to spread batter evenly. Bake for about 1 minute, cover surface with 1 cup sliced apples, then pour another ¼ cup batter over apples. When pancake is browned on the bottom, turn to brown other side. Bake until apples are tender, then fold pancake over like an omelet and remove from pan. Cover with raspberry sauce and serve im-mediately. Repeat process to bake the remaining 2 pancakes.

Yield: 3 pancakes (1 pancake makes 2 servings)

3 large eggs
2/3 cup whole wheat pastry flour
⅛ teaspoon salt
½ teaspoon honey
1 cup milk
3 large, tart apples
1 tablespoon honey
butter for baking
2/3 cup RASPBERRY SAUCE (see Index)

Dessert Crepes,
Fondues,
and Fritters

CHAPTER XI

INTERNATIONAL FAVORITES

INTERNATIONAL FAVORITES

International restaurants have been springing up in most of our large cities and are well patronized. This increased interest in foreign foods seems to have started following World War II, when so many Americans traveled abroad or lived there. They returned with real enthusiasm for what were to them unusual foods and searched out recipes for making them.

Many of the most fascinating dishes are quite simple to prepare. The ones that take more time and patience are so interesting and delicious that they are worth the effort.

In these recipes I aimed at retaining the authenticity of the dish, while using natural ingredients to make it. This was surprisingly easy to do. The overrefined ingredients which are in widespread use here have not been so wholeheartedly accepted in other countries, so many traditional favorites are still made with whole, unprocessed ingredients.

Presentation is a very important part of these creations. As you will see, even a simple dish becomes spectacular if served with an elegant sauce, decorated with colorful, natural fruit, or served with a flaming liqueur.

Soak the apricots in wine or apple juice overnight.

Next day, add honey, then cook fruit in the soaking liquid. Puree in blender, adding more water if necessary.

Apricot Flummery

In the top of a double boiler, beat egg yolk. Gradually add cream and set over hot water. Cook until mixture thickens, then stir in the apricot puree and grated peel. Dissolve gelatin in cold water briefly, then add to hot mixture.

Cook slowly, stirring steadily with a wire whisk until the mixture is thick and pale. Remove from heat and cool. Turn into a wetted mold or individual custard cups. Chill.

When ready to serve, decorate with very thin slices of orange.

Yield: 6 servings

1 cup dried apricots
1 cup sweet white wine or apple juice
1 tablespoon honey
1 egg yolk
½ pint light cream
2 tablespoons grated orange
    or lemon peel
1 envelope gelatin
2 tablespoons cold water

Butter a 1-quart casserole and put 3 tablespoons honey in the bottom. Set aside.

In a mixing bowl, cream butter, then add 5 tablespoons honey. Beat until creamy, then add lemon peel. Beat in the eggs.

Treacle Sponge

Sift flour with soda and add gradually to batter. Stir in lemon juice. Pour into the prepared casserole. Cover with well-fitting lid, wax paper, or foil. Place in large steaming kettle and steam for 1½ hours (see Basic Procedure for Steamed Puddings on page 91).

Turn out onto a warm serving dish or plate, and serve with LEMON CUS-TARD SAUCE (see Index).

Yield: 6 servings

3 tablespoons very light honey
6 tablespoons butter
5 tablespoons very light honey
grated peel of 1 large lemon
    (2 tablespoons)
2 eggs
1 cup whole wheat pastry flour
1 teaspoon soda
1 tablespoon lemon juice

International Favorites

Wash the berries and pick over them carefully, removing blossoms and stems and discarding any berries which are bruised or soft. Place the fruit in a saucepan, add honey and water, and cook very gently until the berries are soft enough to mash. Puree in a blender or force through a fine sieve. Test sweetness and add more honey to taste.

Whip the cream until thick.

Fold the gooseberry puree into the cream, making sure not to overmix. A marbleized effect is desirable and attractive. Chill.

Gooseberry Fool

1 quart fresh, ripe gooseberries
½ cup honey
3 tablespoons water
2 cups heavy cream

Serve in parfait glasses or individual dessert dishes.

Yield: 6 to 8 servings

GOOSEBERRY FOOL is a very old favorite, particularly in England. The berries are still plentiful there, but unfortunately they have almost disappeared from our markets. If you can grow your own or can find them at a farmers' market, you will enjoy the elegant flavor of GOOSEBERRY FOOL.

"Fool" was a term of endearment—we still love recipes where fruit is combined with cream.

International Favorites

345

Put raspberries into bowl of blender. Add honey and lemon juice or Kirsch, and blend until completely pureed. Strain to remove seeds.

Beat cream until it stands in small peaks. Gradually add the wine, beating well. Lightly fold in the raspberry puree so that the cream is streaked and marbled with pink. Turn into individual sherbet glasses and chill.

Raspberry Syllabub

Yield: 6 to 8 servings

A syllabub is a very old dish which started actually as a frothy drink of milk. It is said that the milk was pulled foaming from the cow directly into a bowl of wine set under it.

Now, served as a dessert in a more solid form, it will keep a week (chilled) and is at its best three or four days old.

1 quart fresh raspberries (or 2 packages frozen, drained)
1 to 2 tablespoons honey
2 teaspoons lemon juice or Kirsch
½ pint heavy cream
1 cup sauterne or other sweet, white wine

International Favorites

Select a glass serving bowl about 7 inches in diameter and 3 inches deep.

Cut several pieces of the cake (enough to line the bottom of the dish), and coat them with the raspberry sauce. Arrange coated pieces in the bottom of the bowl. Cover with remaining sauce.

Trifle

Cut the rest of the cake into cubes, and scatter them over the cake slices. Sprinkle half the almonds over the cubes. Pour the sherry over all and allow the mixture to set for about an hour.

Spread half the fruit over the cake, then spoon the custard over the fruit. Next, add the whipped cream, smoothing over the surface. Garnish the cream with the remaining fruit and almonds.

Yield: 6 to 8 servings

1 piece POUND CAKE (see Index) about 8 x 8 x 1 inch
⅓ cup RASPBERRY SAUCE (see Index)
½ cup slivered almonds
1 cup medium-dry sherry
2 cups fresh fruit (raspberries, strawberries, sliced peaches, blueberries, or cherries—or unsweetened frozen fruit, defrosted and drained)
2 cups CUSTARD SAUCE (see Index)
1 cup heavy cream, whipped

International Favorites

Heat butter, water, carob, coffee, and honey in the top of a double boiler over boiling water. Stir until smooth, then add egg yolks and mix thoroughly. Add rum, remove from hot water, and cool slightly.

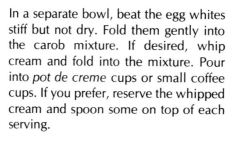

Carob
Pot de Creme

In a separate bowl, beat the egg whites stiff but not dry. Fold them gently into the carob mixture. If desired, whip cream and fold into the mixture. Pour into *pot de creme* cups or small coffee cups. If you prefer, reserve the whipped cream and spoon some on top of each serving.

Yield: 6 to 8 servings, depending on the size of the cups (I use china coffee cups and fill 6 nicely)

Pot de Creme is a very simple and light, but good and elegant dessert. It can be prepared in advance and stored in the refrigerator (covered) up to 24 hours.

2 tablespoons butter
⅓ cup water
⅓ cup carob powder
1 tablespoon instant coffee granules
1 teaspoon honey, or more, to taste
5 egg yolks
2 tablespoons light rum
5 egg whites
½ cup heavy cream (optional)

International
Favorites

Although in our country, canned Bing cherries are usually used to make CHERRIES JUBILEE, we prefer to use fresh or home-canned cherries of any variety, as they do in European countries where cherries are more abundant and popular than they are here.

Cherries Jubilee

Place cherries, honey, and water in a saucepan, and simmer over low heat for about 8 minutes. Drain and return syrup to saucepan. Combine cornstarch with water, add to syrup, and cook over low heat until smooth and transparent. Add cherries and stir until cherries are heated through. Pour warmed Kirsch over cherries and ignite.

Serve immediately: plain or over vanilla ice cream.

Yield: 4 to 6 servings

It is said that the original recipe for CHERRIES JUBILEE was created by the renowned French chef, Escoffier, in honor of Queen Victoria's jubilee. Today it is still a spectacular favorite, especially if prepared in a chafing dish and presented directly from the dining table or buffet.

1 quart fresh cherries, washed and pitted
¼ cup honey (or to taste, depending on sweetness of cherries)
2 tablespoons water
1 teaspoon cornstarch or arrowroot flour
1 tablespoon cold water
¼ cup warmed Kirsch

International Favorites

Melt butter in skillet and saute the onions until tender but not brown. Remove from pan and set aside.

In the same pan, melt 6 tablespoons of butter, and stir in the flour, making a smooth thick roux. Add scalded milk and salt and stir until thick and smooth. Add onions and set aside.

Croque-Monsieur

Butter each slice of bread on one side. On the unbuttered side, place a slice of cheese and a slice of ham. Cover with another slice of bread with the butter on the outside. Grill in heavy skillet, pressing together as you would a grilled cheese sandwich.

Cut each sandwich into 4 squares and place in an oven-proof dish or on a cookie sheet. Top each with a tablespoon of the sauce, then sprinkle generously with grated cheese. Glaze under broiler until browned.

Yield: 12 servings

The classic *Croque Monsieur* is made with ham as indicated in the above recipe. If you prefer, slices of chicken may be used in place of the ham.

Sauce
1 tablespoon butter
2 finely chopped onions (about ½ cup)
6 tablespoons butter
6 tablespoons whole wheat flour
2 cups scalded milk
¼ teaspoon salt
dash of nutmeg

Sandwich
1 tablespoon butter
12 slices whole-grain bread
½ pound swiss cheese, cut into 6 slices
    and the remainder grated
    to yield ¾ cup
¼ pound sliced cold ham

International
Favorites

Preheat oven to 325° F.

In a small saucepan, heat the honey and water, stirring until honey is dissolved. Boil rapidly until the syrup is golden brown. Do not stir. Remove from heat and pour into 5 individual custard cups. Allow caramel to cool and set.

Creme Caramel

In a medium-size mixing bowl, combine eggs and egg yolks. Beat very lightly with a whisk, then add milk and honey. Stir until mixed evenly. Add vanilla. Strain.

4 tablespoons honey
2 tablespoons water
2 whole eggs
2 egg yolks
2 cups milk
1 tablespoon honey
1 teaspoon vanilla

Pour custard into cups on top of the caramel. Set the cups in a baking pan and add enough hot water to come halfway up the sides of the custard cups. Bake in preheated oven for about 25 minutes, or until center of custard is set.

Yield: 5 servings

12 ounces cottage cheese
1 cup heavy cream
1 teaspoon honey
2 cups fresh strawberries, raspberries, peaches, or currants
1 teaspoon lemon juice
1 teaspoon grated lemon peel
1 tablespoon honey, or to taste, depending on the sweetness of the fruit

Rub cottage cheese through a sieve into a mixing bowl. Stir in the cream and honey, and beat with an electric beater at medium speed until mixture is thick.

Press the cheese mixture into 6 individual *coeur a la creme* molds, or a muslin-lined bowl-shaped sieve. (The container you use must have holes or perforations to allow liquid to drain.) Place molds or sieve over a pan or bowl, cover with plastic wrap, and allow to drain in the refrigerator overnight.

When ready to serve, combine fruit, lemon juice and peel, and honey.

If using molds, unmold the cream onto individual serving plates, surround with fruit, and serve immediately. If using sieve, unmold mound of cream onto the center of a large serving plate and surround with fruit. Cut into six wedges, and serve immediately on individual serving plates.

Yield: 6 servings

Coeur a la Creme

International Favorites

In the top of a double boiler, beat egg yolks until foamy, then add the honey and salt and beat until smooth. Place over hot water, add milk, and cook, without boiling, until custard is thick. Add flavoring and strain into a serving dish.

Beat egg whites until foamy. Continue to beat while adding honey very slowly. Beat until mixture is very stiff and smooth.

Oeufs a la Neige

In a deep, open skillet, heat, to simmering, enough water to reach a depth of about 1½ inches. Using 2 dessert spoons, shape egg whites into egg-shaped mounds and slide them into the simmering water. Be sure they do not touch bottom.

Poach "eggs" about 1½ minutes on each side. Carefully remove from pan with a slotted spoon and place on paper towels to drain. When all "eggs" have been poached, set them to float on the custard and chill for several hours, uncovered. Do not store for a long period or "eggs" might begin to weep. When ready to serve, decorate with Raspberry Sauce.

Yield: 6 servings

Most recipes for *Oeufs a la Neige* recommend poaching the egg whites in milk, which tends to produce a gummy, sticky meringue. Poaching in water yields a light, tender meringue which holds up very well and is easy to prepare.

8 egg yolks
¼ cup warmed honey
pinch of salt
2 cups milk, scalded
1 tablespoon brandy, rum, or your favorite liqueur or 1 teaspoon vanilla
5 egg whites
1 tablespoon warmed honey
¼ cup RASPBERRY SAUCE (see Index)

Strawberries Romanoff

This is a perfect dessert to be created and served by the hostess from a teacart or dining room table while guests look on and admire.

Arrange, on a large tray, a dessert dish two-thirds full of fresh, whole strawberries (about 2 quarts), washed, hulled, and drained. In another medium bowl, place 1 pint VANILLA CUSTARD ICE CREAM (see Index), softened slightly. Spoon two cups of whipped cream into a third bowl. On the side, stand a bottle of rum or Cointreau and a tiny pitcher containing juice of one lemon.

Carry the tray to table or cart. Work the ice cream gently with a large silver fork, then fold in the whipped cream. Toss until partially mixed. Pour about ¼ cup of rum or Cointreau and the lemon juice over the cream and mix gently. Spoon mixture over berries, toss lightly, and serve immediately on individual serving plates.

Yield: 6 to 8 servings

Peches Celestial

Peel peaches, cut into halves and pit. In a wide, shallow saucepan, combine water, honey, and ginger. Heat and stir until well mixed, then add peaches and poach gently for about five minutes, or until peaches are soft but not mushy. Cool the fruit and then chill it. When ready to serve, arrange two peach halves on each dessert plate, spoon one tablespoon of the juice over each half, then fill the centers with yogurt, sour cream, or whipped cream. Sprinkle nuts or seeds over each portion.

Yield: 6 servings

6 large, ripe peaches
3 tablespoons water
1 to 3 tablespoons honey, to taste
⅛ teaspoon ground ginger, or about ½-inch chunk of ginger root
1 cup yogurt, sour cream, or whipped cream
⅓ cup chopped nuts or sunflower seeds

Poire Belle Helene

Boil together honey, vanilla, and water for 5 minutes.

Halve, peel, and core the pears. Poach in the syrup until tender (do not over-cook). Allow pears to cool in syrup, then drain and chill.

When ready to serve, place about 2 tablespoons of ice cream in the bottom of individual dessert dishes, put 1 pear half on the ice cream and top with about 1 tablespoon of carob sauce.

Yield: 6 servings

¾ cup honey
1-inch piece vanilla bean
2 cups water
6 fresh pears
1 pint OLD-FASHIONED VANILLA CUSTARD ICE CREAM (see Index)
½ cup BASIC CAROB SAUCE (see Index)

International Favorites

Sift flour and salt into bowl. Gradually add water to make a stiff dough. Turn onto pastry board.

Place the oil in a bowl and spread a little of it on the palms of your hands. Knead the dough, gradually adding more oil until you have a smooth, elastic ball. Roll the ball of dough in the remaining oil to cover all sides. Place in a bowl, cover with a cloth, and allow to stand in a warm place for about 2 hours.

2⅔ cups unbleached flour
1 teaspoon salt
½ cup warm water
2 tablespoons olive oil
cornstarch for dusting pastry board

Filo **Pastry**

Divide the dough into 10 parts and roll to ¼-inch thickness on a pastry board dusted with cornstarch. Cover with a cloth and let set for 10 minutes.

Cover a table or counter top with a smooth cloth and lift rolled dough onto it. Put your hands, palms down, under the dough and gently stretch the dough with the backs of your hands, working your way around the table until the dough is stretched as thin as tissue paper. For moist *filo*, using scissors, cut dough immediately into desired size pieces; if you prefer dry *filo*, allow it to stand for about 10 minutes before cutting.

Yield: 10 12 x 16-inch sheets

International
Favorites

Baklava

Preheat oven to 350° F. and butter a 12 x 8-inch stainless steel baking pan. (Do not use glass.)

Cut pastry sheets in half, making 20 12 x 8-inch sheets. Brush 7 pastry sheets with butter and layer the sheets into the pan. Combine walnuts, honey, and cinnamon. Spread one-quarter of the mixture over *filo* sheets in pan. Cover with 2 more sheets of buttered *filo*, then add another one-quarter of the walnut mixture. Repeat until you have used a total of 13 sheets of *filo* and all of the walnut mixture. Brush remaining 7 sheets of pastry with butter, and place on top of sheets in the pan.

With a very sharp knife, cut pastry to form 16 diamond-shaped pieces. Top with remaining butter and bake in preheated oven for about 50 minutes, until top is crisp and golden brown.

When the *baklava* is baking, in a small pan combine remaining ingredients, heat to boiling, then lower heat and simmer mixture for 8 to 10 minutes. Remove the *baklava* from oven and top immediately with hot syrup. Cool.

Yield: 8 servings

10 sheets *FILO* PASTRY (see Index), each 12 x 16 inches
½ cup melted butter
1 cup finely chopped walnuts
¼ cup honey
½ teaspoon ground cinnamon
½ cup honey
½ teaspoon ground cloves
½ teaspoon finely grated orange peel
1 teaspoon lemon juice

Preheat oven to 350° F.

Crumble cheese into a large bowl. Add parsley and nutmeg and mix well.

Melt 1 tablespoon butter in a small saucepan, then blend in flour. Add milk and cook over low heat until mixture boils and thickens. Stir 1 tablespoonful of hot mixture into the egg, then add the egg mixture to the hot mixture in the saucepan. Cook for about 2 minutes over low heat, stirring constantly. Add mixture to cheese and blend well.

Bourekakia
(small cheese pastries)

Place 1 sheet of *filo* pastry on a sheet of wax paper on large cutting board or flat counter top. Brush with butter, then add another sheet of pastry and continue stacking layers until all pastry is used. Cut into 5-inch squares.

Place heaping tablespoonful of cheese mixture in center of each square and fold to form triangle. Moisten edges and press together firmly on three sides to enclose cheese mixture securely. Place on ungreased baking sheet.

Brush tops with melted butter and bake in preheated oven 30 to 35 minutes or until tops are crisp and golden brown.

Yield: 4 servings

¼ pound feta cheese
2 teaspoons chopped parsley
dash of nutmeg
¼ cup butter, melted
1 tablespoon whole wheat flour
½ cup milk
1 egg, well beaten
4 12 x 16-inch sheets *FILO* PASTRY
  (see Index)

International
Favorites

Preheat oven to 350° F.

On a sheet of wax paper placed on a flat counter top, brush *filo* sheets with butter, and stack flat one above the other, using about 2 tablespoons butter.

2 12 x 16-inch sheets *FILO* PASTRY
(see Index)
¼ cup melted butter
¾ cup chopped toasted almonds
2 tablespoons honey
⅛ teaspoon salt
1 egg, well beaten
½ teaspoon finely grated orange peel
¼ teaspoon ground cinnamon
2 tablespoons honey
2 tablespoons water
½ teaspoon finely grated orange peel
¼ teaspoon ground cinnamon
2 teaspoons lemon juice

In a small bowl, combine almonds, honey, salt, egg, orange peel, cinnamon, and the remaining butter. Spread mixture over *filo* sheets.

Flogheres
(almond pipes)

Beginning with the long side of the pastry, roll tightly into one long roll. Slice into 8 portions and place on an ungreased baking sheet. Bake in preheated oven for about 40 minutes or until golden brown.

While the rolls are baking, combine honey, water, orange peel, and cinnamon in a small saucepan. Bring to boiling, lower heat and simmer for 20 minutes. Remove from heat and add lemon juice. Pour over rolls as soon as they are removed from the oven.

Yield: 8 almond pipes

International
Favorites

Combine yogurt, orange peel, cinnamon, cloves, and salt in a large bowl. Blend brandy and soda. Add to yogurt mixture. Gradually stir in flour to make a smooth dough. Cover and set aside for 2 hours.

In a heavy skillet, heat about ¼ cup oil. Drop dough by the tablespoonful into hot oil, and bake until deep golden brown, turning once to bake second side (about 3 minutes on each side). Drain puffs on absorbent paper and layer into crystal bowl. Top each layer with sesame seeds.

Loukoumades
(sesame honey puffs)

In a small saucepan, combine honey, water, and cinnamon. Boil 5 minutes, then turn heat down to simmer until all puffs have been baked.

Blend in lemon juice and brandy and pour over puffs in bowl. Serve immediately.

Yield: 4 to 6 servings

Classic *Loukoumades* are fried in deep fat. This adaptation is prepared using a minimum of oil, making it more healthful and still retaining its delicious flavor.

1 cup plain yogurt
¼ teaspoon finely grated orange peel
¼ teaspoon ground cinnamon
dash of ground cloves
½ teaspoon salt
2 tablespoons Metaxa or Cognac
½ teaspoon soda
1½ cups whole wheat pastry flour
¼ cup oil for frying
½ cup honey
2 tablespoons water
¼ teaspoon ground cinnamon
1 teaspoon lemon juice
1 teaspoon Metaxa or Cognac
1 tablespoon toasted sesame seeds

International Favorites

In a deep bowl, combine dry ingredients thoroughly. Add eggs, milk, and oil and beat with whisk, hand beater, or electric beater until ingredients are well blended.

Pancakes

¾ cup whole wheat pastry flour
¼ teaspoon salt
¼ teaspoon soda
¼ teaspoon ground cinnamon
2 eggs
1½ cups milk
1 tablespoon oil
additional oil for cooking pancakes

In a 6- to 7-inch skillet with sloping sides, heat a teaspoon of oil over moderate heat. Pour about 3 tablespoons batter into the pan and tip pan immediately back and forth to spread the batter quickly over entire surface of pan.

Cook for a minute or two until pancake's surface is no longer shiny, then carefully turn and cook the other side for a minute. Place each cooked pancake on a plate, and proceed with remaining batter. Very lightly reoil pan as necessary.

Alebele (Goan)
pancakes with spicy coconut filling

Combine all ingredients thoroughly by mixing with a wooden spoon, then by hand.

Filling

2 tablespoons honey
2 tablespoons molasses
1 tablespoon melted butter
⅛ teaspoon salt
1 cup finely grated fresh coconut or grated, unsweetened coconut
1 teaspoon grated, fresh ginger
½ teaspoon anise seed

Spread a tablespoon of the filling on the lower third of each cooked pancake and roll it up but do not tuck in the ends. Arrange the filled pancakes on a platter and serve immediately or cover platter tightly with plastic wrap and set aside at room temperature until ready to serve.

Yield: 12 to 15 filled pancakes

International Favorites

369

Clean carrots and dice coarsely; add 1 quart milk and blend, one-half at a time, in electric blender (or grate carrots on a fine grater and combine with milk). Scald remaining quart of milk in a very large, heavy skillet, uncovered. Add carrot mixture; boil 15 minutes.

Stir in saffron, cinnamon, cardamom, honey, salt, 4 tablespoons butter, raisins, and ground almonds. Lower heat and simmer gently until mixture is almost dry, 1 to 2 hours, possibly longer. Stir frequently. Mixture should reduce to half its original volume and be thick enough to coat a spoon heavily.

Add remaining tablespoon butter; heat 10 more minutes or until all moisture is absorbed. Chill 4 to 5 hours.

When ready to serve, combine whipped cream, honey, and orange water, beating until well blended and stiff. Divide dessert into small individual serving dishes, top with flavored whipped cream, and garnish with toasted almonds.

Yield: at least 8 servings

Halwa Gajjar
(sweet carrot dessert)

1½ pounds tender, young carrots
2 quarts whole milk
$1/16$ teaspoon saffron
½ teaspoon ground cinnamon
seeds of 4 cardamom pods, crushed
¾ cup honey
1 teaspoon salt
5 tablespoons butter
½ cup golden raisins
1½ cups whole almonds, ground in
    blender or nut grinder
2 cups heavy cream, whipped
1 tablespoon honey
1 tablespoon orange flower water
½ cup chopped toasted almonds,
    for garnish

International
Favorites

3 tablespoons unsalted butter
½ cup grated, unsweetened coconut
2 tablespoons honey
2 medium-size ripe but firm bananas,
cut into rounds ¼-inch thick
1 cup plain yogurt
⅛ teaspoon salt
½ teaspoon finely crushed
coriander seeds

In a heavy skillet, melt butter but do not brown. Add coconut and honey and stir; gently stir in sliced bananas and cook for several minutes. Remove skillet from heat and add about 2 tablespoons of the yogurt.

Place the remaining yogurt in a small serving bowl and blend the skillet mixture, salt, and coriander into it, combining gently but thoroughly. Cover tightly and refrigerate at least 1 hour before serving.

Yield: 4 to 6 servings

Kela Ka Rayta
(yogurt with banana and grated coconut)

1 pint plain yogurt
½ teaspoon ground coriander
seeds of 3 cardamom pods, crushed
⅛ teaspoon ground cloves
¼ teaspoon salt
1 tablespoon honey
2 cups fresh orange sections

Combine yogurt, coriander, cardamom, cloves, salt, and honey. Mix well. Stir in orange sections. Chill several hours before serving.

Yield: about 8 half-cup servings

Narrangee Dhye
(orange yogurt)

International
Favorites

Kheer
(cinnamon nut pudding)

Combine milk, rice flour, honey, salt, and cinnamon in a large, heavy saucepan. Cook over medium heat, stirring constantly until mixture thickens and boils. Remove from heat.

Stir in pistachios, coconut, and orange flower water. Cool to room temperature. Spoon into 6 sherbet glasses; chill thoroughly.

Whip cream with 1 tablespoon honey until stiff. Top each chilled pudding with whipped cream and sprinkle with toasted almonds.

Yield: 6 servings

This is a soft pudding, not too sweet, with an unusual combination of flavors.

3 cups milk
4 tablespoons rice flour
⅓ cup honey
¼ teaspoon salt
½ teaspoon ground cinnamon
⅓ cup chopped pistachio nuts
¾ cup toasted, grated coconut, unsweetened
½ teaspoon orange flower water
½ pint heavy cream
1 tablespoon honey
chopped, toasted almonds for garnish

Poothena Chutney
(minted pineapple chunks)

Combine in a small saucepan, the pineapple chunks and juice, honey, spearmint, cardamom, coriander, chili powder, garlic powder, and salt. Heat to boiling; boil for 5 minutes.

Blend in butter. Cook, stirring constantly, until one-half of the liquid remains and pineapple chunks are well glazed. Cool slightly before serving.

Yield: about 3 cups

1 can (1 pound, 13 ounce) unsweetened pineapple chunks
2 tablespoons honey
1 tablespoon spearmint leaves
seeds of 4 cardamom pods, crushed
1 teaspoon ground coriander
½ teaspoon chili powder
¼ teaspoon garlic powder
½ teaspoon salt
2 tablespoons butter

International Favorites

1½ cups diced fresh oranges
2 cups halved, fresh, seedless grapes
2 bananas, thinly sliced
1 can (1 pound, 13 ounces) pineapple chunks, drained of juice
1 fresh papaya, peeled and diced, or one small can cubed papaya
2 tablespoons fresh lemon juice
2 cups plain yogurt
1 tablespoon honey
¼ teaspoon salt
seeds of 4 whole cardamom, crushed

Combine oranges, grapes, bananas, drained pineapple chunks, and papaya in a large bowl. Gently add lemon juice. Chill ½ hour.

Combine yogurt, honey, salt, and cardamom. Chill.

To serve, spoon fruit into sherbet glasses; top with chilled yogurt mixture.

Yield: 8 servings

Raitas
(fruit with yogurt)

Preheat oven to 375° F. and grease a shallow 8-inch round or square baking dish.

Place the peach halves in the prepared baking dish.

8 large, peeled peach halves (fresh or frozen)
1 peach half, mashed
½ cup natural cookie crumbs
1 tablespoon honey
1 tablespoon soft butter
1 egg yolk
2 tablespoons slivered almonds
2 tablespoons Marsala

Mix the mashed peach half, cookie crumbs, honey, butter, and egg yolk. Fill peach halves, using about 1 tablespoon of mixture per half. Dot with slivered almonds. Pour Marsala over the tops and bake in preheated oven for about 25 minutes.

Serve warm or cold.

Yield: 8 servings

This classic way with peaches is typical of lovely Piedmont at the foot of the Italian Alps.

Peaches
Piemontese

International
Favorites

Slice cake horizontally into three slices and place base layer of the cake on a serving plate. With a wooden spoon, force cheese through a coarse sieve into a medium-size bowl. Beat until smooth. Add cream, honey, and Strega or orange juice, and continue to beat until well blended. Fold in the chopped fruit and peel.

Combine carob syrup and raspberry sauce. Mix well.

Cassata Siciliana

Spread the base layer of the cake with half the ricotta mixture, then spread the cheese with half the carob-raspberry mixture. Place second layer of cake on top of first layer, then repeat layers of cheese and carob-raspberry mixture. Top with the third cake layer.

Press the filled cake gently to make it firm, then cover and refrigerate for several hours.

Combine carob syrup and honey, then fold carefully into the whipped cream. Spread evenly over the top, sides, and ends of the *Cassata*, swirling the topping attractively. Cover and refrigerate up to 24 hours.

Yield: 8 to 12 servings

1 9 x 5-inch POUND CAKE (see Index)
1 pound ricotta cheese (2 cups)
2 tablespoons heavy cream
2 tablespoons honey
3 tablespoons Strega or orange juice
3 tablespoons chopped, dried apricots
1 tablespoon finely grated lemon peel
2 tablespoons BASIC CAROB SYRUP (see Index)
2 tablespoons RASPBERRY GLAZE (see Index)
¼ cup BASIC CAROB SYRUP (see Index)
2 tablespoons warmed honey
1 cup heavy cream, whipped

International Favorites

½ cup Marsala
3 egg yolks
1 to 2 tablespoons honey
2 tablespoons water
¼ teaspoon almond extract
1 cup heavy cream, whipped
2 tablespoons chopped,
toasted almonds

In the top of a double boiler, put Marsala, egg yolks, honey, water, and almond extract. Place over simmering water. Beat constantly with a wire whisk until mixture is warm and begins to thicken. Do not allow to boil.

Remove from water and beat until mixture becomes smooth and thick. Fold in whipped cream and mix carefully.

Spoon into individual custard cups, cover, and freeze for about 6 hours.

When ready to serve, remove from freezer, and sprinkle with chopped, toasted almonds.

Yield: 4 to 6 servings

Spumoni

6 egg yolks
2 tablespoons honey
4 tablespoons Marsala

Put egg yolks into a heavy, round-bottom bowl. Beat until thick and light. Add honey. Set into a saucepan half-filled with hot (not boiling) water. Beat constantly over very low heat using a hand beater or whisk. Slowly add the Marsala and beat until mixture is thick.

Pour into sherbet glasses, and serve warm or very cold.

Yield: 4 to 6 servings

Port or sherry may be substituted for Marsala in this recipe.

Zabaglione

International
Favorites

Biscuit Tortoni

In a small saucepan, combine honey and water. Bring to a boil, stir to dissolve honey, then cook over high heat, uncovered, for about 5 minutes until consistency of syrup. Cool slightly.

In the top of a double boiler, beat egg yolks with electric beater at medium speed until yolks are light and fluffy. Add syrup slowly and continue to beat until mixture is smooth. Place over hot, not boiling, water and cook, stirring constantly, until mixture is very thick. Add sherry and cook 1 minute longer, then remove from heat and allow to cool.

When custard is cooled, fold in whipped cream. Pour into 8 5-ounce souffle dishes or small sherbet glasses, and place in freezer for 3 or 4 hours.

When ready to serve, allow to set at room temperature to soften for several minutes, then top each serving with about ½ teaspoon almonds.

Yield: 8 servings

⅓ cup honey
2 tablespoons water
5 egg yolks
¼ cup dry sherry
2 cups heavy cream, whipped
2 tablespoons finely chopped almonds

International
Favorites

½ cup BASIC CAROB SYRUP
   (see Index)
2 tablespoons honey
¼ cup butter
4 egg yolks
½ teaspoon vanilla
6 egg whites
pinch of salt
3 tablespoons warmed honey
¾ cup whole wheat pastry flour
½ cup APRICOT GLAZE (see Index)
   rubbed through a sieve
1 cup heavy cream, whipped

Preheat oven to 350° F. and line 2 9-inch layer pans with wax paper.

In a small saucepan, heat carob syrup with honey and mix until smooth. Add butter and stir until melted. Do not cook. Remove from heat and cool.

Sacher Torte

In a small mixing bowl, beat egg yolks very lightly with a fork. Beat in cooled carob mixture and add vanilla.

In a separate bowl, beat egg whites with salt until foamy. Add honey gradually, about 1 teaspoon at a time, and continue to beat until whites are stiff.

Mix 1 cup of whites into the carob mixture, then fold the carob mixture into the remaining whites. Sift flour over mixture, and fold until all whites and flour are distributed evenly through the batter. Do not overmix.

Pour the batter into the prepared pans and bake in preheated oven for 20 to 25 minutes.

International Favorites

Remove from oven, turn cake out onto wire rack, and remove wax paper. Cool. Meanwhile, prepare topping.

Topping

¼ cup BASIC CAROB SYRUP
   (see Index)
1 cup heavy cream
¼ cup honey
1 egg
1 teaspoon vanilla

In a heavy saucepan, combine carob syrup, cream, and honey. Cook over low heat until smooth and starting to thicken (about 5 minutes).

In a small bowl, beat egg lightly. Stir in 3 tablespoons of carob mixture, then pour back into remaining carob in saucepan. Cook very slowly (do not boil) for 3 minutes. Remove from heat and add vanilla. Cool.

Place one cooled cake layer on a wire rack with a tray underneath. Spread evenly with apricot glaze, then place second layer on top.

Pour or spoon carob glaze over top and sides of torte, spreading evenly.

When cake is completely cooled and topping is set, transfer to a serving plate and put into refrigerator to harden for several hours.

When ready to serve, remove from refrigerator and allow to warm to room temperature. Serve with whipped cream on the side.

Yield: 8 servings

This popular torte is believed to have been created in 1832 by Franz Sacher, a chef to Prince Metternick. Later, when Sacher opened the Hotel Sacher, his little torte was largely responsible for the hotel's instant success. For generations Hotel Sacher guarded the recipe. Today there are many versions of the recipe, and in recent years a seven-year court battle raged in Vienna to determine who can claim to serve the authentic *Sacher Torte*.

Cream butter, add honey, and blend together until light and fluffy.

Force the hard-cooked egg yolk through a sieve, and add to the butter-honey mixture. Add beaten egg yolk, citrus peel, vanilla, and salt. Mix well, then sift flour and add to dough. Form into a ball, wrap in plastic wrap, and chill for about an hour (not longer or it becomes too stiff to handle).

Viennese Apricot Foldovers

Roll out the dough on a floured board to form a 15-inch square about ⅛ inch thick. Cut into 3-inch squares, place 2 teaspoonfuls of apricot glaze in the center of each square and fold dough over to form a triangle. Seal edges by pressing firmly with your thumb or the tines of a fork. Place on a large, buttered, floured cookie sheet and chill for a half-hour.

Preheat oven to 350° F.

Brush the top of each triangle with egg white, cut a small gash in the center of each folded edge, and bake in preheated oven for 12 minutes.

Remove from baking sheet carefully, and cool on wire rack.

Yield: 1 dozen foldovers

⅔ cup butter, softened
⅓ cup warmed honey
1 hard-cooked egg yolk
1 raw egg yolk, lightly beaten
½ teaspoon grated orange
    or lemon peel
1 teaspoon vanilla
¼ teaspoon salt
1¼ cups whole wheat pastry flour
⅔ cup APRICOT GLAZE (see Index)
1 lightly beaten egg white for coating

International Favorites

2 egg yolks
1 teaspoon vanilla
½ teaspoon finely grated lemon peel
1 tablespoon whole wheat pastry flour
4 egg whites
pinch of salt
1 tablespoon warmed honey
1 tablespoon COCONUT SUGAR
(see Index) for decoration

Preheat oven to 350° F. and butter an 8 x 10 x 2-inch baking dish.

In a medium-size bowl, combine yolks, vanilla, and lemon peel. Mix well. Sift flour over mixture and fold gently.

In another bowl, beat the egg whites with salt until foamy. Continuing to beat, add honey slowly and beat until whites are stiff enough to hold their shape.

Stir ½ cup whites into yolk mixture, then fold yolk mixture into the rest of the whites. Do not overmix.

Spoon souffle into prepared casserole, forming three large mounds piled high in the dish. Bake in preheated oven for 10 minutes, until lightly browned.

Remove from oven, sprinkle with coconut sugar, and serve immediately, directly from the baking dish.

Yield: 6 servings

This delightfully simple dessert is delicious, light, and very easy to prepare.

Salzburg Souffle

In a medium-size mixing bowl, beat butter until light and creamy. Add honey and continue to beat. Stir in almonds.

Mix flour and salt and add to batter. Stir in rum. Chill batter in refrigerator for about 20 minutes.

Viennese Almond Cakes

Preheat oven to 350°F. and dust a cookie sheet with flour.

With your hands, roll dough into balls about the size of large marbles and place about 2 inches apart on prepared baking sheet. Bake in preheated oven for 15 minutes, or until lightly browned.

Remove from oven and top with coconut sugar. Cool on wire rack.

Yield: 4 to 5 dozen cakes

½ cup butter
¼ cup honey
½ cup ground almonds
¾ to ⅞ cup whole wheat pastry flour
⅛ teaspoon salt
2 tablespoons rum
3 tablespoons COCONUT SUGAR
  (see Index)

Combine apricots, apple juice, and water in a 2-quart saucepan. Allow to stand several hours or overnight. Place over very low heat and cook, covered, until tender (20 to 25 minutes). Cool slightly.

Apricot Kisel

Place mixture in a blender and puree. Add honey and lemon peel. Mix well until honey is completely dissolved. Pour into individual dessert dishes and refrigerate at least 4 hours before serving.

Yield: 6 servings

1½ cups dried apricots
2 cups unsweetened apple juice
2 cups water
2 tablespoons honey
1½ teaspoons grated lemon peel

International Favorites

1 package dry yeast
½ cup lukewarm milk
2 tablespoons honey
2 cups whole wheat flour
½ teaspoon salt
4 eggs, beaten
½ cup butter, softened
2/3 cup currants
¼ cup honey
2 tablespoons water
¼ cup dark rum (or to taste)
½ cup APRICOT GLAZE (see Index)
1 cup heavy cream, whipped
fresh fruit for garnish (orange slices
and large, dark grapes
are attractive and tasty)

Stir the yeast into the milk and add honey. Mix well, then set aside in a warm place for about 20 minutes until mixture becomes frothy.

Meanwhile, stir together flour and salt. Add eggs, butter, and currants. Mix until well combined, then add yeast mixture and mix again until smooth, using a wooden spoon to knead about 5 minutes.

Grease well a 6-cup *kugelhof* mold (this is a rounded mold with a hole in the center, similar to a tube pan) with butter. Spoon the dough into the mold—it should come halfway up the sides. Cover with a dampened towel and set in a warm place to rise for about 1 hour.

The dough should double and rise almost to the top of the pan.

Preheat oven to 400° F.

When cake has risen, place in the center of the oven and bake 10 minutes. Reduce heat to 350° F. and bake for 25 minutes longer.

Remove from oven and allow to rest for 5 minutes. Turn out onto a wire rack with a tray underneath.

Place the honey and water in a small saucepan. Heat until blended and syrupy, stirring constantly. Add rum and pour over the warm *baba*, soaking it thoroughly.

Warm the apricot glaze and add a little water (if necessary) to thin to the right consistency for brushing, then brush generously over the *baba*. Cool.

Transfer to a serving plate, and decorate with colorful, fresh fruit, attractively arranged with whipped cream.

Yield: 12 servings

The dough for the *baba* is not a sweet dough–the cake depends upon the glaze for its distinctive appeal.

Baba au Rhum

Charlotte Russe

Line a 1-pint charlotte mold or small casserole with ladyfingers. Cut the ladyfingers to fit together as tightly as possible along the bottom and sides of the mold.

Soak gelatin in water.

In a small mixing bowl, combine egg yolks and honey; stir until smooth and creamy.

In the top of a double boiler, scald milk with vanilla bean and gradually pour it over the egg mixture, stirring briskly. Return mixture to double boiler and place over hot water. Cook, stirring constantly, until smooth and thick. Remove from heat and discard vanilla bean. Add gelatin and stir until dissolved. Cool.

Fold in whipped cream (reserving ½ cup for decoration) and pour pudding into prepared, lined mold. Chill.

When ready to serve, unmold onto a serving plate and decorate lightly with whipped cream.

Yield: 4 to 6 servings

about 20 single LADYFINGERS (see Index)
1 envelope unflavored gelatin
2 tablespoons cold water
4 egg yolks
3 tablespoons honey
1 cup milk
1-inch piece of vanilla bean
1 cup heavy cream, whipped

International
Favorites

Preheat oven to 350° F. and grease an 8 × 8-inch pan.

Cream butter, add honey, and mix well. Beat in eggs, one at a time. Gradually fold in farina, cinnamon, and almonds. Pour into prepared pan and bake in preheated oven for 30 minutes.

½ cup butter
1/3 cup warmed honey
2 eggs
1 cup farina, uncooked
½ teaspoon cinnamon
½ cup finely chopped almonds
¼ cup honey
¼ cup water

Remove from oven and cool 15 minutes.

Simmer the honey and water for 10 minutes and pour over the baked mixture. Cool and cut into squares or diamonds.

Yield: 8 servings

In place of the honey syrup glaze, cake icing may be drizzled over the *halva* before it has cooled completely.

Halva

Preheat oven to 375° F. and grease an 11 × 7-inch oblong or a 10-inch round baking pan.

In a medium-size mixing bowl, beat egg, then add honey and yogurt and mix well.

1 egg
2 tablespoons honey
2 tablespoons yogurt
1½ cups whole wheat pastry flour
1 teaspoon soda
¼ teaspoon salt
6 tablespoons melted butter
2 pounds fresh plums
1 tablespoon honey

Sift together flour, soda, and salt. Add to the egg mixture. Stir in butter and press dough into prepared pan, covering bottom and sides.

Cut plums into ½ to 1-inch sections and press into the dough sidewise. Drizzle honey over the fruit and bake in preheated oven 30 to 40 minutes.

Yield: 8 servings

Swiss Plum Cake

International Favorites

Sift flour and salt into a medium-size bowl. Make a well in the center. Put the butter, yolks, honey, and lemon peel into the well. With a wooden spoon, mix the ingredients together. Add water and work into mixture until dough is smooth. Form into a ball, dust with flour, cover with a cloth, and allow to stand for 40 minutes.

Swiss Flan

Butter and flour a 9-inch flan ring or pie pan. Roll dough very thin and press into ring. Spread cheese evenly over dough.

Preheat oven to 350° F.

In a bowl, beat eggs until light. Add butter, salt, nutmeg, and milk or cream. Pour over cheese in pastry shell and bake in preheated oven for 20 to 25 minutes, until custard is set and lightly browned.

Yield: 1 9-inch flan

Pastry
2 cups whole wheat pastry flour
pinch of salt
½ cup butter, cut into small cubes
2 egg yolks
1 tablespoon honey
1 teaspoon finely grated lemon peel
2 teaspoons ice water

Filling
2 cups grated Emmenthal cheese
4 eggs
2 tablespoons butter
pinch of salt
dash of nutmeg
2 cups milk or light cream

International
Favorites

Hungarian
Crepe Cake

Preheat oven to 350° F. and lightly grease a shallow, ovenproof serving dish.

Combine applesauce and lemon juice.

Place a *crepe* on prepared dish, and spread with about 2 tablespoons applesauce mixture. Continue to layer applesauce and *crepes,* ending with a *crepe.*

Combine apricot glaze and rum.

Brush top and sides of *crepe* cake with glaze. Sprinkle almonds on top. Place in preheated oven for about 30 minutes.

Yield: 8 servings

Crepe cake may be prepared in advance and heated in the oven when ready to serve.

1 recipe BASIC *CREPES* (see Index), baked in advance
2 cups very thick applesauce, made with honey or unsweetened apple juice
2 tablespoons lemon juice
1 cup APRICOT GLAZE (see Index)
2 tablespoons rum
¼ cup toasted, slivered almonds

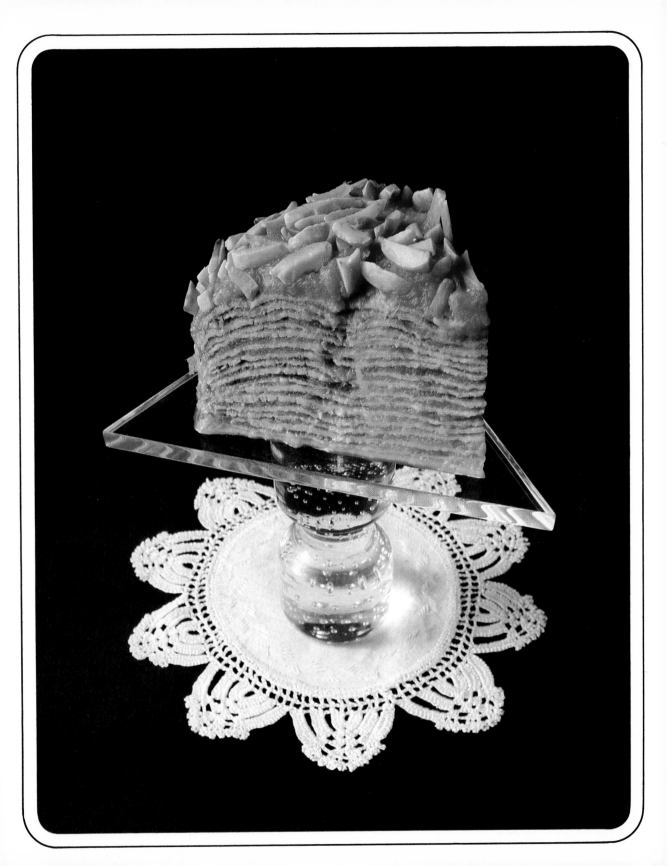

CHART FOR FREEZING DESSERTS AND SNACKS

Food	Preparation for Freezing	How to Package	Recommended Storage Life	Thawing and Serving
Mousses and Cold Souffles	Prepare desired recipe in freezer-proof serving dishes.	Cover tightly with foil. Use inverted foil pan, or make foil collar to protect delicate surface.	1 month	Thaw in refrigerator for 8 hours.
Fresh fruits to be used later in desserts or fillings	Berries, currants, grapes, cherries: Wash, dry well, and fast-freeze on trays. Seedless grapes can be left whole; skin and seed others. Chill cherries in ice water for one hour, then pit.	Seal in bags, cartons, or glass to prevent leaking when thawing.	12 months	Can be eaten partially thawed, or thawed for toppings, fillings, syrups, or cooking.
	Grapefruits, lemons, limes, and oranges: Peel, section, and pack dry or with a bit of its own juice. Also can be packed in syrup made with juice and honey.	Seal in bags, cartons, or glass. Leave room for expansion when packed in syrup.	12 months	Thaw 1 to 2½ hours at room temperature.
	Apples: Peel, core, and slice. Place in cold water while slicing to prevent browning. Pack slices with a little lemon juice, puree with honey, or pack in honey syrup.	Seal in bags or cartons. Leave room for expansion when packed in syrup.	8-12 months for slices with lemon juice 4-8 months for puree or syrup-pack	Thaw at room temperature and use in pies, puddings, sauces, and ices.

390

Fruit	Preparation	Packaging	Storage time	Thawing
Apricots	Peel, halve, and pack in honey syrup, or puree with honey.	Seal in bags or cartons. Leave room for expansion.	12 months for syrup-pack 4 months for puree	Thaw at room temperature and use in dessert recipes, sauces, and ices.
Bananas	Mash with honey and lemon juice—½ cup honey and 3 tablespoons lemon juice to 3 cups banana.	Seal in cartons.	2 months	Thaw unopened carton for 6 hours in refrigerator. Use in dessert recipes, cakes, and breads.
Coconut	Grate or shred and moisten with coconut milk.	Seal in bags or cartons.	2 months	Thaw at room temperature, drain off milk, and use as fresh coconut.
Melons	Cut into slices, cubes, or balls, sprinkle with lemon juice, and cover with a light honey syrup.	Seal in plastic or waxed carton, leaving room for expansion.	12 months	Thaw unopened package in refrigerator. Use fruit while still frosty.
Nectarines and peaches	Peel peaches (optional for nectarines), cut into halves or slices, and brush with lemon juice. Pack in honey syrup, or puree, adding 1 tablespoon lemon juice to 1 pound fruit. Sweeten with honey to taste.	Seal in plastic or waxed containers or jars. Leave room for expansion.	12 months	Thaw in refrigerator for 3 hours. Use in dessert recipes, fillings, or toppings.
Pineapple	Use only ripe fruit. Peel and cut into slices or chunks, or crush fruit.	Freeze crushed pineapple in plastic or waxed cartons. Separate slices or chunks with wax paper or plastic wrap, and seal in bags or cartons.	12 months	Thaw at room temperature and use as fresh fruit.
Rhubarb	Trim to desired length and wash in cold water. Blanch for one minute, then wrap in plastic or foil.	Seal in bags or cartons.	12 months	Thaw at room temperature or can be cooked while still frozen.

continued on next page

Chart for Freezing Desserts and Snacks (continued)

Food	Preparation for Freezing	How to Package	Recommended Storage Life	Thawing and Serving
Custards, Puddings, and Hot Souffles	*Not Recommended:* Custards separate. Milk puddings become mushy or curdle. Hot souffles lose texture, and may curdle. Clear gelatin becomes granular and murky. (Gelatin in creamy mixtures and mousses can be frozen.)			
	Creamed gelatin puddings: Prepare desired recipes in freezer-proof serving dishes.	Cover tightly with foil. Use inverted foil pan or make foil collar to protect delicate surface.	1 month	Thaw in refrigerator for 8 hours.
	Whipped Cream: Whip heavy cream, and drop from spoon onto wax paper-lined cookie sheet. Freeze firm.	Separate mounds with wax paper and seal in bags or containers.	3 months	Place frozen mounds on puddings and desserts. Cream will soften at room temperature in 15–20 minutes.
	Fruit puddings: Prepare desired recipe and allow to cool.	Cover tightly with foil, and seal in bag or large plastic container.	2 months	Thaw at room temperature, serve cool or reheat by baking or stewing.
	Icebox cakes: Prepare as usual, and chill in refrigerator overnight. *Note:* Filling may soak into cake.	Wrap tightly in foil, and place in rigid container for added protection.	1 month	Thaw in refrigerator and serve.
Cakes, Buns, and Dough-nuts	Tortes and upside-down cakes: Bake as usual, cool thoroughly.	Wrap tightly in foil or plastic bag, and place in rigid container for added protection.	2 months	Remove wrapping and thaw at room temperature.

Note:
Fillings and icings may make cakes soggy. Butter icings freeze best. Chill cakes with icing in refrigerator to harden icing before wrapping and freezing.

	Preparation	Wrapping	Storage	Thawing
	Angel and sponge cakes: Bake as usual, cool thoroughly.	Wrap in foil or plastic bags.	4 months	Thaw in wrapping at room temperature. If frosted or filled, thaw, loosely covered, in refrigerator.
	Fruitcakes, flavored cakes, gingerbread, and spice cakes: Bake as usual, cool thoroughly.	Can be left in baking tin or taken out with care. Wrap in foil or plastic bag. If desired, place in sturdy container.	4 months for fruitcakes and flavored cakes 2 months for spicecakes and gingerbread 2 months if frosted	Thaw in wrapping at room temperature. If frosted or filled, thaw loosely covered in refrigerator.
	Buns, breakfast cakes, and muffins: Bake as usual, cool thoroughly. If iced, chill to harden icing before packing.	Pack serving-size quantities in foil or plastic bags. If iced, separate layers with wax paper.	4 months 2 months with icing or filling	Thaw in wrapping at room temperature. If iced, thaw, loosely covered, in refrigerator.
	Baked doughnuts: Bake doughnuts and allow them to cool. Don't apply butter or coconut sugar.	Seal in plastic bags or containers with wax paper between layers.	1 month	Reheat frozen doughnuts in oven, then butter and sprinkle with coconut sugar.
Cookies Unbaked	Drop cookies: Prepare dough from desired recipe.	Seal dough in lightly greased plastic or waxed containers.	6 months	Thaw in container at room temperature until dough is soft. Bake as usual.
	Bar cookies: Prepare dough and press into baking pan.	Seal baking pan in foil or plastic wrap.	6 months	Bake without thawing.
	Refrigerator cookies: Prepare dough and shape into roll.	Seal rolled dough in lightly greased foil or plastic wrap.	6 months	Thaw at room temperature just enough to slice roll, then bake.
Cookies Baked	Bake as usual, cool thoroughly.	Seal in rigid containers with wax paper between layers. Fill air spaces with crumpled wax paper or plastic wrap.	6 months	Thaw in package at room temperature.

continued on next page

Chart for Freezing Desserts and Snacks (continued)

Food	Preparation for Freezing	How to Package	Recommended Storage Life	Thawing and Serving
Pie Crusts	*Unbaked*: Pie crust freezes very well, and it's much more convenient to make one large batch of pie crust and freeze shells for future use. Freezing unbaked pie shells actually enhances their flavor and makes them crisper and flakier.	Press dough into pie plates, and seal in bags or containers. Shells can be stacked into each other with greased wax paper between layers.	2 months	Use same as fresh pie crust.
	Baked: Prepare dough, press into pie plates, and bake.	Wrap individual pie crusts in foil or plastic wrap, and seal in bags or containers.	4 months	Thaw in wrapping at room temperature before filling. Heat in low oven if using a hot filling.
Fruit Pies	*Unbaked*: Brush bottom crust with egg white to prevent sogginess. Sprinkle lemon juice on light-colored fruits. Do not slit top crust.	Cover with inverted foil or paper plate. Seal in foil or plastic wrap.	2 months	Do not thaw. Unwrap and cut vent holes in top crust. Bake in medium oven until done.
	Baked: Bake as usual and cool quickly.	Cover with inverted foil or paper plate. Seal in foil or plastic wrap.	4 months	Unwrap and heat frozen pie in medium oven, or thaw at room temperature in wrapping, and serve.
Sauces, Glazes, and Syrups	Sauces, glazes, and syrups freeze well. Only custard sauces cannot be frozen.	Pack serving-size portions in plastic containers or jars. Leave room for expansion.	6 months when using fresh fruit 1 month when using fruit juices, flavorings, and pudding mixtures	Heat in double boiler, or thaw in container in refrigerator and serve cold.
Pastry	*Unbaked*: Freezing unbaked dough improves the flavor and aroma of the pastry, and makes it crisper and flakier. Roll the dough and form it into squares.	Wrap squares of dough in wax paper, then seal in foil or plastic wrap.	4 months	Thaw slowly at room temperature, then bake as fresh pastry. Do not refreeze pastry baked from frozen dough.

Breads with Yeast	*Baked:* Bake as usual and allow to cool.	Pack in plastic or cardboard boxes with wax paper between layers. Fill air spaces with crumpled paper.	6 months	Thaw at room temperature in wrapping, then ice or add filling.
	Unbaked: The dough can be frozen, but it will rise more slowly when thawed. Allow dough to rise once, then shape for baking. Brush dough with olive oil or butter to prevent toughening of the crust.	Wrap in foil or plastic wrap, and seal in bags or containers.	2 months	Thaw in a moist, warm place. Fast thawing will enhance light texture. Allow dough to rise before baking.
English Muffins and Cornbread	*Baked:* Bake as usual and allow to cool.	Seal in foil or plastic wrap.	1 month	Thaw in wrappings at room temperature, or reheat frozen loaf in medium oven for 45 minutes.
	Bake as usual and allow to cool.	Wrap serving-size quantities in foil or plastic wrap, and seal in bags or containers.	10 months for muffins 4 months for cornbread	Muffins: Thaw in wrapping at room temperature for 30 minutes, then toast. Cornbread: Thaw in wrapping at room temperature.
Quiches	Prepare and bake as usual. Freeze on a cookie sheet without wrapping to avoid spoiling the surface.	Wrap in foil or plastic wrap, and seal in rigid containers.	2 months	Thaw in loose wrappings at room temperature, and serve cold, or reheat.
Pizza	Prepare and bake as usual.	Leave pizza on baking plate, and seal in foil or plastic wrap.	1 month	Thaw at room temperature for one hour, then thoroughly heat in a medium oven.
Crepes and Pancakes	Prepare as usual, and cool thoroughly. Do not add fillings or toppings.	Separate pancakes with wax paper, and seal in foil or plastic wrap.	2 months	Thaw in wrappings at room temperature to separate them. Heat in a low oven, or cover with a cloth and steam.

INDEX

A

B

R

S

T

U